PEER COUNSELING

Skills and Perspectives

PEER COUNSELING

Skills and Perspectives

Vincent J. D'Andrea
and
Peter Salovey

Science and Behavior Books
Palo Alto, California

Library of Congress Card Number 82-062926

ISBN 0-8314-0064-1

Printed in the United States of America

CONTENTS

FOREWORD

This is a timely book. Volunteerism has regained value and virtue in its own right. On the state and national levels, cutbacks in funding for various helping services may well spark a renewed interest in self-help groups. Many support and academic services face the close scrutiny of those who must decide what our institutions will afford to do. Many have also become aware of the so-called wellness movement, where responsibility for personal and community health rests less with the professionals and more with the lay people.

Peer counseling is relevant to each of these developments. It helps people help themselves. Training does not cost much, and peer counselors are often volunteers. Peer counseling skills—listening attentively, understanding others, recognizing and dealing with feelings, suspending judgment, nonverbal communication, paraphrasing, and recognizing the important and relevant in personal dialogue—are practical and transferable.

There are also some less easily defined skills. How can one locate, for example, that evasive boundary beyond which individuals must be responsible for helping themselves—the boundary beyond which the helper ought not go?

Many roles and jobs in our society depend on people with such skills—skills that are not often learned well in the classroom setting. For this reason, I am pleased that the authors have not limited the scope of application of the concepts and information to students and campuses. Much of their training can easily be incorporated into community programs that use volunteers to provide needed services not available in more formal, funded programs.

Peer counseling programs are not a panacea for all economic ills. Nor should such a program be used as a basic building block for an effective student affairs organization, for example. It cannot be a substitute for a clinically solid counseling service or a responsive and competent community clinic or center. In a similar way, community self-help groups, drop-in centers, and hotlines provide important adjuncts to more traditional clinics or centers.

Let me turn to my area of expertise, the college student community. I cannot imagine a good student-affairs program without peer counselors integrated into its fabric of counseling and social programs. Peer counselors have much to offer and deserve a presence in our medical, personal counseling, academic advising, residential advising, and career planning programs.

The campus with a good peer counseling program benefits significantly. It is important that students know they are assuming responsibility for their own affairs. Most students learn they can be independent of home, family, and adolescent structures. In fact, they probably would develop independence (maybe even more) if they did not attend college. But independence is not enough. The real challenge is to develop interdependence—the webs of social and personal relationships—and learn how to give and receive the help and support of friends and peers. Peer counseling programs provide the opportunity to learn, practice, and appreciate interdependence.

A related benefit is the sense of community that often flows from a strong tradition of students helping students and students taking responsibility collectively for their own affairs. Having made such an investment in it, those students regard and refer to their college as THEIRS.

Students in such programs also learn about making referrals and providing helpful information. To do this, they learn about the texture and missions of the campus's academic and support services.

The personal benefits to student peer counselors are real. For many, those benefits add up to an effective way of testing their own vocational interests and skills. Further, what is learned can be transferred to life after college: the experience of being part of a helping group may well lead to an increased awareness of needs in the communities where those graduates live and work.

Finally, good peer counseling programs possess another important yet often understated or overlooked virtue. They offer constructive means for students to serve and do good. That alone is reason enough to pay close attention to the theories and practices of Dr. D'Andrea, Peter Salovey, and their colleagues. Their work, aptly described in this book, has resulted in enormous benefits to Stanford and its students for over a decade.

James W. Lyons
Dean of Student Affairs
Stanford University

PREFACE

This book is a handbook in the sense that it provides specific materials for peer counselor skills training; it is also a guide to program development, and it treats specific issues such as gay peer counseling and cultural and ethnic factors in peer counseling.

The bulk of the text consists of listening, counseling, and crisis-intervention skills training modules. The book can be used as a single text, supplemented with videotaped materials, or used in conjunction with existing counseling texts.

One of the important virtues of this book is that it provides, in one volume, materials which are understandable to the high school, junior college, and college student. Unfortunately, most counseling texts are aimed at the graduate-student level and must be "watered down" by the instructor for use in peer counseling training programs.

This manual, however, represents a practical, replicable, and easily grasped training program geared to a wide variety of peer counseling interests, including crisis counseling, academic and residence advising, career planning, contraception counseling, and ethnic peer counseling, as well as general psychological support. It is written for the student or community worker who might work in a drop-in counseling center, staff a neighborhood hotline, or counsel peers in a residence-hall setting.

We believe this book will have broad appeal, both on campuses and in the community; it duplicates little of the counseling literature. It may be the first book that specifically addresses in a comprehensive manner all the issues involved in peer counselor training.

The introduction addresses the questions of the kind of training needed, the amount of time needed, and the kinds of goals that are appropriate. It discusses the concerns of professional counselors in dealing with student groups, and it evaluates a specific part of our training program. The rest of the book is essentially a syllabus for the course and a compilation of materials in areas that have proven to be of major importance to peer counselors. We do not claim that our approach is unique; however, we do believe it to be useable by others who may be looking for such a compilation to supplement their own efforts. We also hope this book will serve as a jumping-off place for individuals in many programs; may they continue to discover new ways of enabling students to help other students.

Vincent J. D'Andrea
Peter Salovey

ACKNOWLEDGMENTS

To Allen Ivey and Norma Gluckstern, whose pioneering work in developing microcounseling skills attracted our attention, and who have graciously and generously encouraged us to "develop our own style."

To Martha Martin and Bill Leland, who were instrumental in working to develop the Bridge in 1971, and gave of their time and talents to establish peer counseling at Stanford.

To Andrew Gottlieb, Matt Wolf, Steve Hibschman, Don Gallagher, Lee Rowen, and Sue Crissman, student teachers who contributed much to the form and content of the training programs at the Bridge and other peer counseling efforts.

To Joan Evans, Mike Boyd, and the Riverside California Suicide Hot Line for the suicide checklist and I.Q. test.

To Jim Lyons, Jim McClenahan, Dave Dorosin, Thom Massey and Patricia Brandt, whose administrative support and continued encouragement have been of invaluable help in developing peer counseling at Stanford.

To Peggy Smith and Barbara Binkley, whose teaching expertise in communication skills helped to refine and develop our training materials, in particular our videotape modules.

To Fritz Bottjer, whose skill and technical expertise enabled us to produce high-quality videotape modules and who gave generously of his time in other ways.

To Herant Katchadourian, Mike McHargue and Cary Walker, whose efforts put peer counselor training courses in the catalogue, giving impetus to peer counseling programs to increase the academic merit of their offerings while substantively adding to the quality of services offered to students.

To all the hundreds of peer counselors and student coordinators whose many contributions over the years have refined our training and service programs to their present form.

To Brent Davis and Rain Blockley for editorial comments.

To Mary Cunha and Win Vetter, whose cheerful and competent translation of our atrocious handwriting into beautiful typescript has earned our thanks and respect.

To all, many many thanks.

CONTRIBUTING AUTHORS

Fritz Bottjer, Ph.D., is media specialist at Counseling and Psychological Services, Cowell Student Health Center, Stanford University

David Dorosin, M.D., is Director, Counseling and Psychological Services, Cowell Student Health Center, Stanford, and Clinical Professor of Psychiatry, Department of Psychiatry and Behavioral Sciences, Stanford University School of Medicine.

Sam Edwards, M.S.W., is on the staff of Counseling and Psychological Services, Cowell Student Health Center, Stanford University.

Andrew Gottlieb is a graduate student, Department of Psychology, University of Washington, Seattle.

Richard N. Jacks, Ph.D., is Director, Counseling Center, Whitman College, Walla Walla, Washington.

Alejandro Martinez, Ph.D., is clinical psychologist, Counseling and Psychological Services, Cowell Student Health Center, Stanford University.

Franklin Matsumoto, M.D., is a psychiatrist practicing in Menlo Park, California; consultant to Cowell Student Health Service and to Job Corps Programs in Western USA; and Clinical Associate Professor of Psychiatry at Stanford.

Peter Nye, M.S., is a graduate of the Computer Music program at Stanford University, and a senior counselor in the Gay Peer Counseling Program there.

Jane Pao, M.S., is a staff counselor at Counseling and Psychological Services, Cowell Student Health Center, and consultant to Asian-American student programs at Stanford University.

Peggy Smith, Ph.D., is Assistant Professor of Counseling Psychology, San Francisco State University.

Alice Supton is an Assistant Dean of Student Affairs, Office of Residential Education, at Stanford University.

Matthew Wolf, Ph.D., is a clinical psychologist practicing and teaching in San Rafael and San Francisco.

Laraine Zappert, Ph.D., is staff psychologist, Counseling and Psychological Services, Cowell Student Health Center, and Research Associate at the Center for Research on Women, Stanford University.

INTRODUCTION

We include this introduction to *Peer Counseling: Skills and Perspectives* because it identifies many of the issues that need to be considered when a peer counseling center is first established. What kind of training is needed? How much professional supervision is necessary? What kinds of services will the center provide? What are the benefits to the counselee? What is learned by the counselor? We hope you find the questions raised in this chapter useful in clarifying the goals, values, and needs of your counseling center.

This section is based on the presentation by Drs. David Dorosin, Vincent D'Andrea, and Richard Jacks at the 1977 meeting of the American College Health Association. It discusses the rationale for establishing a college peer counseling center, the way one particular counselor training program was developed, and the data used to evaluate that training program's effectiveness.

A PEER COUNSELING TRAINING PROGRAM: RATIONALE, CURRICULUM, AND EVALUATION

Some years ago, a number of student groups came to us interested in peer counselor training. This opportunity immediately raised three questions: (1) How much staff time—a scarce resource—should we expend in this activity? That is, would it be a "wise investment" of professional time, and by what criteria should we decide? (2) Since ethnic minority groups, contraception counseling groups, drug counseling groups, and even university staff were interested in such training, what might constitute a "core curriculum" that would be applicable to such a variety of interested groups? (3) How could we evaluate the quality and impact of the training?

In this book, we would like to share the answers we arrived at: why we felt this program would be a good investment of professional time, what we decided should be the content of the curriculum, and how we determined the program should be evaluated.

Rationale

Even before the inception of the program, the idea of students helping students had been important to us. For example, we had spent time in selecting and orienting residential staff, facilitating interactions between professionals from our staff and residential staffs, and collaborating in the establishment of a student-run drug crisis center in the late 1960s.[1] In the last three to four years there has been a marked increase in interest among student groups.

The first organized group to become interested in peer counseling was a group of students called "the Bridge," who were concerned about the drug problem on campus and attempted to offer alternatives to drug use. This group set up a crisis intervention, information, and counseling center which devotes itself to the welfare of other students.

Another strong theme of the Bridge has been one of affiliation—coming together as a group for a common purpose. Through such affiliation comes mutual support, heightened individual confidence, sharing of information, and collective action.

A third theme has been the gaining of a better and clearer sense of self through participation in counselor training. One of the results most commonly reported by counselors involved in the Bridge program has been a clearer sense of self and a heightening of self-esteem. Through practicing openness and self-disclosure, through the ongoing support of the group, and through fulfilling a valued role in the group, many have found the experience of being a peer counselor an important one in going from youth to adulthood.

A fourth theme within the Bridge is the providing of meaningful adult roles for young people, something that our society seldom does. A meaningful role is one that involves responsibility for others: the adult is expected to assume such responsibility, whereas the youth, in general, is not. The peer counseling experience offers a chance to fulfill an adult role to those who are interested in careers as teachers, counselors, psychologists or doctors, or in other professions that involve responsibility for another person.

A fifth theme of the Bridge is one of providing greater social and interpersonal skills. For some, the peer counselor training is "intimacy training" that might be important in one's own personal life. For others, it teaches social skills that might be useful in one's work role. Through the training and interaction, the peer counselors themselves have been

---

[1]Wolf, M.; D. Dorosin; and V. D'Andrea. "How to Be There When You're There: A Guide to Handling Student Problems in the Residences." Counseling and Psychological Services, Stanford University.

able to achieve a better understanding of individual psychology, of group processes, and of ways of facilitating communication and interaction.

A sixth and last theme in the Bridge is the learning of adaptive and coping intrapersonal skills. These coping skills, as formulated by White,[2] involve cognitive, intrapsychic mechanisms and behaviors for dealing both with environmental situations and with emotional and maturational states in oneself. The peer counselors learn these skills from others—by observing, by identifying, by learning precepts, by training, by following examples, by coaching. Most people learn such skills as a part of everyday life, but in peer counselor training we feel that there is a heightening of this "normal" process.

The Training Course—Process of Choice and Content

As more student groups began to express interest in peer counseling, we began to review our training program more systematically with two major questions in mind: (1) What kind of training program would provide the best content and potential for evaluation? (2) What program might have a sufficiently broad appeal so that we would not have to redesign the training program for each group?

A committee of students and staff—mostly staff—was organized. This committee reviewed the rationale for and the mechanism of the peer counselor training. Tapes were reviewed, literature was read, and people were interviewed. The committee then drew three major conclusions: (1) There is a broad interest in peer counseling among students, both in using peer helpers and in becoming peer helpers. (2) The microcounseling technique of Ivey[3] seems most suitable as a basic model for training peer counselors. (3) Basic skill training should be required for every student who wishes to be a peer counselor; specialized training should also be required for those wishing to be a part of a special-interest peer counseling group (e.g., Health Service, Career Counseling and Placement Center, and so on).

The content of the course in basic skills is based on the microcounseling technique: students learn skills and use videotape to get immediate feedback in role playing. The basic course consists of six two-hour sessions. Each session focuses on a specific skill: (1) basic attending skills,

---

[2]White, R. W. "Strategies of Adaptation: An Attempt at Systematic Description," in *Coping and Adaptation*, eds. Coelho, Hamburg, and Adams. New York: Basic Books, 1974.
[3]Ivey, A. E. *Microcounseling: Innovations in Interviewing Training.* Springfield: Charles Thomas, 1974.

(2) open invitation to talk, (3) paraphrasing, (4) reflection of feeling, (5) summarizing, and (6) integration of all skills.

Each session begins with a videotaped mini-lecture and demonstrations of the specific skill to be learned that day. The students then practice and view each other's role plays. They then discuss their experiences, paying attention to what is effective or ineffective in peer counseling.[4]

Evaluation

We have attempted to evaluate three separate aspects of this program: (1) the attitudes of the trainers and trainees about the training, (2) the effectiveness of the training, and (3) the quality of the actual counseling done by people who took the training.

Attitudes of trainers and trainees about the training. Evaluation forms filled out by trainers and trainees at the end of each session have been consistently positive. The trainees report growing feelings of competence, personal growth in relationships with peers, and increased ability to apply the new skills to real-life situations.

There was some criticism of the original lecture tapes—criticism focusing on a lack of diversity. We subsequently modified the videotapes, using more people, using both negative and positive models in the role plays, and increasing the variety of topics. Feedback on the new videotapes has been much more positive.

Effectiveness of the training. Three training groups were selected in the spring of 1975 for this more formal evaluation: six males from the Gay People's Union, eight females from the married-students' housing area on the campus, and eight Chicano students from the university. We first had each trainee do a seven-minute videotaped interview of a "standard client." At the end of the training program, we videotaped the same trainees interviewing the same clients. The videotapes were then presented to a group of raters consisting partly of professionals on the training staff. No trainer evaluated people whom he or she had actually trained. The trainees were evaluated on each of the various skills taught in the training.

The results of these evaluations are shown in Figure 1. The post-training videotapes showed a higher frequency of open questions, paraphrases, reflections of feeling, and summarizations, and they showed a lower frequency of topic jumps and closed questions. There was also a significant increase in the overall quality between the pretraining and post-training evaluations.

Quality of counseling done by trainees. A second evaluation study was undertaken in the Career Planning and Placement Center on the campus.

---

[4]Ivey, A. E., and N. Gluckstern. *Basic Attending Skills: An Introduction to Microcounseling and Helping.* Amherst, MA: Microcounseling Associates, 1974.

Skills Profile—Average of All Subjects' Response per Opportunity Ratio for Pre and Post Video Tapes

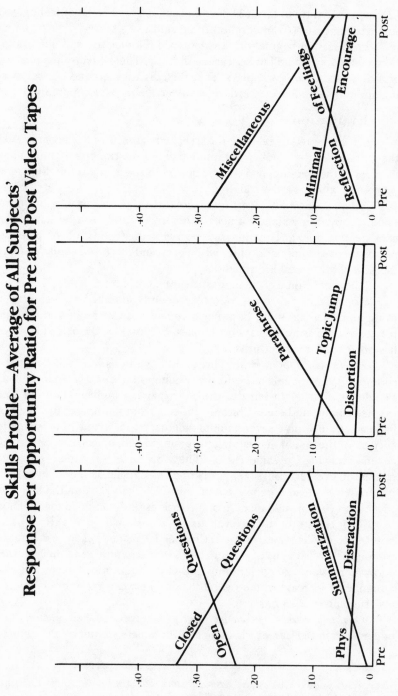

In this study, students coming to the center were randomly assigned to either peer or professional counselors. Prior to their counseling session, students were asked to complete a questionnaire which addressed the following areas: (1) previous experience with the center; (2) attitudes and opinions regarding the relative value of peer versus professional counseling along five dimensions on a Likert scale; and (3) a checklist indicating their preferences for types of services available (peer or professional) by types of problems and issues presented.

Following their interview, subjects completed two questionnaires. The first asked them to rate counselor behavior and activity along specific and nonspecific dimensions. The second replicated the pre-interview questions.

The results showed that subjects tended to rate peer counselors more highly after their interview. This was especially so for assessments of general counseling skills displayed by the peer counselors. Professional counselors were rated more highly along dimensions having to do with greater and more specific information displayed, but there was little change from the initial ratings along counseling dimensions.

We interpret this to mean that after meeting with peer counselors, students tended to rate them more highly. This generalized to perceptions of peer counselor competence in noncareer counseling areas (e.g., personal, crisis, problem-solving).[5]

CONCLUSIONS

1. There is broad student interest in peer counselor training.
2. University and college counseling centers should encourage interested students to develop peer counseling services to supplement the existing professional counseling service.
3. A peer counseling service should be operated and evaluated with the same care as a professional clinical service.
4. A peer counseling service is a valuable addition to a campus clinical service but does not replace the existing professional service.

[5]Jacks, R.; F. Bottjer; and V. D'Andrea. "Student Perceptions of the Relative Competence of Peer and Professional Counselors in a Career Counseling Setting." Stanford University, 1978 (unpublished study).

Part I

PEER COUNSELING SKILLS

Chapter 1. What Is Peer Counseling?

A. Definition
B. The Eight Commandments
   1. Be Nonjudgmental
   2. Be Emphathetic (Not a Brick Wall)
   3. Don't Give Personal Advice
   4. Don't Ask Questions that Begin with "Why"
   5. Don't Take Responsibility for the Other Person's Problem
   6. Don't Interpret (When a Paraphrase Will Do)
   7. Stick with the Here and Now
   8. Deal with Feelings First
C. Becoming an Effective Counselor
   1. Learning the Listening Skills
   2. Role Playing to Practice Skills
   3. Co-counseling for Sharpening Skills
D. References

1.

What Is Peer Counseling?

Peer counseling is the use of active listening and problem-solving skills, along with knowledge about human growth and mental health, to counsel people who are our peers—peers in age, status, and knowledge. Peer counseling, then, is both a method and a philosophy. The basic premise behind it is that people are capable of solving most of their own problems of daily living if given the chance. The role of the counselor in peer counseling is not to solve people's problems for them but rather to assist them in finding their own solutions. Peer counselors don't tell people what they "should" do, nor do they give advice; peer counselors generally do not interpret or diagnose. As *peer* counselors, we are not professionals and we cannot assume that we know what a person is thinking or feeling any better than that person does. Rather, by using the active listening and counseling skills that will be presented in this book, the peer counselor helps the counselee clarify his or her thoughts and feelings and explore various options and solutions.

Peer counseling is actively practiced in many settings. Most colleges and universities have drop-in peer counseling and crisis intervention centers; many cities have telephone crisis and suicide hotlines run by nonprofessional counselors; self-help group activities may include large amounts of peer counseling among participants; and in the business world many companies are training supervisors in peer-counseling skills to increase their ability to understand and help solve the work-related problems of their colleagues. Since the late 1960s, peer counseling (as opposed to professional counseling) has been used with increasing acceptance and success in various situations. In fact, in a recent review by J. A. Durlak (1979), nonprofessional (peer) counselors were seen as effective as professionals in helping people cope with many of the hassles of daily living. Thus, as listeners, clarifiers, and information providers, peer counselors can play an important role in assisting others with significant problems.

THE EIGHT COMMANDMENTS

Whether you are simply listening to another person's problems, actively helping someone make a critical decision, or counseling someone during a crisis, there are eight important rules that should be kept in mind. We call these rules "commandments" not because they cannot be broken, but because they apply so consistently across so many of the counseling situations in which you will find yourself. We will first list all eight commandments and then discuss each:

1. Be Nonjudgmental
2. Be Empathetic (Not a Brick Wall)
3. Don't Give Personal Advice
4. Don't Ask Questions that Begin with "Why"
5. Don't Take Responsibility for the Other Person's Problem
6. Don't Interpret (When a Paraphrase Will Do)
7. Stick with the Here and Now
8. Deal with Feelings First

Be Nonjudgmental

Being nonjudgmental is basic to effective peer counseling. As a peer counselor, you will undoubtedly be exposed to problems and situations quite foreign to your own experience and style of life. You may even find yourself thinking, "This person is really strange" or "If I were this person, I would do X." It is important, however, to remember that you are *not* that person, and that what you would do if you *were* the person is not particularly relevant. Stick with the listening and counseling skills, helping the counselee to clarify and perhaps solve his or her problem. Don't try to "size the person up," diagnose him or her, or compare the person's problem or background to your own. Let's look at some examples:

Counselee: I have this problem. Every time I'm on a date, I get very nervous and say stupid things.

Judgmental response: It sounds to me like you are not particularly experienced in sexual matters.

Nonjudgmental response: How does it feel to be nervous?

or

So you tend to feel nervous in dating situations.

Here's another example:

Counselee: I find that I'm attracted to other men. (*Counselee is male.*)

Judgmental response: So, you have latent homosexual tendencies. That's really strange, although I'd imagine it's quite common.

Nonjudgmental response: Tell me more about your feelings toward other men. (*Note: words like "gay," or "homosexual," are not used unless the counselee uses them first*).

or, if the counselor *is* uncomfortable in this situation:

Nonjudgmental response: This is a situation that I'm not entirely comfortable talking about. Could I find a different counselor for you?

The last response brings up an important question: Are there any situations that you would feel uncomfortable talking about? That is, are there any topics about which you would find it very difficult to remain nonjudgmental? If so, these situations should be identified and you should decide what you want to do when they come up. Most likely, you'll want to refer such counselees to another peer counselor. But perhaps—through role playing, discussion, etc.—you could learn to be nonjudgmental in that situation. Just because you are personally opposed to abortion, for example, does not mean you couldn't nonjudgmentally counsel someone who is considering having one. The counselee is *not* you, and it is important not to let your own values and experiences interfere with your effectiveness as a peer counselor. If you think that they will, however, you should help the counselee find a different counselor.

Be Empathetic (Not a Brick Wall)

Empathetic counselors, no matter what their training, orientation, or level of experience, are much more effective than counselors who are not empathetic. By empathy, we mean the ability to see a problem from the counselee's point of view and, accordingly, to be warm and supportive. Or, as Barbara Okun (1976) puts it, empathy is the understanding of another person from that person's frame of reference. Empathy, she says, underlies the entire counseling relationship.

Just what do we mean by being empathetic? In the counseling situation you need to do more than see the world through your client's eyes. You need to show the counselee that you are doing this. Empathy is demonstrated every time you accurately paraphrase something the counselee has said, every time you use a minimal encourager (smile, nod, uh-huh, etc.), and every time you maintain eye contact.

Being empathetic also means adopting a counseling style that suits the counselee. Animated clients should be counseled in an "upbeat" way; depressed, quiet, or shy people should be treated in a softer, more gentle manner. An effective peer counselor must learn to adjust his or her behavior so that it accurately reflects the mood and style of the counselee.

The worst approach to peer counseling is to be a brick wall—to let your client express all kinds of feelings and thoughts without your showing any kind of response at all. Unfortunately, old Hollywood films depicting therapists as ancient, bearded Viennese men who do little more than sit behind their clients' heads and grunt once in a while have perpetuated the brick-wall-is-good-therapeutic-style myth. Unless you're a highly skilled traditional psychoanalyst (and even if you are), providing little empathy is not a productive way to deal with the thoughts and feelings that people bring to a peer counseling session.

Don't Give Personal Advice

When speaking with a friend about a problem he or she might be experiencing, we often offer our opinion—in the form of advice—about what he or she could do to solve the problem. Likewise, we are often tempted to give advice to a counselee; but in this case it is important to refrain from doing so. No matter how empathetic we may feel, we do not have the same thoughts, feelings, and experiences as our counselees. As a result, advice coming from our own experience with situations similar to those of our counselee is generally inappropriate.

Trying to give advice during a counseling session usually leads to the unproductive exchange that Eric Berne (1964) called the "Yes-But Game." For example:

Counselee: My roommate disturbs my studying by having his stereo too loud.

Counselor: Well, have you tried talking to him?

Counselee: Yeah, but it doesn't seem to work.

Counselor: How about telling his girlfriend?

Counselee: Yeh, but she would be on his side.

Counselor: Hey, have you tried putting a sign on the stereo that says "No loud music after 10 P.M."?

Counselee: Yeah, but . . .

As you can see, advice is not all that easy to give.

We have found that when the counseling session is structured so that the counselee generates alternative solutions on his or her own, the counselee is much more likely to act on any decision made during the session. The counselee feels that he or she has the ability to solve his/her own problems. On the other hand, recommendations made by the counselor are frequently not followed, and when they are it is often with a sense of resignation or helplessness.

Giving advice should not be confused with providing information. Often peer counselors have access to vast stores of information about community resources, mental health services and agencies, support groups, classes, and the like, and one of the important functions of the peer counselor is to dispense such information. Information should be passed along in a tentative but straightforward way, not cloaked in advice. For example:

Good: We've received some information about self-help groups for weight control. Would you like me to send you a brochure?

Bad: Have you thought about joining Weight-Watchers? I could send you their brochure.

Sometimes counselors feel that if their advice is taken by a counselee and it "works" then they were justified in giving it. Such Machiavellian thinking about ends and means, however, does not lead to effective counseling in the long term. When counselees receive advice, they are deprived of the opportunity to develop their own brain-storming and decision-making skills. Furthermore, giving advice extends the unproductive dependent relationships that clients so often have with professional counselors to a new domain—peer counseling. When such a dependent relationship exists, we can really no longer say that we are helping a *peer* to solve his or her own problems.

Don't Ask Questions that Begin with "Why"

Why shouldn't peer counselors ask questions that begin with "why"? Generally, we have found that "why" questions put counselees on the defense, making them feel as if they are being interrogated. "Why" implies that an explanation is being demanded rather than simply that more elaboration is desired. It is easy to rephrase "why" questions into less threatening language, and we encourage counselors to do so whenever possible. For example, compare the tones of the two dialogues that follow.

DIALOGUE 1:

Counselor: How are you feeling?

Counselee: Sort of depressed.

Counselor: Why are you feeling depressed?

Counselee: Well, my wife left me six months ago, and I just lost my job.

Counselor: Why did your wife leave you?

Counselee: How the hell should I know? She's a bitch I guess.

Counselor: Why do you think your wife's a bitch?

Counselee: Look, stop playing Perry Mason with me . . . You're the doctor, why don't you answer the questions?

DIALOGUE 2:

Counselor: How are you feeling?

Counselee: Sort of depressed.

Counselor: What do you mean by "depressed"?

Counselee: Well, ever since my wife left me, I feel down in the dumps; I can't eat . . . can't sleep . . .

Counselor: Tell me more about that.

Counselee: Well, six months ago my wife and I had a big fight about . . .

In the first example, the counselee seems unsettled and angry, put off by the barrage of "why" questions. On the other hand, in the second dialogue the counselee appears relaxed, and is having little difficulty responding to the counselor's questions. "Why" questions are not particularly productive in counseling; it would serve us well to drop the word from our vocabulary when a counselee comes to talk. Why not?

Don't Take Responsibility for the Other Person's Problem

As peer counselors we must ask ourselves frequently, "How can I be most helpful in this situation?" Unfortunately, counselors often make the mistake of equating helpfulness with assuming personal responsibility for the welfare of the counselee. It is important to remember that the client comes to you with his or her problem, looking for help in solving that problem. By using the skills presented in this book, you can try very hard to help the counselee. But ultimately, the problem is not yours, it is his or hers, and (s)he must come to the final decision about what to do.

Your responsibility as a peer counselor is to provide as empathetic and supportive a counseling environment as possible and to help the other person deal with the thoughts and feelings he or she might be having regarding the problem at hand. Your responsibility is *not* to solve the other person's problem(s). If problems get solved—fine. But if not, you will have been very helpful simply by allowing the counselee to express his or her thoughts and feelings. In fact, often counselees simply want someone with whom they can talk; they are not expecting to get their problems *solved* at all! If you are using this book as part of a counselor training course for a particular agency or counseling center, we encourage you to discuss as part of your course exactly how much responsibility you are expected to take as a peer counselor. Are there any situations in which you might make a decision for your counselee's "own good" without consulting him or her? What do you tell counselees who insist on your solving their problem for them?

Don't Interpret (When a Paraphrase Will Do)

Interpretation occurs when you go beyond the information given and infer something about the counselee—his or her unconscious motivations, personality characteristics, or social situations, for example. Although the section on interpretation in chapter 3 discusses some of the legitimate uses of carefully worded, tentative, nonaccusative interpretations, we will also stress in the next chapter that interpretations usually do not need to be made. Paraphrasing the information provided by the counselee is generally sufficient to encourage him or her to continue speaking. Interpretation in peer counseling is similar to advice giving: both tend to be gratuitous and counterproductive. Generally, the counselee is interested in getting his or her thoughts and feelings clarified rather than in listening to your explanations about the motives for his/her behavior. Compare the two dialogues that follow:

DIALOGUE 1:

Counselee: I have this problem with my mother; I feel guilty every time I ask her to do me a favor.

Counselor: Sounds like you have some unresolved feelings toward your mother.

Counselee: Well, I don't know . . .

Counselor: It seems that your guilt might be a projection of some kind. Are you jealous of your father?

Counselee: No. What are you driving at anyway?

Counselor: Just a hunch . . . What kinds of dreams did you have as a boy?

DIALOGUE 2:

Counselee: I have this problem with my mother; I feel guilty every time I ask her to do me a favor.

Counselor: You have guilt feelings when dealing with your mother?

Counselee: Yes; I can't seem to ask her for anything without feeling terrible.

Counselor: Tell me more about these feelings.

Counselee:	Well, I feel ashamed . . . and anxious. I get nervous and flustered. I can't even ask her to pick up a newspaper for me on her way home from work.
Counselor:	So you're feeling guilt but also anxiety. Is that right?

Notice that in Dialogue 1, the counselor is attempting to interpret the counselee's behavior in terms of some kind of underlying motive, whereas the counselor in Dialogue 2 is merely paraphrasing information that's "on the table." We believe the second approach is much more likely to help the counselee express and clarify his or her thoughts and feelings regarding the problem. There is less chance of distracting the counselee with inaccurate interpretations. Even if interpretations are correct (and this determination is typically impossible to make), they can still be distracting and counterproductive. Behavioral and humanistic therapists agree: work toward clarification and change rather than "insight" during initial counseling sessions.

Stick with the Here and Now

Since the goal of peer counseling is to help clients solve their own problems by encouraging them to express and clarify their thoughts and feelings about them, it is not particularly useful (especially at first) to spend large amounts of time mulling over the person's early childhood experiences or discussing individuals who are not in the room. Instead, it is most productive if the counseling situation is kept in the present and if the counselee (rather than anyone else) is the focus of attention.

There may be times when you wish to leave the here and now. For example, it is often useful during problem solving to have the counselee fantasize about the consequences of particular alternatives. Or, when dealing with feelings, you may want to find out the "history" of these feelings: how long they've persisted, what has caused them in the past, etc. Both of these situations—and we're sure you can think of others—are perfectly legitimate times to leave the here and now temporarily. *But* (and this is important) in these examples and in similar situations, significant amounts of time would be spent counseling on here-and-now thoughts and feelings before past feelings or future alternatives are discussed. Perhaps our rule could be more accurately stated as follows: Stick with the here and now, but if you decide to deviate, make sure to deal with the here and now thoroughly and first!

Deal with Feelings First

Since some kind of emotional reaction is associated with virtually every situation discussed in counseling, it is probably most useful to elicit, clarify, and discuss feelings before moving to more cognitive (i.e., problem-solving) matters. One of the first questions we find ourselves asking, after the counselee has explained his or her problem, is "And how does that make you feel?" or "How do you feel about that?" or, as Bob Dylan put it, "How does it *feel* (to be on your own, with no direction home, like a complete unknown, just like a rolling stone)?"

Often a counseling session will involve little more than the expression and clarification of feelings. Since problems don't always need to be solved, peer counselors play a most important role in creating a safe context for the free expression of emotions. People may simply need someone with whom they can share their successes, commiserate about their failures, or cry over their losses.

Problem solving which is attempted before feelings are clarified is generally not successful. The unresolved feelings often get in the way of discussing alternatives and options, and the counseling session can degenerate into a gripe session or a "yes-but" situation. So, deal with feelings. Ask feeling questions, paraphrase and reflect verbal and non-verbal emotions, place the feelings in context, ask *more* feeling questions—and then problem solve.

BECOMING AN EFFECTIVE COUNSELOR

Learning the Listening Skills

In presenting the listening skills, we use a "single skill" approach that has been extensively researched and tested. No one expects you to master all the skills in the beginning; they are arranged so that, as you learn each skill, you can add it to the previously learned skills. The easier skills are presented earlier in the section.

As is true with any skill, whether it be driving a car, playing tennis, or playing the piano, when you begin to use basic attending skills you may feel awkward, phoney, or embarrassed. Do not worry. If you persist in practicing, you will soon feel more natural. Eventually, the newly learned skills will fit unnoticed into your normal repertoire of behaviors.

As you are learning and practicing, remember to give and listen for feedback that is *specific:* in order to learn, it is important to find out exactly what is good and what is bad about what you are doing so that you can focus your learning in specific ways.

It cannot be stressed too much that each of you has an individual style. Each of you differs from the others in your group. Be brave, experiment, and find out what feels most comfortable for you. Give each skill, as you are learning it, a chance to work; ultimately you will find the right blend, or mix, for you. The most important thing to remember is: Be you, and give of yourself.

Role Playing to Practice Skills

After learning about a particular listening skill, it is important to practice it by role playing. You will find, for example, that you may clearly understand the difference between "open" and "closed" questions, but that actually using open questions in a role-played counseling situation is difficult—at first. Role playing is the best way to become comfortable with the skills, to make counseling feel as natural as routine conversation. Not only does role playing let you practice your listening skills, it also allows others—the counselee and observers—to provide you with feedback about your style and skill use.

The purpose of role playing is to give the listener a chance to practice his or her skills, not to provide counseling for the problem-giver—although that may happen as well. It's very important to keep this in mind. To help the listener practice his or her skills, the problem-giver must give an appropriate problem, and must give the listener an opportunity to counsel. An appropriate role-play problem is one that can be effectively counseled in a role-play situation. If you are the problem-giver, you should:

1. Pick a problem that involves YOU—your thoughts and your feelings. "My problem is that my roommate is having a real bummer in her relationship with her father" is not appropriate; "I'd like to talk about my feelings about my roommate" is.
2. Pick a problem that is reasonably well defined, since the role plays are short. While "My life is all screwed up" is a legitimate problem, it would be difficult to solve the problem in just a few minutes. Such things as "I have a problem talking to my lover" or "My roommate wakes me up at 5 A.M. every day and it infuriates me" are better.
3. Pick a problem that is not so heavy that you will get upset by talking about it. Again, role-play practice is for the benefit of the counselor, not the problem-giver. A problem that is likely to upset you is not appropriate for role-play situations. Of course, problems that involve no feelings are not very useful either. Often it is good to choose either a slightly traumatic existing problem or else a problem that you have solved in the past.

Giving the listener an opportunity to counsel is also essential. Give the counselor a chance to practice the skill, to ask questions, paraphrase, and explore feelings. Don't talk on and on without pause for ten minutes, thereby preventing the person from using the skills.

A good way to use role playing to practice listening skills is in groups of three: a problem-giver, a counselor, and an observer. After about ten minutes, the problem-giver and the observer give feedback to the counselor about his/her counseling style and use of the skills. Roles are rotated so that everyone experiences each of the three tasks.

Co-counseling for Sharpening Skills

Co-counseling is an excellent way to hone your counseling tools. Co-counseling is an exercise in which two people agree to meet for a particular time period and alternately counsel each other and give feedback to each other. For example, David and Ellen agree to meet for 90 minutes on a particular day at the coffee shop. During this 90-minute period, David first counsels Ellen (on a specific problem of hers) for 30 minutes, stops and asks her for feedback. Then Ellen does the same for David.

In the context of your peer counseling training course, co-counseling is a useful method for practicing counseling techniques, role playing, developing friendships with fellow counselors, and confronting the possible problems of peer counseling. Your partner can be a classmate, peer counselor, friend, spouse, acquaintance, or anyone with whom you can meet regularly. We suggest that you spend one or two hours meeting with your partner each week. You can play both roles during this time or just the role of counselor or client and then switch roles later in the week. You should feel free to discuss anything you and your partner feel comfortable talking about, and you may utilize any techniques that you think are appropriate.

Invariably, participants in our counseling classes find co-counseling to be one of the most useful aspects of their training. Here are one person's comments:

> My experience with co-counseling was very positive! As the client, I gained a very warm, positive outlet for my problems. I could consistently and constructively deal with my situations in the supportive atmosphere of my counselor-peer. As a counselor, I was able to practice the various techniques which we had experimented with in class. I feel that I improved many of my counseling skills, particularly active listening. My co-counseling partner was a close friend, and through our counseling experience we added a new dimension to our relationship by establishing a very positive pattern of interaction.

Try co-counseling this week and see if you share the feelings of this person. If you are using this book as part of a peer counseling training course, ask your instructor to set aside some time at the beginning of your next class meeting to discuss everyone's co-counseling experiences.

References

Berne, E. *Games People Play: The Psychology of Human Relationships.* New
        York: Random House, 1964.
Durlak, J.A. Comparative effectiveness of paraprofessional and profes-
        sional helpers. *Psychological Bulletin* 86 (1979): 80–92.
Okun, B. *Effective Helping: Interviewing and Counseling Techniques.* North
        Scituate, MA: Duxbury Press, 1976.

Chapter 2. Listening Skills

2.

Listening Skills

Listening skills have broad applications. Many of you may find that you use them quite naturally. Good listening is about 50 percent of counseling, and you should find it a useful tool with family, with friends, and at work. Good listening is a means of support, of helping another person explore what s/he is thinking and feeling. Good listening, therefore, may help another person solve or clarify a problem.

A word of caution about what good listening is NOT: It is not doing all the talking. It is not giving advice. It is not manipulating. It is not taking the responsibility for the other person's problem and its solution.

Keep in mind that this book does not teach you how to become a therapist. Listening is only part of helping, but it is a crucial part.

We hope this section will demystify the skills of active listening. These skills can be defined, taught, and learned. One does not have to be superhuman to grasp them. In fact, some of you may find you have acquired one or more of the skills quite naturally, while others need to be learned. What is most important is a sincere desire to understand other people accurately and to be more aware of these skills, skills that do facilitate interpersonal interactions.

The material in this chapter is based on the work of Alan Ivey. Materials used in composing this chapter were written by Andrew Gottlieb, Peggy Smith, Peter Salovey, and Vincent D'Andrea. Gottlieb is responsible for the outlines in the chapter, and the remaining material is based on teaching manuals prepared variously by Gottlieb, Smith, Salovey, and D'Andrea, all adapted from Ivey.

FIRST SKILL: NONVERBAL AND MINIMUM VERBAL ATTENDING BEHAVIOR

Nonverbal attending skills are the foundation on which all the other skills are based. Sometimes called "the art of listening with your mouth closed," this set of skills will help you be a more effective and empathetic listener.

Although we are not consciously aware of it much of the time, our body language is a critical part of how we relate and what we communicate. Of particular interest in this regard are eye contact and body posture.

Good eye contact is important but complex. Different cultures and subcultures, even different individuals, have different "standards" for good eye contact. Be sensitive to another person's comfort; good eye contact says "I am with you" but is not invasive. With practice, you will come to know when you are engaging in appropriate eye contact.

Just as eye contact varies from person to person or culture to culture, so does *personal space.* Being the right distance from another person is part of appropriate posture. In addition, an open, relaxed stance without extraneous, distracting movement is part of an ideal posture. Once again, it is important to remember to "be you" and to stay with a posture with which you feel comfortable.

The last element of basic attending is verbal following. Verbal following is different from ordinary conversation, where each person may be pursuing his/her own line of thought. In using verbal following, you must let the other person determine the course of conversation while you simply respond or ask questions. Keep interruptions to a minimum and avoid "topic jumping" or changing the subject. Although it may be difficult at first, also avoid giving advice or judging the other person's motives, thoughts, and behavior. Avoid sharing your personal experiences or "comparing notes." Remember, you are not responsible for solving the problem!

Summary—*Nonverbal Attending*

1. Eye Contact—Look at the person most of the time.
    —Communicate caring: "I am with you, I'm listening."
2. Body Posture—Be comfortable, be relaxed, lean forward slightly.
    —Be aware of personal distance.
    —Avoid distracting gestures or fidgeting.
3. Facial Expressions—Don't be a brick wall!
    —Display appropriate empathy
4. Following the Counselee's Lead—Don't interrupt, don't change the subject.
    —Listen, don't talk.
    —Don't share experiences: "Oh, I've been there . . ."

SECOND SKILL: THE OPEN QUESTION

This section concentrates on what we call "the open invitation to talk." In this section we speak of "open" and and "closed" questions. Open questions are questions that encourage a person to talk without feeling defensive. Closed questions are the kind asked by a census taker, a doctor, a lawyer, or a parent: in most cases, it is understood by both parties to the conversation that very specific information is requested and that the answer to the question will be very short. Examples of closed questions are: "Did you do that last Monday?" "Is it true that there are three people living here?" "How long have you been here?"

There is nothing wrong with using a closed question if you need to—and if the counselee is amenable. However, such questions do tend to cut down communication, and if used unadvisedly they can lead to frustration for the counselee. Especially frustrating are questions that begin with "have you tried" or "do you think" or "what do you think," since such questions are really sneaky ways of giving advice or airing your opinion.

Open questions, on the other hand, are phrased for the purpose of exploration. An open question allows the counselee to direct the flow of conversation, to bring up more data and deal with it in more depth. Open questions serve several functions: they can begin the interview; they may encourage the counselee to elaborate on a point or explore a point further; they may elicit specific examples to clarify what is being said; and they may allow the counselee to focus on his/her feelings.

Open questions often do something further: they lead the conversation into a more personal, here-and-now, "internal" mode in which the counselee assumes responsibility for feelings and behavior. This contrasts with the anecdotal, "external" style of conversation, in which others are blamed for what is happening.

As the counselee is allowed to speak more personally, there is a greater chance s/he will be able to find solutions to problems.

Example: Internal mode

Counselor: How are you today?

Counselee: I'm feeling kind of down, like everything is going wrong. I'm not much fun to be with . . .

Example: External Mode

Counselor: How are you today?

Counselee: I'd be okay if it weren't for the people at my house. They get on my nerves and make me feel like climbing the walls.

"How," "What," and "Could you say more about" are appropriate
beginnings for open questions. Examples of open questions are: "What
could you have done then?" and "How did it happen that you were there
at that time?" One especially good kind of question is, "What would you
like to have happen?" or "If you could have things just the way you wanted, what would they be like?" This type of question gives the counselee
permission to fantasize, and answering the question often triggers a new
insight, a new alternative.

Be careful of using "why." Beginning a question with "why" often
puts the other person on the defensive. It seems to call for an explanation,
a justification. Using "why" is good if one is asking how something works
("Why does the apple fall down?") but it is not very effective in other
cases. Many times, a "why" question can be rephrased so that it asks essentially the same thing but does not elicit the defensive response. For example, try saying to yourself, "Why did you do that?" and then "How did
it happen that you did that?" and see which sounds better to you. Or compare "Why are you here now?" with "What brings you here now?"

As a peer counselor, you need to be sensitive to the "temperature"
of your interview. If the counselee seems anxious or if conversation is
dying, open questions can stimulate the interchange. If you, the counselor,
are feeling flooded with information, use closed questions to cool down
and slow the flow. But be careful: some questions that sound like open
questions are really "coolers"—"Exactly what kinds of sexual activities
do you engage in with your spouse?" is an example. On the other hand,
some seemingly closed questions can unleash a flood; for example, "Are
you thinking about a divorce now?"

Minimal encouragements also move the conversation along. They
may be either verbal (such as "Go on," "Uh-huh," "I see," "Yes," or
a repetition of the last few words the counselee has said—for example,
"So little time . . . ?") or nonverbal (such as nodding, smiling). The important part is that they be brief and natural to you. Again, by experimenting
you should be able to find your own best style. Many times an encouragement or the simple restatement of something already said has a powerful
effect, so do not be afraid to limit yourself to the use of minimal encouragements if you want to keep the conversation going.

Although we do not often think of it in this way, *silence* is a useful
minimal encouragement. Practice using silence instead of asking a question and see what occurs! Being patient and not asking questions to fill
silence allows the counselee to think, talk, and explore.

Summary: Open Questions

AN OPEN QUESTION is one that:

1. can't be answered by one or two words.
2. usually starts with "how" or "what."
3. encourages the person to talk.

A CLOSED QUESTION is one that:

1. can be answered by "yes" or "no" or by one word.
2. starts with "is," "do," "have," etc.
3. discourages the person from talking and slows the flow of conversation.

USES OF OPEN QUESTIONS:

1. Beginning a Conversation
   — "What would you like to talk about?"
   — "What's going on with you?"
2. Clarifying and Elaborating
   — "How is this a problem for you?"
   — "What do you mean by __?"
   — "What is it about the situation that bothers you?"
3. Working with Feelings
   — "How do you feel about that?" (Make sure you get a feelings answer!)
   — "What is (a feeling) like for you?"
   — "How do you feel right now?" (Helps people bring feelings into the here and now.)
   — "What would you like to say to him/her?" (Helps people get in touch with feelings about other people.)
4. Problem Solving
   — "What options do you have?"
   — "What have you thought of doing?"
   — "How do you feel about each of these options?"
   — "What's the best thing that could happen?"
   — "What's the worst thing that could happen?"
   — "What do you think will actually happen?"

DON'T:
   — ask questions to satisfy your own curiosity.
   — ask "why . . . ?"
   — ask long complicated questions with lots of dependent clauses and other grammatical junk.
   — give advice in a question (*e.g.* "Have you tried talking to him?")

DO:

— keep questions clear and simple.

— keep questions in the here and now and with the person.
  (Don't counsel someone who's not in the room.)

THIRD SKILL: PARAPHRASING

Each of you has observed the use of the paraphrase and has probably used paraphrasing, perhaps without noticing it. Newscasters often repeat in their own words what was said during interviews. When you take notes in a class, you probably paraphrase the instructor's lecture. When you send a telegram, you condense the message into as few words as possible—again, a form of paraphrase. A paraphrase reflects the essence of the verbal content; it expresses briefly the facts of the situation, but pares away details. This skill is a bit sophisticated, taking more concentration and more practice than the open questions described earlier.

The paraphrase has three main functions: (1) A paraphrase acts as a perception check, to verify that you have understood what the other person has said. This is especially helpful if you are confused, or if you feel you may be identifying too closely with the person's situation. If you have heard correctly, the counselee may respond to your paraphrase by saying, "Yes," or "That's it," or "Right." (2) A paraphrase may clarify what the counselee has said, especially if you pick up trends, set up dichotomies, or list priorities. As an active listener with some objectivity, you may see these trends and priorities more clearly than the counselee. (3) A good paraphrase can demonstrate that you have what Carl Rogers calls "accurate empathy." Accurate empathy is a nonjudgmental reflection of another person's world view; it is "walking a mile in another's shoes."

It is important that a paraphrase be brief; it should almost always be shorter than what was originally said. Make the paraphrase tentative, so that if it is not right, the counselee feels free to correct you. It is crucial that you know when you have not heard correctly. You might end with "Is that right?" or something similar. Watch out for endings like "isn't it" or "aren't you," since they turn the paraphrase into a closed question. Standard openings for a paraphrase are: "In other words . . ." or "So I hear you saying . . ." You will discover other openings with which you feel comfortable.

What is especially tricky about paraphrasing is that if you parrot back exactly what you heard, you are not being terribly helpful and may even be irritating; on the other hand, if you add too much of your own perceptions, you may be putting words into the other person's mouth. The former is called a "restatement"; the latter is an "interpretation." While both restatements and interpretations have their appropriate place, they are both quite advanced tools and neither of them should take the place of the paraphrase. With a little practice, you will be able to tell the difference between restating, paraphrasing, and interpreting.

Summary

A PARAPHRASE is a brief, tentative statement that reflects the essence of what the person has just said.

A GOOD PARAPHRASE:

1. captures the essence of what the person said. It leaves out the details.
2. conveys the same meaning, but usually uses different words. (Sometimes, though, the wording used by the counselee will be so apt that you will use some of the same words.)
3. is *brief.* That is, your paraphrase should be shorter than what the person said.
4. is clear and concise. Your paraphrase should help clarify things, not confuse them.
5. is tentative. You want the counselee to feel comfortable about disagreeing with or correcting your paraphrase if it is inaccurate.

REASONS FOR USING PARAPHRASE:

1. *to check perceptions*
   When you paraphrase what you think the person has said, he or she can react to your paraphrase and tell you whether it is accurate or inaccurate.
2. *to clarify what the person has said*
   Hearing an accurate paraphrase of what they have just said helps counselees clarify for themselves what they are thinking and feeling. Often a paraphrase will bring up new thoughts and feelings.
3. *to give accurate empathy*
   An accurate paraphrase demonstrates to the person that you are listening, and that you understand. In effect, a good paraphrase says, "I am with you."

DO:

— Keep it brief and keep it tentative!
— Use standard openings like:
   — "Let me see if I've got it right . . ."
   — "Sounds like . . ."

— "I think I hear you saying . . ."

— "So, in other words . . ."

— End by asking, "Is that right?"

THE CONTINUUM

restatement	paraphrase	interpretation
(OK)	(Best!)	(Avoid, for now)

FOURTH SKILL: WORKING WITH FEELINGS

Working with feelings is difficult for two reasons. First, people are taught not to discuss feelings openly; feelings are too private, or too embarrassing, or too powerful to deal with directly. Second, partly as a result of this training, what a person says may not coincide with—or may not be "congruent"—with what s/he is communicating nonverbally, and nonverbal communication is more directly a reflection of feelings. Nevertheless, a timely reflection of feeling can be quite useful, since it gives the counselee "permission" to own his/her feelings—it gives validation to the emotional as well as the cognitive expression.

Since talking about feelings is a limited experience, our vocabulary may be equally limited. When working with the feelings of a counselee, avoid pejorative or evaluative terms, and stick to more specific, simple, expressive words. This is a sensitive area, and you will want to refrain from interpreting what you sense or putting the counselee on the defensive.

There is a vast difference between saying "you feel . . ." and "you feel that. . . ." The former is a genuine reflection of feeling, while the latter moves into more cognitive areas. Say to yourself, "I feel happy" and then, "I feel that today is going to be a happy day," and you will notice the difference.

It is of paramount importance to notice both verbal and nonverbal expressions when working with feelings. (Sometimes you may even get two dissimilar verbal or two incongruous nonverbal messages.) While you may not always want to comment on discrepancies you notice, it is helpful to use this information as a cue for your own behavior. Be sensitive, again, to when it would be appropriate to point out congruence or lack of it—and when it would be judgmental or threatening.

The four basic steps in working with feelings are:

1. Identifying the feelings
2. Defining and clarifying the feelings
3. Acknowledging the feelings and taking responsibility for them
4. Dealing with feelings

Identifying the Feelings

There are three ways to discover what someone is feeling. You want to be able to use all three and to learn when each is most appropriate.

Ask Feelings Questions

The main question is, "How do you feel?" Sometimes it is more effective to substitute "What emotions do you feel in relation to that?" Try to help the counselee stick to the here and now. Talking about feelings in the past tends to turn into storytelling. Even when the situation deals with a past event, the counselee has here-and-now feelings about what happened.

It is essential that you get feelings for answers rather than thoughts. Statements that begin with "I feel that" or "I feel like" usually are expressions of a thought. Statements that begin with "I feel" usually express feelings.

If the counselee gives you a nonfeeling answer, paraphrase it and then ask the feeling question again.

Counselor: How do you feel about that?

Counselee: Well, I fell like I should be angry at her.

Counselor: So you think you *should* be mad at her, but how do you actually *feel?* What emotion or emotions are you experiencing?

Counselee: I'm pissed-off at her and frustrated that I haven't told her.

Paraphrase Spoken Feelings

It's not always necessary to pry feelings out of people. Some people express their feelings quite openly. When someone does express feelings, it's a good idea to paraphrase them. This tends to clarify for the person what s/he is expressing.

Counselee: I get so angry when my sister comes to visit for the holidays and all she does is complain.

Counselor: So you're feeling angry, is that right?

Reflecting Feelings

Reflecting feelings is one of the most effective methods for bringing up feelings, but it is also one of the trickiest and most easily abused. The term "reflecting feelings" is slightly misleading, because what you actually reflect are a person's nonverbal expressions of feelings.

For example, a woman comes in for counseling and you notice that her face and body seem very tense. There are two ways you could react:

1) "You seem to be angry."
2) "You seem to be very tense."

The first response reflects a feeling but is an interpretation. The woman might be nervous or scared and not angry at all. The second response is much better. It makes note of the actual nonverbal message the woman is expressing, and it does not make a judgment or interpretation; it is not a conclusion in any sense. One of the most effective ways of using reflection of feelings is to reflect the counselee's nonverbal messages, and then ask, "What are you feeling?" This opens the conversation rather than closing it.

Remember that reflection of feelings deals with emotions, while paraphrase deals with content and data. Sometimes the two may seem very similar, particularly if you are talking about an emotional situation. Discuss the differences with your trainers until you are sure you understand them. When you are role playing as the counselee, use a situation you have lots of feelings about.

Defining and Clarifying Feelings

Once you've elicited a feeling such as "I'm upset," it is important to find out what that means to the person. This process of definition is particularly important when the feeling expressed is a "global" one, such as "I'm depressed," or "I'm lost," or "I feel good."

Good questions for defining and clarifying feelings are:

—   What does [being mad] mean to you?
—   What is being [nervous] like for you?
—   How does that feel physically?
—   What other ways would you use to describe what you're feeling?

What often happens as you define and clarify feelings is that other feelings come up. These also can then be defined and explored. Don't assume that you know what it means if counselees say, "I'm depressed, angry, sad, down, confused," etc. Define and clarify what their feelings, words, or expressions actually mean in *their* world.

Counselee: I feel depressed.

Counselor: How do you experience that depression?

Counselee: It's like a numbness, a not wanting to do anything.

Counselor: So you feel numb?

Counselee: Yes, I feel like there are all these feelings inside me and yet I can't really feel them.

Counselor: (stays silent)

Counselee: You know, it just feels so numb.

Counselor: Could you describe the numbness?

Counselee: It feels like there's a void within me. It's empty . . . no, it's not, it's full of feelings . . . but they're dangerous . . . they need to be kept under control.

Counselor: What are those dangerous feelings?

Acknowledging the Feelings

In order to deal effectively with his or her feelings, a person must first acknowledge and take responsibility for those feelings. Many people tend to place their feelings outside of themselves, saying things such as, "It makes me feel" or "He made me feel." Although feelings may be associated with external events, they are *not* "out there"; they are within the person. Compare these statements:

"You made me angry when you slept with Cleopatra."

vs.

"I felt angry when you slept with Cleopatra."

The first statement suggests causation, the second, correlation. Statements that begin: "It makes me feel,"

"She makes me feel," or

"One would feel" signal that the person is not owning or taking responsibility for his or her feelings. Statements beginning with "I feel" generally indicate that the person *is* acknowledging and taking responsibility for his or her feelings.

All of this is well and good, but what can a counselor do if the person is *not* taking responsibility?

Counselee: You know, when you're working at a job you don't like, you just can't find any energy for other things. You feel bummed out and you feel disgusted, you know?

Counselor: So you feel bummed out and disgusted, is that right?

Counselee: Yeh, you just can't seem to break out of it, you know?

Counselor: When you say, "You can't seem to break out of it," do you mean "I can't seem to break out of it?"

Counselee: Yes, I just can't get rid of these feelings.

Counselor: What makes you want to get rid of those feelings? etc.

What the counselor here does is first to paraphrase the counselee's statement in a way which puts the responsibility on the counselee. Like many
people, the person being counseled doesn't recognize the distinction and
continues to say "you." The counselor then asks a closed question that
encourages the counselee to acknowledge the feelings personally.

This step is a tricky part of working with feelings. It is important
not to challenge the counselee too directly, but sometimes people simply
refuse to acknowledge their own feelings. When this happens, it may be
necessary to take a different approach (such as a problem-solving or a fantasy approach). It is not useful to force your point of view on the counselee. It is often more constructive to move past or around the issue.

Dealing with the Feelings

Once you have elicited the feelings, defined and clarified them, and have
gotten the person to acknowledge them, then what? The first part of dealing with feelings is to place the feelings in context ("What thoughts and
events are these feelings correlated with?"). Good questions are:

— What brings up this feeling of ——— for you?
— What's the situation when you experience these feelings?

People usually don't experience just one feeling at a time. The question
"What other feelings are associated with ——— for you?" will often bring
up many related feelings.

It can also be useful to relate thought to feelings. A question such
as, "What do you say to yourself when you are feeling ———?" is helpful.

An important part of dealing with feelings is to get the counselee
to express feelings that s/he had previously found difficult to articulate.
Examples of effective questions are:

— How would you like to express this feeling?
— What would you like to say to that person?

It may help to have the counselee pretend that s/he is speaking directly
to the person to whom s/he is expressing the feeling. So rather than have
him or her say, "I'd say that I'm angry and that I never want him to do
it again," have the person stay in the present and say "I'm angry and I
don't want you to do that again!"

If the counselee has difficulty or is uncomfortable with this, questions
such as these may help:

— What's the best (worst) thing that could happen?
— What would you like to see happen?

— How have you dealt with this before?

— What could you do to feel better?

If the situation depicted seems hopeless and the counselee sees no possibility for improvement, then s/he may be really stuck. In such cases, acknowledging this reality and their feelings about it may be more helpful than encouraging a possibly premature course of action.

Finally, the best preparation for working with feelings is to deal honestly with your own. This can be approached by role-play practice or co-counseling sessions specifically devoted to exploring your personal style of dealing with feelings.

Summary: Working with Feelings

Working with feelings is an *essential* part of counseling. It is difficult to explore alternative solutions to problems until the feelings surrounding the problem itself are clarified, vented, and dealt with.

1. Identify the feelings
   a. Ask feeling questions
      — How do you feel about that?
      — How does that make you feel?
      — How do you feel?
      — What feelings does it bring up in you?
   b. Paraphrase spoken feelings
      — So, you are feeling ———, is that right?
      — Sounds like you are really ———.
      — You must feel pretty ———.
2. Define and clarify feelings
   a. Elicit feelings that accompany the one that is primarily expressed
   b. Discover the individual's personal experience of a given feeling (What does the person mean when s/he says, "I feel X"?)
3. Acknowledge the feelings
   a. Assist the counselee in taking responsibility for his/her feelings
   b. Reinforce the counselee for stating feelings in a direct, personal way (e.g., "I feel X" rather than "I feel that one should feel X in this situation, don't you?")
4. Deal with feelings
   a. Relate thoughts to feelings
   b. Further express feelings
   c. Help the counselee express "repressed" feelings through best/worst fantasizing and other open questions

FIFTH SKILL: SUMMARIZATION

A counselor's summary is like a combination of one or more paraphrases and often includes a reflection of feeling. In addition, it tends to cover a relatively long period of time—several statements of the counselee, perhaps even more than one session. A summary attempts to capture the essence of what the person said, to tie together content and feeling, to put things in perspective, and to identify important trends, conflicts, or possible decisions. Even so, it is a good idea to keep the summary brief; being concise leads to less confusion.

With summarization, more than with any other skill, there is the possibility of distortion or interpretation, so be especially sensitive. Constantly check with the counselee to verify that you are not adding to or subtracting from what s/he has said. Be tentative in your remarks.

As you sum up what you have observed as the two of you talked, emphasize the positive aspects of the situation: what has been done, what could be done, what the possibilities for the future are. Dwelling on the negative aspects rarely leads to constructive action, so while you may not be able to ignore them, do not limit yourself to enumerating them!

A good summary has several functions: (1) It acts as a perception check (and is especially helpful if you find you *strongly* identify with—or cannot *at all* identify with—the problem). (2) It directs the course of future interaction, decisions, and planning. Again, you should therefore BE POSITIVE. (3) It clarifies the situation, reflects trends, points out conflicts, and lists priorities.

When should you use a summary? A summary is useful after main events in a counseling session—for instance, after you have explored feelings and are about to go into problem solving.

—   A summary is also good at the end of a counseling session. It ties things together for the person, and gives him or her a clear image of the session.

—   A summary is useful when shifting modes. For instance, after you've found out what the person considers to be the problem, it is useful to summarize and then go on, using an open question and/or exploring feelings.

After a good summary there may be a pause or a sense of "what now?" This indicates that you are ready to move into new territory, and an open question is appropriate at that point. Learn to be sensitive to this forward movement; such sensitivity is one of your goals as an active listener.

Summary

A summary is a larger paraphrase. A summary should capture the essence of what the person said. Like a paraphrase, it is brief and tentative. A summary serves many of the same purposes as a paraphrase. It:

— serves as a perception check

— demonstrates accurate empathy

— clarifies for you and the talker

A summary is not a sequential recounting of what has been talked about. A good summary takes what has been said and puts it into a logical, useable form. It mentions both the thoughts and the feelings and ties them together. A summary helps people see where they've gone and where they're going.

INTEGRATION OF SKILLS

Integration is putting all your skills together and using each when appropriate. This is where the art and the finesse of counseling has its fullest expression.

OPEN QUESTIONS turn on the flow of conversation. They encourage people to talk. They can also direct the conversation.

PARAPHRASING tends to interrupt the flow. Because a paraphrase reflects what a person has just said, it focuses the conversation. Paraphrases fit together well with open questions; first you paraphrase, then you ask an open question.

EXPLORING FEELINGS is useful after the initial problem has been presented. Sometimes, exploring feelings will be a very effective method of counseling. Some people and some types of problems respond less to feelings-oriented counseling, and in these situations you will want to take a different approach. Remember, use what works for the counselee.

REVIEW OF CHAPTER 2: LISTENING SKILLS

A. NONVERBAL AND MINIMAL VERBAL ATTENDING
    — Eye contact
    — Body posture
    — Concerned facial expression and tone (no brick wall)
    — Verbal following (don't topic-jump)
    — Minimal verbal encouragers
    — Head nodding

B. ASKING OPEN QUESTIONS
    — Begin with "how" or "what"
    — Encourage expression rather than yes/no answers
    — Can be used for clarifying, elaborating, working with feelings, and problem solving
    — Should be kept clear and simple
    — Should not begin with "why" or be leading questions

C. PARAPHRASING
    — Essence of what person said
    — Brief and tentative
    — Checking perceptions
    — Clarifying for talker
    — Giving accurate empathy

D. WORKING WITH FEELINGS
    1. Identifying the feelings
    — ask feelings questions and *get* feelings answer
    — paraphrase spoken feelings and reflect unspoken feelings
    2. Defining and clarifying feelings
    3. Acknowledging and taking responsibility for the feelings
    4. Dealing with the feelings

E. SUMMARIZING
    — Larger paraphrase that captures the essence of what has been said and puts it into a logical and usable order.
    — Brief and tentative: "Is that right?"
    — Good for closure
    — Good for shifting modes

F. Integrating Skills
    — Open questions encourage talking and can be directive
    — Paraphrase slows down conversational flow and focuses conversation
    — Feelings should be explored before problem-solving begins
    — Summarization helps to wrap things up

A FINAL WORD ON THE COUNSELING SITUATION

The guiding philosophy for peer counseling is that the counselee is in charge; you are there to help your counselees deal with their emotions and find their own solutions. There are times, however, when something goes wrong in the counseling process itself, and it becomes necessary to talk about it—namely, when you find yourself becoming frustrated, anxious, or angry. Dealing with such a situation requires assertiveness on the part of the counselor, but it is essential that it be dealt with in order to preserve the counseling situation. You can't be an effective counselor if you are wishing you were somewhere else.

Here are some typical situations that make some counselors uneasy:

1. You feel that you are going around in circles and not getting any-
    where. The usual way of dealing with this situation is to pick one area
    to concentrate on and not let the counselee get away from it. But if
    it gets to be too much of a problem, it's a good idea to talk about
    it with the counselee. Expressing your feelings ("I'm getting really
    frustrated because . . .") will get you farther than if you sound as
    though you are accusing the other person ("We're not getting any-
    where because you . . .").

2. The counselee starts crying. This can be an essential part of releasing
    pent-up emotions. Some people find that it helps to reassure the per-
    son that it's okay to cry. Sometimes touching the person, or even giv-
    ing him/her a shoulder to cry on, can be appropriate, depending on
    your style and the situation.

3. The counselee becomes hysterical. Talking to the person calmly can
    sometimes help the person settle down. At times, however, the person
    is so distraught that s/he cannot talk to you at all. In this situation,
    you can stay with the person until s/he settles down and is able to
    talk. You may want to ask whether the counselee prefers to be alone
    for a while or wishes to continue the session at a later time. In any
    case, try to ascertain whether the person wants you to stay. Be pre-
    pared for a rather lengthy session.

    > If you are counseling on the telephone and the person cannot
    > calm down, ask whether it would not be better to talk again in
    > a short while. Try to get the person's phone number so you can
    > return the call in fifteen or twenty minutes. Gently tell the per-
    > son that you cannot talk while s/he is hysterical and that you
    > would be willing either to stay on the line while s/he calms
    > down or to call back at a later time.

4. You are attracted to the counselee or s/he is attracted to you, or both;
    or the person is lonely and would like to have you as a friend. You
    don't have to deal with this situation immediately unless it is getting
    in the way of your counseling. But at some point, you will probably
    have to clarify the nature of your relationship. If the person is coming
    back to see you (or will call you again), and you have the feeling that
    it is not for counseling, you have to decide if this is something you
    are willing to do. If so, it is a good idea to clarify the relationship and
    not get stuck between being the person's counselor (which is some-
    thing of a position of power, even in peer counseling) and being
    his/her friend.

5. A person wants to talk to you to have someone to talk to, rather than to work on problems. If you want to accept this, fine. But if you don't, you can be firm about being willing to talk about problems, but not being willing just to talk. If the person starts attacking you ("I called this place because I thought you cared about people, and here you won't talk to me!"), a good rule of thumb is: DON'T DEFEND YOURSELF. It will only prolong the situation. Instead, keep repeating yourself until the person gets the message.

TAKE CARE OF YOURSELF. AVOID BURN-OUT.

References and Recommended Reading

Egan, G. *The Skilled Helper.* Monterey, CA: Brooks Cole Publishing Co., 1975.

Carkhuff, R. *Helping and Human Relations,* Vol. 1 New York: Holt, Rinehart, and Winston, 1969.

Ivey, A.E. *Microcounseling: Innovations in Interviewing Training.* Springfield, IL: Charles C. Thomas, 1974

Chapter 3. Counseling Skills

3

COUNSELING SKILLS

This chapter concerns itself with techniques usually thought of as beyond listening skills alone: contracts and the contracting process, decision-making skills, confrontation, and interpretation. An understanding of these techniques helps put listening and counseling skills in perspective. As we have taught them, they give the peer counselor additional options, particularly in extended counseling situations and in working with people in crisis. The case illustrations and exercises are designed to give the beginning counselor some guidelines for the types of situations in which these advanced skills might be introduced.

OVERVIEW

Counseling is a process, usually of short duration, involving exploration and discussion of values, beliefs, and attitudes, with self-rewarding behavior as its goal. It is largely a cognitive process. It sometimes involves getting new information to help in problem solving, and its feasibility and outcome very much depend on the individual's intellectual, social-emotional, and maturational level.

To the extent that counseling is a problem-solving process (Krumboltz), it often involves: examining assumptions about oneself and one's world view, potential, ability, etc.; confronting new perspectives on a particular issue; and confronting disregarded or distorted aspects of a problem, such as neglected communication.

Problems best suited to counseling approaches include:

1. Dilemmas—situations where there are confusing choices, value conflicts, or unclear values.

2. Decision making—choosing among various alternatives by clarifying and exploring values, beliefs, and goals, or by verifying information and getting new information. (This process is presented in detail in the section on decision making.)
3. Situational problems—temporary breakdowns of coping skills, as well as challenges to values and belief systems. Examples include relationship problems, acute illness, or sudden loss.
4. Bad feelings associated with dilemmas, impending decisions, or situational problems. These feelings usually center around anxiety or guilt; it is expected that as the situation is resolved, the negative feelings will also subside.

Advice in Counseling:

Unless specific, factual information can be given that is appropriate within the context of the counseling session, giving advice is generally useless. This is so largely because of the types of problems usually brought to counselors:

1. Problems in living: the counselee's experience is more relevant to the solutions than are the counselor's opinions.
2. Situational problems: the counselee's own knowledge of the situation is of most use for predicting the results of any course of action.
3. Longstanding issues: the facts are usually to be found in the person's experience and are usually known only to him/her.

Also, since the counselee's autonomy is a major goal of counseling, offering advice is clearly inconsistent with that goal.

"Responsibility" in Counseling

The counselee expects certain things to occur in the counseling session. He/she expects that the counselor will help him/her:

1. Explore and define problem areas.
2. Gain an increased understanding of his/her beliefs and the relationship between beliefs, feelings, and actions.
3. Act for him/herself on the basis of that increased understanding.

Professional counselors (licensed, credentialed health and mental health personnel) have a certain degree of responsibility to meet these expectations, as determined by explicit agreements (professional, societal, legal). Nonprofessional helpers must define their role and the extent to which they will agree to assume responsibility. This issue is further discussed in the following section on Contracts.

Reference

Krumboltz, J. Excerpts from a talk given at a Counseling and Psychological Services seminar. Stanford University, 1978. (Unpublished communication).

CONTRACTS AND THE CONTRACTING PROCESS

In this book, the term "contract" is used in three different ways: self-management contracts, contracts for exploration, and contracts regarding counselor responsibility. Almost all behavioral and humanistic psychotherapies emphasize contracting as an essential part of the change process.

Self-Management Contracts

Originally developed as a tool of behavior therapists (Homme, 1970), self-management contracting is based on theories of reinforcement, which state that rewarded behavior tends to be repeated. A self-management contract is a specific agreement between two people that emerges from a study of target behavior. The behavior is studied from the point of view of its antecedents (A), the behavior itself (B), and its consequences (C). Focused strategies of intervention can be developed on the basis of "A-B-C"ing such sequences (example on page 40). There is often no punishment if the individual does not meet the terms of a contract, but the reinforcement is withheld and given only after performance of the agreed-on target behavior.

Contracts may be informal (e.g., "If you do A, I'll do B"), or formal, written agreements spelling out the specifics of behavior, reward, and conditions for fulfillment of the contract.

General conditions for self-management contracts include:

1. The contract should be fair.
2. The terms should be clear.
3. The contract should generally be positive, stressing desired change rather than prohibitions.
4. The procedures should be systematic and consistent.
5. At least one other person should participate.
6. The contract should have a legal objective (i.e., it should not specify immoral or antisocial behavior).
7. All parties must agree to the terms.

A Sample Self-Management Contract

Self: Pinocchio

Goal: To reduce my lying   Other: Jiminy Cricket

Agreement

Self: I agree to lie not more than once during each day.

Other: Jiminy Cricket agrees to praise me whenever he sees me telling the truth and will not play with me after I've lied more than once that day.

Consequences

Provided by Self:

If I stick to the above agreement, at the end of each week (ending Sat. at 6 p.m.) I will reward myself with an ice cream. If I do not keep the above agreement during a particular week, I will clean Gepetto's workshop that Saturday evening (no ice cream).

Provided by Other:

Jiminy Cricket will (1) praise me for telling the truth, (2) ignore me when I am lying, and (3) keep me company each week that I keep the contract.

For each week that I fail to keep the contract, Jiminy is authorized to (1) insist that I go to school and (2) limit my access to ice cream and candy.

Signed: Pinocchio

Jiminy Cricket

Review Date: June 10, 1983   Witness: Gepetto

Adapted from Mahoney, M. J., and C. E. Thoresen, *Self-Control: Power to the Person*. Monterey, CA: Brooks/Cole, 1974, p.53.

The use of self-management contracts is widespread in education. It is common for teachers and school counselors to write up contracts with students. In some school systems, parents are taught how to formulate contracts with their children and other family members. Transient behavior and habit problems lend themselves well to this approach. In general, the self-management (A-B-C) approach is best suited for working with specific behavior as opposed to diffuse thoughts and feelings. For example, undesirable habits, problems with social skills, phobias, and sexual problems lend themselves well to this kind of contracting.

Contracts for Exploration

Contracting can also be used as part of a process of exploration, not necessarily as an end in itself. For purposes of this discussion, counseling as a process can be divided into various phases:

1. **Attending Phase.** "Being with" the other person, using basic attending skills (BAS) for understanding and developing a relationship.
2. **Responding Self-Exploration Phase.** The counselor, responding with empathy and understanding through use of BAS, establishes rapport and facilitates self-exploration. Contracting may come into play in this phase. Goals and objectives may be established.
3. **Integrative–Interpretative Phase.** Self-understanding is enhanced by piecing together data, identifying themes and patterns (paraphrasing, interpretation, summarizing). Insight may emerge; self-rewarding behavior may ensue.
4. **Action Phase.** The person, acting on new knowledge, begins behavior change; in a collaborative manner, counselor and counselee work out specific contracts for exploration or behavior change.
5. **Resolution Phase.** Behavior changes successively approximate the goals set through contracting. There may be exploration of other resources with appropriate referral; mutual agreement to terminate counseling work emerges.

Contracts in phases 2, 3, and 4 may be for awareness or change. Contracts for awareness involve an agreement to simply observe behavior, and are often in the nature of experiments to discover elements about behavior that are out of awareness. This process may enable the person to act for him or herself on the basis of increased understanding, or it may help the counselor and client to form reasonable, "do-able" contracts for action. The contracting process becomes one of exploration. Here are a few examples of contracts for exploration:

A woman reported discomfort in greeting other people. She was asked if she was willing to say "hello" to the first ten people she saw the next day, whether she knew them or not. She did, and reported that it got easier to do, and that she became aware of a lot of "chatter in her head" about fears and embarrassment. The avoidance behavior of not greeting people was protecting her from confronting the thoughts, which were successively clarified and examined for their probability. She became more comfortable socially.

A young man reported problems with time management. A "time pie"* was drawn, and he agreed to follow the time-blocking laid out in the pie. To his surprise, he had about four hours a day "left over." This "gap" was related to a general tendency to overestimate the time needed to do things, so that he always felt pressed for time. By challenging some mild feelings of discomfort, he was able to find more relaxation time and get all his work done.

A student reported "freezing up" in small group discussions when she was asked questions by the instructor. She was beginning to question her intelligence, memory, and competence. Among other things, she was asked to track the behavior throughout the day for seven days.** A look at her reporting showed that: (1) the problem diminished for four days (not unusual); (2) it was more apt to occur when she was reporting on material she had already studied some time ago; (3) the events themselves lasted less than a minute (a surprise to her); and (4) she saw a pattern of consistently poor preparation for the seminars. It was decided she would review more completely and practice ahead of time.

It also emerged that she felt flustered in shops when approached by salespeople, or in restaurants when asked to give her order when she wasn't ready. She seemed to have general performance anxiety. By practicing on specific pieces of the general problem, she greatly reduced the anxiety; the more general problem of lack of assertiveness was explored using role-play situations and live practice (in restaurants, shops, etc.).

---

*A circle representing an average 24-hour day. The number of hours the person wants to spend on various activities are subtracted from 24 hours (leaving an average of 8 hours for sleep). This is an excellent class exercise.
**This behavior tracking is usually done in chart form, with a sheet for each day showing time of day, what was happening, what the person said or did, and what happened afterward. Behavior, thinking, and feeling are reported briefly.

A chronically unhappy but reasonably successful male graduate student began to talk about some recent disappointments and regrets. Through a process of tracking a specific example, a pattern emerged: indecision led to turning down invitations for social and recreational events, which led to unhappy idle hours filled with regrets that he hadn't gone somewhere. He contracted to say "yes" to the next invitation. He observed some excitement and anxiety and found he had regrets that he wasn't home working! At this point, it seemed that the "indecisiveness" was serving to make certain that he would experience disappointment no matter what "he didn't choose to do"! This pattern of reporting only sadness and regrets was challenged. He was instructed to report to others only the positive aspects of his experience and to brag about his accomplishments to someone he knew. He reported that he felt very uncomfortable bragging about himself, as though this would be disapproved by others, including the counselor. This pattern was traced to experiences in his family where his excellent grades and other accomplishments were taken for granted; if he did brag, he was told to be modest.

This complex example illustrates how contracting can be used at critical points in counseling to challenge automatic patterns of behavior that are rooted in false assumptions.

Mary Edwards Goulding and Robert Goulding have suggested a set of questions that counselors can ask their counselees to provide a framework for exploration contracts:

1. What do I want to change? What do I want to stop or start doing? Where? When? With whom?
2. How am I now stopping myself from doing this?
3. What am I willing to do to get what I want?
4. How will I and others know when I've done it?
5. How might I sabotage myself?

In this framework:

— The client is asked to be specific about what he/she wants.
— The issue is raised of how the person explains away why he/she isn't doing what he/she wants to do.
— Motivation is explored and challenged.
— An observable, practical end-point is defined.
— Perhaps most importantly, the client is asked to list the various ways in which he/she could avoid working on the contract.

The counselor should pay close attention to the language used by the counselee. Expressions such as "I'll try . . .," "I'll make an effort to . . .," and "I wish I could . . ." are expressions aimed at avoiding the issue or "pleasing" the counselor rather than clear statements of intent. A typical "avoiding" statement might be, "I thought I might like to try to see how I can make some progress in exploring why I can't seem to be able to learn how to be free of my problems."

There is a very important underlying assumption about the contracting process: it is not necessary to *be* different in order to *do* things differently. It is commonly believed that extensive personality reconstruction is necessary in order to change behavior patterns. This belief is simply not true for many of the undesirable habits or behavior patterns that trouble people.

Working on contracts often raises important issues that have to do with habit, learned helplessness, or involuntary reinforcing systems. Contracts lead to an understanding of how people "keep bad feelings going." Helping the client act in his or her own best interest through increased understanding of him or herself leads to further contracts for exploration and action. Much of the time, the counselor encourages the client to challenge old patterns in order both to get information and to change behavior.

Contracts Regarding Responsibility in Counseling

A third kind of contract involves the counselor's responsibility in the counseling situation. When the counselor is licensed, there are explicit statutes and codes spelling out the extent and limits of that responsibility. Licensed health-care workers learn how to contract with clients to clearly define boundaries of responsibility. Contracting should set up a situation of cooperation where both people know what to expect. Lack of clarity can lead to excessive dependency or confusion. Clearly, limits have to be set on what a counselor can do for a client and when and how often the counselor can be available.

What, then, are the responsibilities of nonprofessional peer counselors? Some of these responsibilities might include:

1. That they have information or access to information that will be of use to peers (e.g., on learning or informational resources, career planning information and strategies, contraception information, etc.).
2. That the peer counselor be available at specific times, usually in an office.

3. That confidentiality be maintained unless otherwise agreed to by both parties.

4. That, in the case of personal counseling, counselors acknowledge their competence in certain limited areas (i.e., that they be able to offer good listening, problem-solving techniques, help with clarification of issues troubling a counselee, and opinions or information about referral to other resources). The brochures and descriptions of peer counseling services should spell out explicitly the range of services provided.

Every effort should be made to delimit the boundaries of the responsibility of the counselors so as to protect them and counselees from possibly misunderstanding the counselors' role.

Summary: Contracts

1. The term "contract" may be used in three different ways: self-management contracts, contracts for exploration, and contracts regarding counselor responsibility.

2. Self-management contracting is based on theories of reinforcement. A behavior is studied from the point of view of its antecedents (A), the behavior itself (B), and its consequences (C); focused strategies of intervention are developed on this basis ("A-B-C"ing behavior). Such strategies are best suited for work on behavior, as opposed to emotions and thoughts.

3. Contracting can also be part of a process of exploration, not necessarily an end in itself. Within this framework contracts may be for awareness, for change, or both.

4. An important assumption in contracting is that it isn't necessary to be different to act differently. The "how" of behavior is more important than the "why."

5. Contracts regarding counselor responsibility make specific the expectations of both parties in a counseling relationship. Some aspects of the contract are explicit; other aspects are implicit. These implicit assumptions should be clarified as much as possible to avoid misunderstanding about the responsibility of either party. These principles apply to peer counselors as well as to professional counselors. Clear specifications of the role of the peer counselor, as well as clear program descriptions, serve to clarify expectations about responsibility.

References

Goulding, R. and Goulding, M., *The Power is in the Patient: A TA/Gestalt Approach to Psychotherapy.* San Francisco: T.A. Press, 1978.

Homme, L., *Use of Contingency Contracting in the Classroom.* Illinois: Research Press, 1970.

Mahoney, M. J. and Thoresen, C. W., *Self Control: Power to the Person.* Monterey, CA: Brooks-Cole Publishing, 1974.

Contracting Exercises

1. Choose a partner and review the conditions for a self management contract. Consider with your partner how you might set up a contract with him/her regarding a habit or behavior pattern you want to change. (Use the "A-B-C" approach.) Write up the contract following the format at the beginning of this chapter. Arrange follow-up. Report to larger group on the process and progress.

2. With a partner, review the implicit and explicit contract you have with family, friends, institutions (your school, other groups). Are these contracts all agreeable to you? Are there any you might want to renegotiate or refine?

3. With a partner, engage in a contracting process to explore a behavioral or emotional issue in your life. Use the Gouldings' questions as a guide to exploring the issue, the aim being a contract on which you can report back to your partner.

4. Discuss in a section of large group your understanding of the limits of your responsibility as a peer counselor in your program. Consider writing it down. Does your peer counseling program provide enough of a definition of your role and responsibilities?

DECISION-MAKING COUNSELING SKILLS
by Fritz H. Bottjer

In decision-making counseling, as in counseling in general, the counselor uses basic attending skills to foster precise communication. The counselor must thoroughly understand the client's problem in order to help. This process involves gaining an awareness of the content of the problem as well as the "feeling" of it from the client's point of view.

Open and closed questions focus the client's discussion on issues that require elaboration or clarification. Paraphrase, summary, and reflection of feeling further the client's exposition and act as perception checks, ensuring that the counselor accurately perceives how the client views the problem.

Other valuable functions are served by the counselor's use of basic attending skills. In the process of describing a problem to the counselor, the client may clarify for himself or herself issues that were previously less clear. Sensitive and active listening can often lead the client to see factors previously overlooked. Merely describing one's perceptions and feelings to someone else can change them to some degree, perhaps as a result of self-clarification. Also, the experienced counselor fosters rapport and demonstrates a desire to help by the proper use of basic attending skills.

For many decision-making problems, active listening may be all that is required to provide the type of help desired by the client. Other problems or clients may require additional skills in decision-making counseling.

What are these skills?

The decision-making counseling skills described in this chapter are strategies, exercises, activities, and procedures that may be prompted or suggested by the counselor in certain situations. Each procedure is meant to help the client clarify an aspect of the decision-making process in an unbiased way.

The skills are NOT used to recommend a particular option or course of action to the client. In most situations, exercises should not be initiated by the counselor. Instead, the counselor should describe an appropriate strategy. If the client chooses to engage in this suggested activity, the counselor can further help the client use it properly.

This section is based upon the author's doctoral dissertation, and on work by J. D. Krumboltz and D. Hamel (1977) as well as numerous other authors.

How can these skills help?

Most of the important decision-making problems that are brought to the counseling situation involve many relevant factors. Valuable information can easily be overlooked when a problem is highly complex. A person may become overwhelmed by the importance, magnitude, and/or complexity of the problem. This situation can often lead to (1) making rash or hasty choices, (2) relying upon intuition, luck, or the opinions of others, and/or (3) not being able to make a decision at all. This latter condition can cause secondary problems that can drastically disrupt one's life and further reduce one's ability to make wise decisions.

Systematic procedures for making important and complex choices can provide a workable solution to many of these problems. The counselor's use of decision-making counseling skills can help many clients structure their decision making in an efficient way and make appropriate, responsible decisions.

Decision-making problems often involve long-range planning (such as which major to select or which career direction to pursue). Of course, outcomes are harder to predict for the distant future. The goals, values, or objectives that prompted the selection of an option may change over time. These and other factors can make decision-making strategies difficult to evaluate. Nonetheless, many of the principles shown to be effective in problem solving can be applied to decision-making counseling.

How are these skills used?

The following section lists the skills used in many decision-making situations. It does not list all skills for all combinations of problems, counselors, and clients. It provides instead a beginner's guide for counselors and trainees, and it should be developed and refined through practice and direct application. In it, there are seven major steps, and the first letter of each step goes to form the word DECIDES. (The first "D," for example, stands for "Defining the Problem.")

If a client is seen for several sessions over a long period of time (several weeks or longer), many of the skills may be applicable. Short-term counseling (one or two sessions) renders some of these procedures unnecessary. For most situations it is wise to view the model as a menu of possible activities.

The order in which these elements are presented is a logical one, but it is not the only one. You should select appropriate elements to fit the desires of the client, the direction of the counseling, the nature of the problem, and your own counseling style.

We recommend that the counselor obtain personal experience with the procedures described in this chapter before attempting to suggest their use to clients.

THE D.E.C.I.D.E.S. COUNSELING-SKILLS MODEL

Defining the Problem.

1. Provide a context of acceptance within the decision-making work by the appropriate use of basic attending skills.

    Use encouragements, open and closed questions, paraphrase, and reflection of feeling to establish a working relationship by demonstrating a desire to understand the situation and to provide help.

2. Elicit a clear statement of the problem.

    Use open and closed questions, paraphrase, and reflection of feeling to elicit the client's detailed description of the situation. Elicit discussion about the objective content as well as the emotional content of the problem as perceived by the client. Be sure to find out when the decision has to be made.

3. Recognize and summarize the problem clearly. Check for accuracy.

    When you feel that you understand the most important aspects of the problem, attempt a detailed summary of your impressions with the client. Be tentative. Your summary should be expressed as an attempt to understand rather than as a professional opinion.

    Be sure to include a specific statement of the goals your client hopes to achieve as a result of his or her decision-making work—for example, "You want to have a list of at least five possible graduate schools by the first of December so that you can get all the necessary application forms on time. Is that right?"

    Revise your summary with additional or corrective input from the client. Continue in this fashion until the client indicates that your summary accurately reflects his or her own perceptions of the situation.

4. Establish the fact that responsibility for decision making rests with the client.

    Some clients may appear to want you to make a decision for them. If you have reason to assume that this is the case, clarify your role as helper. You may want to give a rationale as to why you cannot assume responsibility for someone else in his or her decision. Be aware that you probably *WILL* influence the client's decision-making process despite your efforts to remain objective and nondirective.

Exercises

Each of the seven units of the D.E.C.I.D.E.S. model should be practiced sequentially in groups of two or three trainees each. One person assumes the role of the client and presents a decision-making problem. The second person is the counselor and attempts to demonstrate as many of the numbered skills for that unit as possible. The third person, if included, is the observer. After a unit is practiced, the observer leads a brief discussion of how well the counselor demonstrated the skills, how appropriate the skills were for that particular situation, and how the interaction could be improved. Each member of the group should have experience in each role before going on to the next unit.

Remember, the skills presented in this chapter are most appropriate for clients who cannot make a decision, who do not have refined personal decision-making skills, and/or for whom the problem is overwhelming or of great importance. The person assuming the client's role should keep this in mind when choosing and presenting a problem for practice.

"Defining the Problem" Exercises

This first unit is primarily a focused application of the skills you have learned in previous chapters. Be sure to discuss the implications of point 4 (responsibility, objectivity, and directiveness in counseling) to your satisfaction before going to the next unit.

Questions: (1) Can any counseling be truly nondirective? (2) In what situations would active guidance from the counselor be most appropriate?

Establishing an Action Plan

1. Describe the general strategy and/or introduce the various areas of the model as appropriate.

    Your task is to encourage the client to actively gather, weigh, and apply all relevant information in a way that enhances his or her ability to estimate the overall consequences of a given action and as a result to make a more educated choice from available alternatives. Your description may be a simple claim, such as "An informed choice is typically a better choice," or you may want to detail the various steps which could be taken.

2. Ask the client if this approach is acceptable and desirable.

    It is very important that the client approve of the course of action to be taken. This approval may require reaffirmation as each new element is introduced. Consent may sometimes be implied by a client's favorable reaction to such statements as, "It may be valuable to explore . . . ," "What about . . . ?" or "Another way to expand your analysis may be to . . ."

3. Assess how much time and effort the client is willing to devote to the decision-making problem.

    This specification can aid both the client and the counselor in efficiently structuring the overall task.

4. Elicit specific commitments for outside decision-making work.

    Important decision-making problems are often carried outside the counseling session by the client—sometimes to obsessive proportions. A more efficient use of time may result from your help in structuring specific decision-making activities for your client to do outside of the counseling session. The end of a session is an appropriate time to discuss areas requiring additional attention.

    Once an area or activity is mutually identified, elicit a specification of the plan (what, when, for how long, to what goal, etc.). Open-ended questioning can be an effective way to help the client specify the plan—for example, "What can you do to find out more about . . . ?" "How much time can you devote to this exploration (task, exercise, etc.)?" "When can you set aside time for this work this week?" and "When can we discuss your findings, or would you rather work alone from here on?"

    Your goal is to facilitate the types of activities that the client actually wants to do. Be careful that your casual suggestions are not regarded as a strong message to do particular work.

Exercises

For practicing points 1 and 2, the "client" should specifically ask for suggestions as to how the problem can be worked on. Point 4 is obviously a part of establishing an action plan; however, practicing the skills of describing activities and eliciting commitments for outside decision-making work is probably best done after additional skills are presented. Practice point 4 as a part of each unit, beginning with clarifying values.

Clarifying Values

1. Promote a discussion of the relevant personal values involved in the decision-making situation.

    A first task may be to define what is meant by "values." Values represent personal principles, ideals, self-definitions, goals, or motivating guidelines that may underlie certain actions, feelings, and thoughts relevant to the problem at hand. Values can change over time. They may be situation-specific or be altered by influences such as the decision-making procedures you suggest. Some clients may be well aware of their personal values and how these values enter into the situation at hand. Others may not have considered them at all. Use the appropriate basic attending skills to explore the client's values.

2. Elicit and discuss any values that may not have been considered by the client.

Be tentative in your suggestions—for example, "What other personal values do you think may be important in this situation?", "Do _____ or _____ enter into the picture?" The use of examples may be helpful. For a career decision, a client may profitably consider his or her feelings about prestige, security, salary, leisure time, leadership, altruism, variety, entry requirements, responsibility, and location. Other situations may require an exploration of the client's feelings about family ties, being loved or disliked, friendship, respect, obligations of various types, lifestyle activities, and identifications with groups or principles.

3. Prompt thought about weighing values.

Values can be ordered, weighed, and discussed as abstracts or they may be concretely anchored to the presenting problem. Abstract weighing can be insightful and interesting. You may suggest an exercise such as, "If you had, for example, 100 units of satisfaction that you could distribute among those values you have identified as important, how would you distribute them?"

Exercises

When practicing point 3, remember that many forms of comparing values may be appropriate. Try to allow the client to determine (and even initiate) a suitable weighing strategy. Remember to practice point 4 from "Establishing an Action Plan." Valuable outside activities include fantasy exercises. A client in a career-planning situation, for instance, may profit from such activities as writing his or her own ideal obituary or writing mock letters of recommendation from the perspective of significant people in his or her life (boss, spouse, friends). Be creative in your practice.

If out-of-counseling activities are desired by the client, be sure to discuss the outcomes with the client when the exercise is completed. Reweighing of values may also be necessary.

Identifying Alternatives

1. Prompt the consideration of all feasible options. Write them on a work sheet when possible.

A work sheet is especially useful in situations that have many alternatives and/or that involve a great deal of complexity.

Should you and your client desire to use this strategy, summarize each alternative in a few words down the side or across the top of the paper. You may later want to illustrate value by alternative pairing in a graph-like fashion.

2. Brainstorm new alternatives. Generate information sources for establishing new options.

Sometimes the discussion of seemingly unlikely options can lead to the generation of a new viable alternative. Previously discarded alternatives can sometimes be reinstated in the light of new information. Be sure that any suggestion you make is viewed simply as input to the brainstorming, not as your opinion.

Additional information can sometimes create new options. If you think it necessary, suggest that the client gather new information. Feel free to refer your client to information sources if you both feel that it may be profitable. Service organizations may be suitable referrals. If the client agrees that additional information is desirable, commit the client to this task as specifically as possible.

Exercises

In practicing point 2, trainees should assess their knowledge of other information sources. Large-group discussion and input from the instructor can help to increase this knowledge.

Discovering Probable Outcomes

1. Discuss each option in terms of its expected outcome.

Expected outcomes are the client's predictions of what will result after a decision is made and acted upon. Outcomes may be of a situational nature, or they may relate to feelings, values, or conflicts among values. There are usually a number of expected outcomes, both positive and negative in nature, for each option. There may be both short- and long-term *expectations.* Some outcomes may be more probable than others; some may be much less predictable. Discussion of these *expectations* can help the client view the problem in greater depth. Sometimes the probable outcomes expressed by the client may not seem probable to you at all. You may want to gently question or challenge such statements in the interest of clarification.

A fantasy exercise may be a valuable strategy in some situations—for example, "Imagine that it is five years from now. You have lived with your decision (alternative A) for a while now. We meet on the street and I ask you how things are going, what you like about your decision and its effects upon your life. What would you say?"

2. Generate other information sources for estimating outcomes more clearly.

Some expected outcomes may be better estimated with additional information. Suggest likely sources for obtaining such new input and commit the client to gathering information when appropriate.

3. Prompt a discussion of later possibilities for changing course once an option is acted upon.

Few decisions require absolute adherence to a selected course of action if it later proves to have been a poor choice. The consequences of changing action at a later point can, however, vary with the options. An analysis of the potential for later change can provide meaningful input to a decision-making problem. Open-ended questioning can facilitate this analysis—for example: "What if you later find that option A doesn't pan out? Could you change to option B? What consequences would you expect?"

4. Try writing down probable outcomes on a grid.

At this point the counselor can create a "values vs. alternatives" grid with the information gathered so far. Each previously identified value is written on the left side of a piece of paper; alternatives are then written across the top. A grid is drawn. Questions are asked about each alternative with respect to how well each value is addressed by the probable outcome of that alternative. These predictions are then entered (in summary form) in the appropriate space.

The following example of a decision-making counseling session may serve to highlight this approach.

Counselor: There is another exercise that can sometimes help to compare alternatives and probable outcomes. You can construct a grid that shows how each alternative stacks up against the list of values you came up with. It's a way of getting an overview of the important issues all on one sheet of paper.

Client: Tell me more.

Counselor: Okay, first let's use the six values that you previously iden-
               tified as important in this decision. List them one under the
               other on the left margin of a piece of paper spaced from the
               top of the sheet to the bottom. Separate each value with a hori-
               zontal line so that six rows are formed. Now form columns in
               the same way, one for each of the four alternatives that you
               previously identified. Briefly designate each alternative in the
               top margin. This procedure forms a grid which provides a
               space for summarizing the intersection of each value with each
               alternative. Now we fill in the grid with your estimation of
               how well each alternative addresses each value. Are you with
               me so far?

Client: Yes, I get the picture. So for instance, desire for independence
               would be well served by the alternative of taking the full-time
               job with Pressman, Inc., in Cleveland at least with respect to
               living arrangements. But I'm less sure about independence on
               the job. That is a somewhat different issue.

(This client is beginning to explore the complexity of evaluating probable
outcomes by alternative pairings. The counselor may suggest establishing
a new value category if it is perceived to be helpful. The counselor uses
basic attending skills in helping the client to fill in each box [value by alternative pairing] on the grid. Sometimes additional information must be
gathered to accomplish this task.)

Exercises

Constructing a grid is a strategy worthy of considerable practice. Counselors will probably feel awkward at first in practicing this procedure. Initially
the counselor can fill in the grid with the client's help. Begin with a statement such as, "I'm going to write down a few of these things so that I
can organize all of this information." (Ask questions, paraphrase and summarize, check for accuracy, enter the information, and describe what you
are doing.)

     Later, practice ways of describing the process so that the client con-
structs and fills in the grid. Begin with a statement such as, "In this case,
it may be helpful to organize a work sheet to enter all of this information."
(Describe process further.) "Would this be something you would like to
do?" (Describe how to construct grid.)

     Trainees should gain firsthand experience in organizing a complex
decision-making problem in grid form. With practice, this strategy will
become part of the counselor's normal repertoire.

Alternative / Value Categories	Full Time Work at Pressman Inc.	Half-Time Work Half-Time Law School (C.U.)	Full Time Work ¼ Time Eve. Law School (S.C.U.)	Full Time Law School (C.U.) With Student Loans
20[1] Living Arrangement Independence (next few years)	10[2] 20 X 10 = (200)[3]	2 20 X 2 = (40)	10 20 X 10 = (200)	5 20 X 5 = (100)
15 Personal Independence	9 15 X 9 = (135)	5 15 X 5 = (75)	4 15 X 4 = (60)	5 15 X 5 = (75)
10 Money (Next few years)	8 10 X 8 = (80)	5 10 X 5 = (50)	7 10 X 7 = (70)	4 10 X 4 = (40)
25 Money (later potential)	7 25 X 7 = (175)	10 25 X 10 = (250)	10 25 X 10 = (250)	10 25 X 10 = (250)
15 Prestige, Self-concept, Approval from others	6 15 X 6 = (90)	8 15 X 8 = (120)	7 15 X 7 = (105)	9 15 X 9 = (135)
15 Security (peace of mind aspect more than job security)	8 15 X 8 = (120)	7 15 X 7 = (105)	9 15 X 9 = (135)	6 15 X 6 = (90)
Totals 100	**800**	**640**	**810**	**690**

[1] The numbers assigned to the value categories (value weights) obtain from the exercise described on page 00. That is, 100 points are distributed among the identified values according to their relative importance to the client.

[2] Each intersection of a value category and an alternative is assigned a number from 0 to 10 according to how well that particular value is likely to be fulfilled by the alternative it intersects. For instance, this client felt that full-time work at Pressman, Inc. would allow the maximum amount of "living arrangement independence" over the next few years.

[3] Value weights are then multiplied by the numerical estimate of potential fulfillment, and summed up for each alternative.

Eliminating Alternatives Systematically

1. Prompt the integration of all values, alternatives, and expected out-
    comes. Review the decision-making work sheet if it is used.

    If no single alternative seems obviously best to the client and
    no additional preparatory work (such as continued information
    gathering) is desired, suggest a review of all currently available
    information.

    It is often the case that your client's values have shifted some-
    what or that probable outcomes are now viewed in a different
    light. It is important that only the most current information is
    considered in the review. You may want to tell your client to
    feel free to change his/her mind about values or expected out-
    comes.

    It is typically most helpful to let the clients provide their own
    unique integration of the information. You may prompt, ques-
    tion, and tactfully challenge your client's analysis if appropriate.
    Proceed directly to the elimination strategy (point #3) if it
    seems that closure is at hand.

2. Prompt the rating of projected outcomes with respect to each value,
    and summarize for each alternative.

    This strategy can be valuable in some cases, provided that (1)
    two or more options remain equally desirable, and (2) the client
    desires a highly quantitative breakdown of the problem. Make
    sure that the client desires this approach before proceeding.

    The decision-making work sheet is used for displaying this anal-
    ysis. Have the client assign an appropriate numerical value to
    each piece of data. If, for instance, three personal values are rele-
    vant to this problem, first have the client rank their relative im-
    portance on some scale (e.g., by dividing 100 points between
    the three values). The probable outcome of each option is then
    rated with respect to how much it satisfies or conflicts with each
    value. A number is arrived at for each alternative by first multi-
    plying each value's number by the score for each probable out-
    come and then adding these scores for each alternative. (See
    grid on page 56).

    You or your client should feel free to modify this scheme if nec-
    essary. The objective is not to arrive at a decision by picking
    the alternative with the highest number, but rather to stimulate
    meaningful thought about the interaction of the various compo-
    nents involved in the decision.

We continue now with the example begun in the previous section. Assume that the grid has been completed and the client desires a quantitative breakdown of the decision-making problem.

Counselor: Keep in mind that assigning numbers to values and matching them with alternatives is only an exercise to aid you in getting an overall perspective on the problem. It is definitely not a scientific formula for making a decision.

Client: Yes, I understand. In fact I think I am leaning toward an alternative already but I want to see how this works. I've always been a numbers buff but I've never applied math to personal decision making before. I guess I'm just curious to see how the numbers come out. How does it work?

Counselor: Okay. Remember when we divided one hundred points between all of your values? Let's do it again. You may want to make some changes. (The client assigns points to each value so that the total is equal to 100 points.) Now list each value's points on the grid in the appropriate row.

Client: Done. Now what?

Counselor: This gets a little abstract. Okay, now estimate from 0 to 10 (any scale will work) how well each value will be fulfilled by each alternative. So for "living arrangement independence" (this client broke independence into two distinct values)—how well would the Pressman Inc. job satisfy this value?

Client: Oh, completely, I would assume. I could most likely swing a place of my own, so I'd give it a 10 rating.

Counselor: Okay, now what about the second alternative—half time study at C.U. while living at home? How much "living arrangement independence" do you think you would have?

Client: Well, as I mentioned before, it wouldn't be a total zip but not great either. Let's say a 2.

(The client continues in this fashion with the counselor's help until a number is assigned to each cell. Assume that this procedure has now been completed.)

Counselor: Now we simply multiply each value's assigned points by the number you have entered in each box. (Underlining or any other method that distinguishes the new number may be used. Assume that this procedure is now complete.)

Counselor: Now add the numbers in the column for each alternative, and enter the total at the bottom of each column. Each alternative now has a single numerical estimate for comparison purposes. Remember, this exercise doesn't necessarily lead to the "best" alternative. It is simply a way of organizing a lot of material in a small amount of space. You may now want to go over this grid, making changes where appropriate.

3. Eliminate poor alternatives one by one.
    It is sometimes easier to eliminate a poor alternative than to choose the best one from several. Continue to eliminate alternatives until only one remains. Should two or more alternatives be assessed as equal, recycle the appropriate sections of the model (by reclarifying values, gathering additional information, and so on) until one alternative prevails.

Exercises

If counselors are to use point 2 in decision-making counseling, they must be able to describe it to counselees in detail. In your practice sessions, counselors should present elements to the "counselee" a step at a time. Check the counselee's understanding frequently.

Starting Action (when one alternative has been at least tentatively selected)

1. Elicit commitments for specific action on the selected alternative.
    The objective is to help the counselee specify all the necessary actions required to put the decision into effect. Some choices require obvious action; others may require additional detailing of the steps necessary for implementing the decision. Elicit commitments required by the situation and desired by the counselee.

2. Elicit a review of the steps in decision making.
    The counselor can provide a great service by transmitting a general strategy for independently dealing with future decisions. Ask your counselee to abstract the general steps in his or her own words. Contribute where appropriate. Encourage and support statements that reflect the counselee's ownership of the strategies. Be sure to give to the person all credit for arriving at a decision.

Exercises

Trainees may, at first, find it difficult to implement point 2 without appearing pedantic. Therefore, keep the strategy in mind but do not attempt to use it with actual clients until you feel comfortable with it.

Most of the strategies presented in the D.E.C.I.D.E.S. decision-making counseling model may initially seem somewhat stilted or unnatural. Proper selection and use of the skills usually requires considerable practice, so do not become discouraged if you are still unable to use them smoothly by the end of this chapter. Only through further practice and actual experience will you be able to integrate them into your own counseling style.

Summary

The preceeding section describes a method for helping clients with difficult decision-making problems. The seven units of the DECIDES model are: Defining the problem, Establishing an action plan, Clarifying values, Identifying alternatives, Discovering probable outcomes, Eliminating alternatives systematically, and Starting action. Specific counselor actions are described for each unit.

CONFRONTATION

"Confrontation" in counseling means "pointing out discrepancies or incongruities in what clients are saying or doing" (Ivey, 1976). Most schools of therapy have a special technology and point of view about confrontation and give it different degrees of importance; all agree that as a technique, it works best in the context of a good relationship where there is trust and empathy. Confrontation has developed a bad image in counseling probably through reports of methodologies in which it is overemphasized (e.g., in Synanon-type encounter groups).

Within the context of a counseling relationship, confrontation can be of help in giving insight into personal problems resulting from incongruent thinking or behavior. As Ivey reports, "a person is faced directly with the fact that he/she may be saying other than that which they mean, or doing other than that which they say."

Ivey lists the following factors as important facets of confrontation:

1. A confrontation focuses on discrepancies between varying attitudes, thoughts, or behavior.
2. A confrontation focuses on objective data. The more factual and observable a confrontation of discrepancies is, the more helpful it will be. Confrontations are most effective when they are nonevaluative.
3. A confrontation is not a blunt statement of opinion or emotion that disagrees with someone else's. (Ivey, 1976)

Okun (1976) presents a slightly different point of view regarding confrontation. "Confronting involves honest feedback about what the helper really thinks is going on with the helpee." This may involve a focus on "genuineness," e.g., "It seems to me you're playing games here," or, "I feel you really don't want to talk about this." Or, as with Ivey, it may involve a focus on discrepancy, e.g., "On the one hand, you seem upset about not getting the job, but on the other hand you seem kind of relieved.".

The beginning counselor should probably start by using confrontation that focuses on discrepancies in objective facts and observable behavior, rather than on someone's "genuineness." The problem with confrontations based on "gut reactions" (no matter how accurate they might actually be) is that they tend to be personal opinion or to reflect some unexamined prejudice or overreaction on the part of the counselor.

So then, the skills involved in constructive confrontations are:

1. Accurate perception of discrepancies in observable behavior, verbal and nonverbal.
2. The use of "I" statements rather than exclusive "you" statements, which tend to be interpreted as judgmental—e.g., "You are sexist," vs. "I experience discomfort as you talk about your boyfriend; as a man, I'm wondering if you might feel the same way about me." This latter statement blends "I" and "you" remarks to make clear who said what, and where the responsibilities lie. Here's another example: "You say that I seem to understand you, but I don't believe that we are communicating well."
3. The use of responses that convey understanding, such as paraphrasing, reflection of feeling, and sharing of personal reactions.
4. An awareness on the part of the counselor that certain statements by the counselee may trigger responses that are evaluative or judgmental.

Exercises

1. Divide up into groups of three. One person role-plays a confronter, a second the person being confronted, and a third the observer.
    The person being confronted assumes four different characters: a person who is too "agreeable" and complains about being hurt and abused by others, a person who is extremely shy and quiet, a person who is very critical of others and complains of being misunderstood, and a person who seems to live a harried life and complains of pressure and anxiety.

The players assume they know one another in order to simulate a counseling relationship. The observer evaluates and gives feedback based on the criteria given in this section. After the "confrontation," the "counselor" receives feedback from the "counselee" as well. The role-players then switch roles so that all three members can experience each role. When all groups have finished, the whole group reconvenes and considers the following questions: What were people's general reactions to the exercise? What did people learn about being a confronter? What did people learn about being confronted? A group leader should guide this discussion.

2. Class members are encouraged to do the following exercise in and out of class: Confront someone you know about the positive and negative points of your relationship with that person. Avoid "likes" and "dislikes," and focus on actual behavior or attitudes. Take 15 minutes to do so, and then share your experiences with one another. If this exercise is done in a group, members who wish to do so should share their reactions, emphasizing strengths and weaknesses about staying within the guidelines of confrontation.

References

Ivey, A. E., and N. Gluckstern. *Basic Influencing Skills.* North Amherst, MA: Microtraining Associates, 1976.
Okun, B. *Effective Helping.* Belmont, CA: Wadsworth Publishing, Duxbury Press, 1976.

INTERPRETATION

Interpretation is usually considered a key skill in *psychotherapy* rather than *counseling.*

Wolberg (1967) defines interpretation as a skill "by which the more unconscious elements of the psyche are brought to the patient's awareness." He states that "interpretation as a vehicle for insight is particularly valuable in reconstructive psychotherapy, since there is, in this form of treatment, an emphasis on unconscious aspects of mental activity."

In psychotherapy, interpretation is used to bring unconscious motivations into consciousness so that people are more aware and therefore have more options about their behavior and attitudes. Counseling, however, deals more with observable behavior and attitudes, and there is less interest in unconscious motivations and processes.

Interpretation—A Further Definition

Ivey views interpretation as "an act of renaming or redefining 'reality' (feelings, thoughts, actions, experiences) from a new point of view." The object of interpretation is a new understanding for the client. Optimally, this new point of view is a shared one and not just that of the counselor. Since we are all restricted by a particular point of view and tend to give meaning to events from that context, the counselor should be careful not to substitute his/her own point of view for the counselee's.

A graphic representation may further clarify the distinctions between reconstructive psychotherapy and counseling:

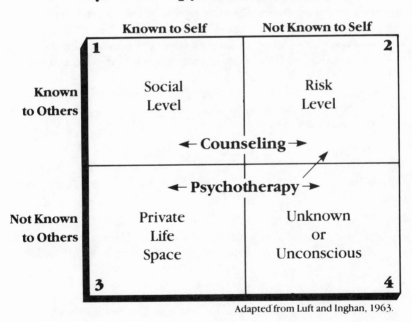

Distinctions between
Psychotherapy and Counseling

Adapted from Luft and Inghan, 1963.

In this diagram, areas 1 and 2 are the province of counseling, while 2, 3, and 4 are the province of therapy; part of the purpose of therapy, in this scheme, is to move materials from 4 and 2 into 3 and eventually into 1. Of course, to the extent that a counselor is working in area 2, s/he may eventually have to do some confronting and interpreting.

Interpretation from the Point of View
of Listening Skills

In the material on paraphrasing, we pointed out that paraphrasing stands
on a continuum between simple restatement and interpretation. Interpretation in counseling involves a mix of open and closed questions, paraphrasing and reflection of feeling. As a counselor interprets, s/he must
necessarily become more directive. For example, in low-level interpretation, the counselor may wait for the *counselee* to interpret reported behavior or experiences as they have been reflected by the counselor; in
mid-level interpretation, the counselor actively pieces together bits of information and asks the counselee to reach some conclusion; and in
strong-level interpretation, the counselor may give the counselee a definite, authoritative interpretation.

Example: A counselee has been describing conflicts with an advisor;
she describes a "waiting game" in which she seems to seek advice but is
prepared to resist if the advisor gives it.

Low-level interpretation: "So, it seems as though you're in a stalemate;
you want direction, but you rebel against it."

Mid-level: "You know, as you talk about the situation, I'm reminded
of similar episodes you've reported; they all seem to involve a tug-of-war
with older people. What do you think?"

Strong level: "You know, it seems like you have difficulties with authority figures, and you tend to regress to very childish behaviors when
you must deal with them."

Counselee:	"Yes, and I'm torn up by it. . . ."
Counselor:	"How do you feel when your advisor pays attention to you?"
Counselee:	"I feel he will then expect more of me. . . . it's always been like this with teachers . . . I just can't relax, but I need that recognition from them—it's like that with my father, too. . . ."
Counselor:	"How so?"
Counselee:	"I always felt I had to jump up and down to get his atten-tion, then I was pissed that it wasn't spontaneous with him. . . ."
Counselor:	"So what might you conclude?"
Counselee:	(Pause) "That I'm treating my advisor as if he were my father, or that I want him to be my father. . . . ?"
Counselor:	"You want him to do the right thing by you without your asking. . . ."

Counselee: "You know, I've thought the same thing in about the same words . . ."

Counselor: "So how much longer do you want to struggle with this?"

Counselee: (Thoughtful) "I do act that way . . . and I do want to have a different relationship. . . ."

Counselor: "Let's explore this a bit more. . . ." (At this point, the counselor and counselee might explore the issue from a different perspective.)

From these examples, it should be clear that paraphrasing and questioning are very important for interpreting. For the counselor to be confident about a possible interpretation, s/he must stay with the material put out by the counselee; in other words s/he must be tentative, just as with paraphrasing. The counselor must learn to perceive patterns and to inquire about their meaning with the counselee. Like an incomplete or awkward paraphrase, an inelegant interpretation may still be of use; the client should feel free to correct the inelegance and perhaps elaborate on the interpretation.

Aspects of Interpretation

1. A useful way to practice making interpretations is to look for an appropriate metaphor in order to begin finding ways to frame the interpretation.

    "This person is behaving as though _____."
    "This person views _____ as if _____."
    "This person generates _____ by _____."

    By searching for such metaphors, you will begin to get a sense of how to frame a statement so that it will be of interest to your client. One of the objectives of active listening is to be able to understand the client's world view.

    Example: A male counselee is describing general feelings of annoyance and resentment toward the people with whom he shares a house. He feels uncomfortable about this, but can rationalize and justify his feelings very well. He goes on to discuss how he opted out of the "Secret Santa" plan at his house, then felt left out, angry, and sad when others got gifts, however trivial. He has given other examples of situations in which he acted in "selfless," apparently "generous" ways, only to feel sad and angry later.

    The counselor sees that the counselee puts up an appearance of not needing anything from anyone, locks himself into a pattern of deprivation through denial of needs, and then experiences sadness and resentment. The counselor might generate metaphors as follows:

"This person is behaving as though *he has no needs.*"
"This person views *"being given to"* as if *it's not allowed.*
"This person generates *sadness and anger* by *denying needs.*"

The counselor then begins to try to frame these ideas in ways that will be meaningful to the client and will offer him alternative explanations for his sadness. Counselor and client could then begin to examine patterns of behavior in order to develop a strategy of challenging the undesirable pattern. They might explore the circumstances under which it was permissible for the client to express his needs at home. In this particular case, this exploration brought out the fact that in his large family, the client did not have his needs met, and had learned to deny those needs while feeling sad. The existence of a "shadow family" in his residence had triggered this old reaction.

2. Interpretations are ideally made by the *client,* on the basis of feedback from the counselor. The interpretations are then called "insights." Whenever possible, the counselor tries to stimulate the client to think through problems by restating, paraphrasing, summarizing, emphasizing important connections, and exploring with questions. Leading the client to the brink of an insight is the highest form of interpretation.

   Example: A woman in counseling comes to a session feeling depressed and sad. She describes her feelings as having come on suddenly. After some exploration, it doesn't appear that there is anything current to account for this sudden sadness. The counselor notices that she is wearing an unusual ring he hasn't seen before and asks about it. The client stares the ring; she says that it's her mother's ring. She had put it on that morning without thinking; it is the anniversary of her mother's death. Her sadness intensifies and they are then able to work on her grief.

3. Interpretations are made within a frame of reference that may either be personal, reflecting an individual world view, or be based on the theory of a school of psychology and therapy.

   Interpretations made from a personal point of view may be fairly informed, or they may be more intuitive. It's common for people to interpret from an informed base of knowledge for others with whom they have long-term relationships. People who share common experiences in life may have empathy for each other's situation and therefore be able to interpret for each other accurately and intuitively. Many relationships have this kind of rapport.

The problem with interpretations from an informed point of view is that they may be projections and are often prejudiced and stereotyped. The danger of making assumptions about how other people feel or think has been discussed in the sections on paraphrasing and reflection of feeling. The best way to avoid forwarding your own opinion is to follow what the other person is saying and to be aware that *their* world view is being examined, not yours.

Another aspect of this same problem is the counselor's own sensitivity to certain issues. A client in the midst of describing a problem may trigger uncertainties or doubts in the counselor. Most counselors learn that there are certain issues or problems about which it is difficult for them to remain an objective listener. Some examples:
— relationship problems between the sexes
— suicidal crisis
— death of a parent, friend, or sibling
— reports of violence or threats to life

Interpretations are most effective when they reflect a respect for the world view of the client and are devoid of accusations or moral judgments. In working with clients, it can be difficult to avoid making judgments or having a strong or even negative reaction to what the client is saying; needless to say, these reactions should not be expressed. The counselor must stay with the counselee, maintain an understanding attitude, and develop cues for framing interpretative interventions. In short, the counselor must keep a good rapport with the counselee.

Various schools of therapy use interpretation with different emphases; as mentioned, it is most intensively dealt with in psychodynamic therapies. The similarity among all the various schools is that they represent highly organized points of view that involve a belief system (the body of theory on which is based the therapy or counseling) and a technology (the techniques by which the school goes about assisting clients in self-understanding and behavior change).

In order of the relative importance they attach to using interpretation, the major schools and their tenets may be summarized as follows:

Psychoanalytic–Psychodynamic (Freud, Jung, Adler, Horney, and Sullivan): Behavior is determined, choices are illusory; behavior reflects conflict between desires and defenses. The unconscious is more important than consciousness, and we can only know the unconscious through interpretation of such things as symbols, dreams, fantasies, slips of the tongue, and so forth.

Existential–Humanistic (Rogerian, Gestalt, and some aspects of Rational Emotive therapy): Behavior is not determined, free will exists, choices are actual, anything which reduces the power of the past is therapeutic; the goal is to live in the present, to choose, and to act for satisfaction within ethical constraints. For example, Perls and Rogers view people as organisms striving for psychological health, reality as subjective and idiosyncratic, and psychological health as harmony between a perceived real self and an idealized internal self. They emphasize congruence between feelings and behavior, and their therapy is primarily with feelings rather than with cognitions, which are distrusted.

Transactional Analysis: Freudian but not psychoanalytic. All behavior is determined by "life script" development. Increased understanding of this "matrix" of behavior brings about increased freedom of choice and behavior change through abandonment of early decisions that led to faulty script formation; behavior is consistent and repetitive, with understandable goals accessible to rational analysis and choice.

Cognitive–Behavioral (Meichenbaum, Bandura, Thoresen, Beck): Cognitive behavior therapy concerns itself with elucidating those patterns of thinking that are associated with unwanted behavior. Focus is on patterns of thinking that tend to be black-or-white, overgeneralizations, "should" statements, and so forth, by which individuals become trapped in nonproductive, self-critical thinking.

Behavioral (Skinner, Wolpe): Behavior is learned; the conditions of learning appear to be more important than the behavioral outcome; reinforcements and contingencies seem fixed, both in and out of awareness. A study of reinforcers, contingencies, and outcomes leads to an analysis of behavior and a shaping of new behavior based on changes in reinforcers and contingencies in the awareness of the individual.

Summary—Interpretation

1. Interpretation is a skill most often used in psychodynamic, reconstructive therapies; it is also appropriate in intensive counseling (Rogerian, Humanistic, Transactional).
2. Interpretations in dynamic therapy are used by the therapist to bring out unconscious elements of the psyche.
3. Ivey defines interpretation as the act of renaming or redefining reality from a new point of view with the goal of bringing new understanding for the client.
4. Generating alternative explanations as metaphors is a useful way to practice making interpretations.

5. Interpretations should be couched in simple language and offered in a tentative manner.
6. Ideal interpretations are made by the counselee and are termed "insights."
7. Before making an interpretation, be reasonably sure of the accuracy of your assumptions and thoughts; interpretations offered in a haphazard manner can change the relationship with the counselee.
8. The timing of an interpretation is important. Part of being helpful with interpretations is knowing when the counselee is close to understanding a particular issue.
9. Try not to let personal issues intrude into interpretative comments. Focus on the client's world view and interpret *that.*
10. Interpretations should always reflect a respect for the attitudes and beliefs of the counselee. Avoid accusations or moral judgments.

Exercises

1. Each person in a small group looks around the room for an object that catches his/her interest. Each person then tells about the object as though it were him/her—e.g., "I am an ash tray. I am round and flat and shiny. People use me to put hot things into. At the end of the day I feel dirty." When each person has finished, the group leader asks the group members to consider how their descriptions of the objects are like them or some aspect of their lives.
2. A volunteer member of a small group is asked to report a dream. Each group member is asked to interpret the dream silently; next, the dreamer asks various people for their interpretations and then comments on them. The leader asks the group members to consider whether their interpretations reflect either some aspect of themselves or some current concern.
3. Either in class or as an assigned exercise outside class, students pair up with one another and take turns talking about an issue of interest or concern to them. The listener practices interpreting and getting feedback. It is important to spend at least a half hour on this exercise and to get immediate feedback before switching roles.
4. In small groups, students take turns describing themselves as though they were an animal or plant of their choice—e.g., "I am a bear; I am big and furry and love sweet things," or "I am a rosebush; I am planted next to a white fence; my roots are deep," etc. Each student is then asked to consider aspects of his/her personification that reveal aspects of him/herself to others.

    Other similar exercises may be created by the instructor as necessary. (Confidentiality and discretion are absolutely essential in these exercises. It must be understood that group members will not gossip about the results.)

References

Ivey, A.E. *Basic Influencing Skills.* North Amherst, MA: Microtraining Associates, 1976. p. 119.

Luft, J., and H. Inghan. "The Johari Window: A Graphic Model of Awareness," *Interpersonal Relationships in Group Processes: An Introduction to Group Dynamics.* ed. J. Luft. Palo Alto, CA: National Press Books, 1963.

Wolberg, L. *The Technique of Psychotherapy,* 2nd ed. New York: Grune & Stratton, 1967.

REVIEW OF CHAPTER 3: COUNSELING SKILLS

A. Overview
    Counseling goes beyond listening; it
    —   is a process of short duration
    —   involves the exploration and discussion of values, beliefs, and attitudes
    —   has self-rewarding behavior as its goal

B. Contracts
    —   involve a specific agreement between two people
    —   consider a behavior, its antecedents, and its consequences
    —   are fair
    —   have clear terms
    —   are stated positively
    —   are systematic and consistent
    —   involve at least one person besides the counselee
    —   should specify legal, moral behavior
    —   are of three types: self-management contracts, contracts for exploration, and contracts regarding counselor responsibility

C. Decision-Making Counseling Steps
    —   Define the problem
    —   Establish an action plan
    —   Clarify values
    —   Identify alternatives
    —   Discover probable outcomes
    —   Eliminate alternatives systematically
    —   Start action

D. Confrontation
   — Point out discrepancies in what people are saying or doing.
   — Perceive discrepancies in observable behavior (verbal and nonverbal) accurately.
   — Use "I" statements rather than "you" statements.
   — Use understanding responses such as paraphrasing, reflecting feelings, and sharing personal reactions.
   — Be cautious of evaluative or judgmental responses on your part.

E. Interpretation
   — Rename or redefine feelings, thoughts, actions, or experiences from a new point of view.
   — Generate alternative explanations for counselee's behavior.
   — Have counselee make interpretations on the basis of clues provided in feedback by the counselor.
   — Be aware of the frame of reference from which an interpretation is shaped.
   — Understand the world view of the counselee.
   — Avoid accusations or moral judgments.

Suggested Reading

Beck, Aaron T. *Cognitive Therapy and the Emotional Disorders.* New York: International Universities Press, 1976.

Freud, S. *A General Introduction to Psychoanalysis.* Garden City, NY: Doubleday, 1943.

Ivey, A.E., and L.S. Downing. *Counseling and Psychotherapy: Skills, Theories, Practice.* Englewood, NJ: Prentice-Hall, 1980. Ch. 11: SS. 8–11.

Chapter 4. Crisis Counseling Skills

4.

Crisis Counseling Skills

A crisis is an emotionally significant event or radical change in a person's life. The central tenet of crisis intervention theory is that some amount of distress is a normal reaction to such changes. All people experience crisis at some point in their lives.

Many crises seem to occur during periods of life change (e.g., from childhood to adolescence, or from adulthood to old age), during periods of increased external stress (e.g., in times of war, unemployment, or disaster), and during periods of decision making. Such crises are normal in human development. It is only when they outstrip the ability of the individual to mobilize his/her personal, social, or environmental resources to deal with the stress involved that crisis intervention counseling becomes necessary.

At a time when a person is experiencing a crisis which s/he feels is out of the realm of his or her experience or beyond his or her ordinary coping strategies, the person may begin to manifest symptoms of anxiety and discomfort, ranging from thought racing, illogical associations, and pressured speech to heightened emotionality, shortened attention span, and vexing self-doubt. In most instances, as the person gains a sense of mastery over the circumstances contributing to the crisis, the confusion and anxiety accompanying it will clear up without intervention.

Occasionally, however, the nature or magnitude of a crisis may so overwhelm an individual's range of coping mechanisms that the interven-

In this chapter, the section on crisis intervention was coauthored by Laraine Zappert and Vincent D'Andrea. The sections on depression and suicide were coauthored by Peter Salovey and Vincent D'Andrea.

tion of an outside person becomes necessary. At that point, it becomes vitally important that the crisis counselor be able to provide some structure for the person in crisis, to help him/her gain a sense of control of the feelings of anxiety and confusion.

What do we mean by coping mechanisms? One of the pioneers of crisis intervention theory, Gerald Caplan, has identified the following characteristics of effective coping behavior:

1. Active exploration of reality issues and search for information.
2. Free expression of both positive and negative feelings and a tolerance of frustration.
3. Active invoking of help from others.
4. Breaking problems down into manageable bits and working them through one at a time.
5. Awareness of the effects of stress and fatigue; pacing efforts and planning accordingly.
6. Active mastery of feelings when possible and acceptance of inevitability when not.
7. Flexibility and willingness to change approach in service of progress.
8. Basic trust in oneself and others and basic optimism about outcome of problem(s).*

The crisis counselor has to perform the dual roles of an active listener and an active collaborator with the counselee in the process of assessing the situation, evaluating the person's resources, suggesting options and alternatives, developing a plan of action, and following up and evaluating the outcome. All of this needs to be done within the framework of thoughtfulness and calm. As Lee Ann Hoff mentions in her book *People in Crisis,* "The necessity of thinking and planning quickly does not eliminate the necessity of thinking and planning. Action without thought is usually fruitless."

The desired outcome of a successful crisis intervention is for the counselee to achieve a sense of active mastery of his or her situation. Because people are more effectively available during crises and because they are highly motivated to resolve their situations, the opportunity for growth and development is very much a part of resolving distress. Crisis counselors should seek to align themselves with the strengths and resources of the individual in crisis, help to identify and mobilize these assets, and ultimately contribute to the individual's sense of self-esteem and efficacy.

---

*Caplan, G. *Principles of Preventive Psychiatry.* New York: Basic Books, 1964. Chapter 3.

Stages of Crisis Development

Caplan has outlined four phases of crisis development that trace the transformation of anxieties and distress into an acute state. They are as follows:

Phase I   A person is faced with an unfamiliar or unanticipated stress which causes an increase in anxiety. During Phase I, the person attempts to use his or her repertoire of usual coping skills to deal with the stress.

Phase II   The usual problem-solving skills fail to reduce the stress and this causes additional anxiety.

Phase III   With the increasing anxiety, a person attempts new coping strategies. The options s/he is aware of and selects may be limited by the anxiety being experienced.

Phase IV   Person is now in a state of extreme distress. The stresses remain unabated and the person feels s/he can no longer cope.

Ideally, crisis intervention should occur before Phase IV so that the person does not reach a state of helplessness and despair. If the person does reach a state of acute distress, it is essential that the counselor provide assurance that options and alternatives are still available, and help the person to choose those most appropriate to her or his needs.

CRISIS INTERVENTION

The cardinal rule in helping an individual who is in a state of distress is: *You help primarily by keeping the person focused on the structuring and organizing of the problem and on definition of possible responses or options.* Second in importance is the joint effort involved in organizing the problem and the associated relationship with a person who is a model of reason, knowledge, and mastery in the acute situation.

Basic skills and rules of thumb involved in handling the situation are:

1. Circumscribing the problem and locating it in time and place. This systematically focuses attention on recent relevant history, on what has happened to the counselee and what connections there might be between events in the here and now or in the recent past, and his or her emotional state at the time. Helping to inventory in sufficient detail the natural history of a crisis generally has a controlling effect on symptoms. By cataloging emotional states and the effects of the disorganized behavior or thinking, you go beyond the limits of the experience into other areas where there is good functioning; in this way the

counselee is able to experience the limits of his or her distress and to gain some control and knowledge.

2. Participating with the counselee in the organization of the problem. This is extremely important, especially in the early and more disorganized phase of the crisis. Here we are interested in what important elements of the individual's life have a bearing on the crisis. One explores the potential for change in various aspects of the situation. What can be changed, and what are some ways and techniques for effecting the desired change? As you work with the counselee and have him/her see how you analyze and organize the situation by surveying potential problems and various solutions, he or she may begin to identify with you as a model and in this way gain greater control.

3. Limiting the duration of the encounter and focusing on growth and development. Throughout the period of problem solving, you should indicate that there will be time limits on working together. In many crisis situations in various settings, visits once or twice weekly of about one-half hour, tapering quickly in length and frequency, seem to work well. Since a high percentage of crises are resolved within 20 days, it is often not necessary to maintain continuous and prolonged contact. You should also indicate that you do not expect to intervene in the problem directly unless, in your judgment, it is deemed necessary. In some instances, it may be advisable to refer the counselee to a physician if symptoms seem to warrant medical attention or to a mental health professional if distress is prolonged.

   Keep the focus on expanding the counselee's resources by the process of taking inventory and exploring options. The possibility of growth and development is greater than the possibility of the crisis becoming a more serious one.

4. Avoiding removal of the counselee from the responsibilities of day-to-day living. Experience indicates that it's best for the counselee not to be removed from work or other occupation during counseling—or to be removed only briefly. In this way, the person acknowledges his/her feelings, including the wish to withdraw, but remains identified with social reality, legitimizes the feelings, and still acts responsibly. Actively making the decision to remain socially responsible is often a powerful influence in maturation and problem solving.

5. Creating a dynamic and renegotiable plan for dealing with a crisis. Any plan that is developed jointly by the counselee and counselor should be flexible. As the crisis situation changes, new options and alternatives may become necessary.

6. Building in a follow-up component. Any intervention plan should include some follow-up provisions that allow the counselor and counselee to evaluate the success of an intervention and to make any necessary adjustments.

When the Professional Can Be of Help

In some cases, a crisis or other critical event in a person's life precipitates a more severe disorder. This is especially true when the individual's history includes previous difficulty either in a school, work, or family context.

The most common problem to be aware of is depression, the feeling of frustration and discouragement which is usually controllable by people but may persist or develop into a more serious problem. In these instances the counselee should also see a mental health professional. When an individual is persistently withdrawn, has been missing significant amounts of work or school time, or complains about a lack of energy and/or disturbances in sleep or appetite, you should direct that person to a physician or therapist.

Relatively few people will require referral to psychiatrists. By keeping in mind the general notions and rules of thumb outlined above, and by discussing and learning from actual situations, many peer counselors have become quite skillful in providing this kind of help.

Case 1

A male student comes in to see you. He appears both agitated and depressed; he claims that he is having increasing difficulty studying because he can't keep his mind on his work. His thoughts keep racing and he is having trouble getting to sleep and staying asleep. He feels as though nothing really matters any more, and he's worried about how this feeling is affecting his schoolwork. Ever since he can remember, he has wanted to be a lawyer, but now he's not sure. When he felt this agitated in the past, he'd taken some of his mother's tranquilizers and they helped him get some sleep. Since he doesn't have tranquilizers at school, he's starting to drink at night, but it hasn't helped his sleep much and leaves him with a bad hangover the next morning.

As a crisis counselor, what is your response?

Some possible approaches:

1. Get a clearer definition of the problem. Get more history regarding the onset of his agitation and depressed feelings. Explore events occurring at the time of onset. (In this case, the onset coincided with his taking the Law School Aptitude Test.)
2. Explore his feelings about significant recent events. Explore how the student feels about the prospect of law school. (The student revealed that he was very ambivalent about becoming a lawyer and felt a strong desire to become a musician. He expressed concern about his parents' reaction. He reported that he felt unable to discuss this with parents, but did mention a sister.) Explore his support system. (The student accepted the counselor's suggestion that perhaps he could discuss his

career concerns with his sister and/or an advisor with whom he had
a good relationship.)

3. Discuss more appropriate coping strategies to use for insomnia in-
    stead of using alcohol.

    a.   Discuss the use of relaxation techniques as aids in falling asleep.
    Provide help in learning the skills and/or provide information on
    where they can be learned.

    b.   If necessary, recommend that the student be evaluated by a physi-
    cian for short-term sleep medication as well as a more complete diag-
    nostic assessment of his depression.

Case 2

You receive a phone call from a young man who is upset and concerned
about the woman he dates. For the past two weeks or so she's been very
cold and aloof, refusing to answer his phone calls and spending increasing
amounts of time alone. When she does speak to him, she claims she needs
time to think and be by herself. He wouldn't ordinarily be worried, but
in talking with her roommate, he learned that the woman was talking
about ending it all and killing herself. Her roommate and the man are
both quite concerned and they have come to you for help.

As the crisis counselor, what is your response?

Some possible approaches:

1. Ask the man to encourage the woman to come in and see you. While
    discussing this with him, allow him an opportunity to vent some of
    his own feelings of anxiety and concern. By providing support and
    structure for him, you enable him to be more in control of his own
    feelings and anxieties, and you indirectly help the young woman in
    crisis. Talking with the man also provides an opportunity to assess
    how much support he can provide in the situation and what other re-
    sources are available to the woman.

2. Mobilize the best resources for encouraging the woman to come in
    for a face-to-face meeting. These resources may include the young
    man or the roommate. It is important not to involve unnecessary peo-
    ple in the process.

3. If the woman will not agree to come in, she may agree to phone you,
    at which time you could encourage her to come in and talk about how
    she's been feeling. You can best assess her strengths and resources
    in a face-to-face meeting and determine the extent to which she is in
    crisis.

During your first meeting with her you learn that she's a sophomore,
pre-med, with serious plans for a career in medicine. A friend of hers had

made a suicide attempt with tranquilizers while in high school. The young man she dates is leaving to begin graduate school in the east in January. She's gotten a positive pregnancy test a week ago and her religious beliefs oppose abortion.

What are some of your options in developing an intervention plan?

1. Provide ample opportunity for the woman to explore her feelings about her situation: the young man, the abortion, her religious concerns. While she should feel free to discuss these feelings and issues, the contact should not be open-ended. A time-limited contact will avoid obsessive machinations that may heighten her sense of helplessness. As a crisis worker, you may have to be more active than would ordinarily be appropriate in a counseling role. Structuring an interview, providing a time frame, or suggesting alternatives are all part of the repertoire of skills used in crisis intervention.

2. Assess the risk of her attempting suicide. Ask whether the woman is having feelings of wanting to harm herself. It may be necessary to do a full assessment of suicidal risk, including finding out whether she has a plan, assessing the lethality of the plan, eliciting admission of prior suicide attempts, and so on, as outlined in this chapter's section on suicide.

3. Explore alternatives. Let her describe and evaluate her options as she sees them, and then perhaps suggest some she has overlooked—e.g., abortion versus adoption versus raising the child, seeking religious counseling on religious issues, and so on.

4. Provide assistance and information about the options chosen. If abortion is the option chosen, provide help in locating a physician through referral to appropriate services. While it is important to be helpful during a crisis, it is equally important that the counselee have an active role in developing a plan of action: "doing for" should not be substituted for "doing with." It is essential that a crisis intervention plan enhance the person's sense of active mastery and not foster unnecessary dependence.

5. Arrange for a follow-up visit. A good crisis intervention plan always includes some follow-up to assess and evaluate how well the plan is working and to determine if further counseling is necessary or desired.

Summary: Crisis Intervention

Crisis intervention is a specialized counseling approach used when a person's usual ways of coping with stress become ineffective or begin to break down. Counseling in crisis situations (such as suicide, death, severe loss, or trauma) calls for action on the part of the counselor without relieving the person of the responsibility of finally solving the problem. Organizing the problem into components and systematically exploring possible solutions is the key to crisis counseling. Maintaining flexibility about alternatives is important, as is a clear follow-up plan. Awareness of social resources and networks is also important in crisis intervention. In many settings, crisis counselors utilize a team approach for mobilizing resources and sharing the problem solving.

References

Caplan, G. *Principles of Preventive Psychiatry.* New York: Basic Books, 1964, Ch. 3.

Huff, L. *People in Crisis.* Reading, MA: Addison-Wesley, 1979.

Suggested Readings

Delworth, U., and T. Rudow. *Crisis Center Hotline: A Guidebook to Beginning and Operating.* Springfield, IL: C. Thomas, 1972.

Lester, D., and G. Brockopp. *Crisis Intervention and Counseling by Telephone.* Springfield, IL: C. Thomas, 1973.

DEPRESSION

Depression has often been referred to as "the common cold of mental disorder" and, like the common cold, it occurs in varying intensities. In this section we will discuss some of the symptoms of depression. It should be kept in mind, however, that "depression" can mean different things to different people. To one individual, being depressed might mean being tired and draggy; to another, it might mean unhappiness coupled with tension or fear. To speak of "depression" is to speak of a very idiosyncratic notion: we each conceptualize and experience depression in different ways.

This section will focus on the "normal" periods of depression experienced by all of us at different times in our lives. This "normal depressed mood" is typically experienced when one encounters losses such as the breakup of a love relationship, the death of a close relative or friend, a failure at work or school, or a sudden rejection. These events that often leave us depressed are clearly within the range of normal human experience.

This usual sort of depression is very different from the more serious affective disorders diagnosed by hospital psychiatrists and psychologists. The affective disorders—often called unipolar depression (or neurotic and psychotic depression) and bipolar disorder (or manic-depressive psychosis)—are usually chronic mental disorders that must be treated by professionals. As peer counselors, we are much more concerned with depression as a reaction to traumatic (but normal) life events. Individuals experiencing extreme or long-term depression are best referred to mental health professionals.

What are the common symptoms of depression? They may easily be divided into four groups: physical, emotional, cognitive, and behavioral.

The most common physical symptoms of depression are changes in eating and sleeping patterns. Although depressed individuals occasionally eat *more* than they otherwise would, depression is generally characterized by a lack of interest in food and a weight loss that can sometimes be alarming. Sleeping habits may also be disrupted. The depressed person might have difficulty falling asleep, sleep irregularly, awaken early in the morning, or occasionally not be able to get out of bed at all. Fatigue is the most common complaint of depressed individuals. Other physical symptoms that can accompany depression include constipation, frequent urination, loss of interest in sex, dizziness, and frequent headaches.

The emotion or affective symptoms of depression are also easily recognized. Depressed people feel helpless, hopeless, and generally unhappy. They may also feel worthless, guilty, lonely, ashamed, or useless. Sadness, however, is the most common affective state and is usually accompanied by crying. The depressed person's day is characterized by these feelings of sadness, which are usually most intense in the morning hours. Some depressed individuals also feel anxious or agitated; this is, in fact, quite common. Also, depressed people often experience no gratification from interests and activities that previously brought them satisfaction. Work, hobbies, recreational activities, and close friends no longer seem exciting or interesting.

The perceptions or thoughts that accompany depression are particularly apparent to the peer counselor, because they are generally quite evident in the depressed person's conversation. The depressed person often has a very negative self-image, considering him or herself inadequate or incompetent. Past failures or disappointments may be exaggerated and thought of as highly significant. These thoughts are often accompanied by self-blame and guilt for one's troubles, and for the problems of others, for which the depressed person mistakenly takes responsibility. Finally, the depressed person thinks about the future with great pessimism. The smallest obstacles seem like great hurdles; potential gains are viewed as dreaded failures.

Depression is associated with some obvious changes in behavior. Depressed persons are often very passive, having little motivation to initiate any kind of activity. In severe cases, routine tasks like grooming or changing clothes are difficult to initiate. Depressed individuals also can suffer from psychomotor retardation and lethargy. They walk and speak slowly and react to stimuli after long delays. Depressed people are slow to initiate physical and mental activity: they seem to move slowly and avoid problem-solving tasks. This avoidance seems to result from acute indecisiveness. Decisions are viewed as overwhelming; outcomes appear frightening.

Example

Lately Dave hasn't had much of an appetite. He has turned down a couple of good offers to go out for food and fun with friends, saying that he has a lot of work. He acknowledges to himself that he feels pressured and unsocial. Without intending to, it seems, he is hiding his true feelings so as not to "bother" his friends. When he sits down to work, he is unable to concentrate for more than a few minutes. He feels bored, and he wishes his life were more interesting. He also wishes that people would drop by to say hello more often. He wonders what it is about him that puts people off. He's been doing a lot of introspection during the last several days, and it makes him sleepy. He takes naps instead of working—another recent habit.

Dave's mother is in a dilemma. She is agonizing over whether to divorce his father. The lines of communication between her and her husband have been rapidly closing up. She also doesn't like the fact that her husband pushes Dave so hard about succeeding in life. Dave is the only one she can talk to; he seems to be both understanding and objective.

How should we, as peer counselors, deal with depressed clients?

1. Discover more precisely what an individual means when he or she says, "I'm depressed." As we've already mentioned, depression is experienced differently by different people. Is the person anxious? Immobile? Feeling guilty? Fatigued? Cynical? Helpless? What specific thoughts, feelings, and behaviors does this person label as "being depressed"? It is important to focus on *specific problems*. If the person says "I'm so depressed," narrow down what is wrong, using questions like: "What specifically is bothering you?"
2. Explore events in the depressed person's life that are controllable (like what to do each day) rather than events that he or she cannot control (like ending world hunger singlehandedly).
3. Concentrate on small steps that the individual can actually take. Motivating the depressed person to do small tasks—like writing a letter, doing the laundry, or going to the supermarket—can sometimes help the person begin to regain his or her sense of personal worth and efficacy.
4. Use a step-by-step approach to motivate the counselee to initiate larger tasks. Break complicated tasks, like finding a job or changing living situations, into small subtasks and ask how he or she would go about starting some of these smaller tasks.
5. Another approach that can motivate depressed individuals is behavioral contracting (see Chapter 3, Part 2.). Make an agreement with the person that s/he will accomplish certain tasks, and encourage the use of self-reward for completing the task. For example, "Would you agree to do X and call me when you do it?" Try to find what kinds of things the person enjoys doing, and pair them with the accomplishment of more mundane, yet important, tasks. It is very important that you give him or her much positive feedback for even the smallest steps in the right direction.

Using these principles as a starting point, let's imagine how a counseling session with Dave, the person in the scenario, might proceed.

Dave has decided to get some peer counseling, so he walks over to the counseling center. You are on duty, and he asks to speak with you.

Dave: Do you have a few minutes? I'd like to talk.

You: Sure. What's on your mind?

Dave: Well, I'm not able to concentrate on my work, and I don't seem to care about much at all.

You: So, you're having trouble concentrating and caring. And how are you feeling?

Dave: I feel sort of numb and a little depressed.

You: Numb and a bit depressed. . . . What do you mean by depressed?

Dave: I think I should be enjoying myself, but I can't generate any interest in having fun.

You: And how do you feel about that?

Dave: Like everything is kind of futile and not worth the hassle of working out.

You should continue to elicit feelings from Dave. He says he's depressed, but remember: depression is a unique set of thoughts, feelings, and behaviors for every person. After talking about Dave's feelings some, try to focus on what *specifically* is bothering him.

You: So everything seems futile. What do you mean by "everything?"

Dave: My friends want me to have a good time with them, but I don't think it'll help me feel any better. I used to like my classes, but school is seeming more and more artificial and pointless. I can't even return my overdue library books . . . . Just too much hassle.

You: Your friends are trying to cheer you up?

Dave: Yes, but they don't know how depressed I really am, and I don't think they'll be able to.

You: You mentioned that school seemed "artificial." Could you say more about that?

Dave: It seems that the more intense classes get, the less I can see their relation to the real world.

You: I hear what you're saying and we will talk about it some more. The intensity of school life can be very frustrating. What else, outside of school, is going on in your life?

Dave: I feel sort of stuck between my parents. They aren't talking to each other—they say it all to me. My mom thinks that my dad doesn't care about her, and it's tearing him up, but he can't tell her. He's sort of like me . . . very sensitive, but he makes people think he's always objective and logical. I just try to listen to them both because I know they need a sounding board—and I'm it.

So, Dave is feeling depressed, and his depression revolves around school and a pending crisis at home that is being dumped on him. At this point, you should continue to explore both of these issues with Dave: his parents and school. When you sense that Dave has been able to disclose his thoughts and feelings fully, try to move the conversation toward those things from which Dave still gets pleasure. What could he be doing to make himself feel better and thus be better able to cope with his parents and with his schoolwork?

You: You've made things pretty clear for me, Dave. I understand why you are feeling depressed. What kinds of things do you still enjoy doing?

Dave: When I'm not sleeping, I've been doing a lot of reading. I'm afraid I'm sort of retreating that way, though. That bothers me.

You: How does that bother you?

Dave: It seems like I should be doing something more constructive.

You: What kinds of things would be more constructive?

Dave: Organizing my studies or doing my laundry or practicing the violin or something.

You: Okay, so those would be constructive things to do . . . but would they make you feel better?

Dave: I've wanted to just go out and play on these nice days, shoot some baskets or throw a frisbee. But when I've got that kind of energy, I feel I ought to study, so I just stay inside.

At this point, you and Dave should discuss some specific ways in which he can deal with his parents. What could he tell them? How should he respond to their demands without feeling guilty? How can he help them? Where should he draw the line? Also, you may want to discuss Dave's frustrations about school. What could he be going to make his school experience more meaningful?

Finally, it is time to wrap things up for this session. Dave feels like he got a lot off his chest and would like to talk some more next week. It is probably a good idea to end on a positive note with some kind of contract specifying behaviors he should focus on in the coming week.

Dave: I'm glad you were so easy to talk to. I feel a lot better. Can I stop by again in a few days to let you know how I'm feeling?

You: Okay. I agree to talk in a few days . . . In the meantime, would you be willing to do a few things?

Dave: Like what?

You: Well, how about getting a few of those little things done that have been on your mind?

Dave: Like my laundry and returning those books to the library? Okay. Sounds pretty easy right now.

You: Sounds great to me. And when you finish that, why don't you go out and shoot some hoops for an hour or two and then I'll see you again on Friday. Okay with you?

Dave: Great. It'll sure feel good to clear up some of these hassles and get some exercise.

You: Okay. See you Friday!

Dave: Bye.

This entire process should take at least an hour to complete. Don't rush things—they will unfold with only a little prompting. In this session, you have:

—   elicited Dave's feelings

—   gotten a handle on how Dave feels when he says he's depressed

—   discovered some causes for his depression

—   discussed some strategies by which Dave can deal with his problems

—   motivated Dave to take some small steps toward resuming his "normal" lifestyle.

—   ended on a positive note; Dave feels better and an agreement has been reached whereby Dave will start getting his life back together, reward himself with a pleasurable activity, and talk to you again in a few days.

This supportive, problem-solving approach is suitable to many situations where there are manifestations of depressed feeling and thinking. If Dave reported continued inability to concentrate, if he felt increasingly hopeless and guilty, if he was waking up early in the morning and unable to get back to sleep, a consultation would be called for. In particular, if he began to have thoughts of harming himself in some way, a no-suicide contract would be called for, as well as discussions with a referral to a professional. This issue is discussed in the following section on suicide.

Summary: Depression

1. An approach, based on good listening and supportive problem-solving, which focuses on feelings and behavior change can be very helpful to many persons experiencing depression.

2. Eliciting accurate and complete information is important.
3. Familiarity with the varied expressions of depression is helpful in estimating the seriousness of the problem.

SUICIDE

Although suicide calls to peer counselors are relatively uncommon (compared to other types of counseling calls), suicide is not an infrequent oc-
currence. About 28,000 suicides are reported each year, with an additional 50,000 unreported or misclassified.* In the entire population of
the United States, suicide is the *tenth* most frequent cause of death.
Among fifteen-to-nineteen-year-olds it's the *third* leading cause of death,
and among college students it is *second* only to automobile accidents.

Fifteen out of every 100,000 students kill themselves each year.**
And since there are about ten times as many suicide attempts as completed
suicides, it is estimated that in the United States 5 million people are alive
today who have attempted suicide.

Certain segments of the population seem particularly suicide-prone.
Divorced and widowed men and women have particularly high rates of
suicide, and although women are three times more likely to attempt suicide than men, men succeed in killing themselves three times more often
than women. Typically, suicide attempters are young (age 20 to 30) females, while committers are older (over 40) males. These sex differences
are probably due to the different methods that men and women use in
attempting suicide. While men often use guns or jump off buildings,
women typically overdose with pills or cut their wrists. This difference
reflects prescribed sex-role behavior (for example, men more often own
guns than women). Since it takes longer to die from taking a drug overdose or slashing one's wrists than from shooting oneself or jumping from
a building, women who attempt suicide are often discovered still alive and
rushed to hospitals.

Some individuals, particularly adolescents, commit suicide in order
to punish others. Often they are trying to manipulate others (usually parents) into feeling guilty and inadequate. This motive for suicide is called
the "ultimate revenge." Some individuals kill themselves because of extreme anger. Occasionally, when people feel they have been abused by
a loved one, they want to kill that person. At times, this "murder" impulse
is directed toward the self. A third, although rare, cause of suicide is psy-

---

*Some automobile accidents, plane collisions, drownings, and deaths of the ter-
minally ill are actually suicides.
**The rate of suicide among nonstudents of the same age is lower: 10 per
100,000.

Suicide Facts

Expected incidence: 10/100,000 population ages 18-25

Student incidence: 15/100,000 student population

In the 15- to 19-year old age group, suicide ranks as the third most frequent cause of death (after automobile accidents and cancer).

In the U.S. population, suicide is the tenth most frequent cause of death. About 28,000 Americans commit suicide each year, with estimates ranging to 50,000 per year.

Profiles

	Attempters	**Committers**
Sex	Female (F:M = 3:1)	Male ("older, white, unemployed male in poor health, divorced and living alone") (M:F = 3:1)
Age	20-30	40 +
Method	Barbiturates	Gunshot
Reason	Marital problems, depression	Health, marital problems, depression, psychosis, alcoholism

Twelve percent of all suicide attempts are by adolescents. Ninety percent of these attempts are by females.

The following are typical indicators that a person may be considering suicide:

—Loss

—Social isolation

—Suicidal act as communication

—No other options perceived

—Poor interpersonal capacities

—Marital isolation

—Disturbed communication

—Help rejection

Sources: *Statistical abstract of the U.S., 1980.* Washington, D.C.: Dept. of Commerce, Bureau of Census, pp. 78–79.

McIntire, M. S. and Angle, C. R., *Suicide Attempts in Children and Youth.* New York: Harper & Row, 1980, pp. 1–13.

chotic behavior, such as trying to fly out of a window. A fourth reason that some people commit suicide is a desire to determine their own destinies. For example, a terminally ill patient may save her sleeping pills by hiding them under her mattress, and then, after several weeks, take them all at once, reasoning that she doesn't want to lie around waiting for a painful death from cancer. Another motive for suicide is the "trial by ordeal." In this instance, individuals are "testing fate," figuring that if they are supposed to live, they'll just wake up; if they're not supposed to live, they won't.

The most common motive for suicide, however, is a complete absence of other alternatives, and this is the most useful way for peer counselors to conceptualize suicide. An individual cannot imagine any other way to avoid his or her "painful" life, and believes that it is impossible to change. *The person feels out of options, hopeless, and helpless.*

Suicide is often the result of severe or prolonged depression. Of course, most depressed individuals do not try to kill themselves, and not all victims of suicide are depressed before killing themselves. In fact, very severely depressed individuals often do not have the energy or motivation to take their own lives. A person who is somewhat depressed and sinking rapidly is most vulnerable to suicide. The person in the depths of depression generally is not.

Counseling the Suicidal Person

For most peer counselors, suicide counseling occurs on the telephone rather than face to face. The procedure described in this chapter was specifically designed for telephone counseling, and it might be useful to keep a copy of the check-list near your hotline for easy reference. However, the procedure can also be used for face-to-face interaction. (Another exercise in using these steps can be done by reviewing appendix B, which is a transcript of telephone counseling with a suicidal man.)

Step 1: Defining the Problem

If you suspect that the person you are talking to may be thinking of suicide, you should frankly ask whether s/he is considering suicide as an option. Counselors are often afraid to ask this question. They worry that they might be putting ideas into their clients' heads. Nonsense! No one will ever answer the question with, "No, I wasn't considering suicide, but that's a good idea, I think I will kill myself, thanks."

If an individual is considering suicide, s/he will appreciate your frank discussion of the topic. If the person is not considering suicide, you can simply continue with your usual counseling strategies.

Often clients will give you clues that they are seriously considering suicide. If you detect any of these clues, ask "Is suicide an option that you

Depression and Suicide Risk

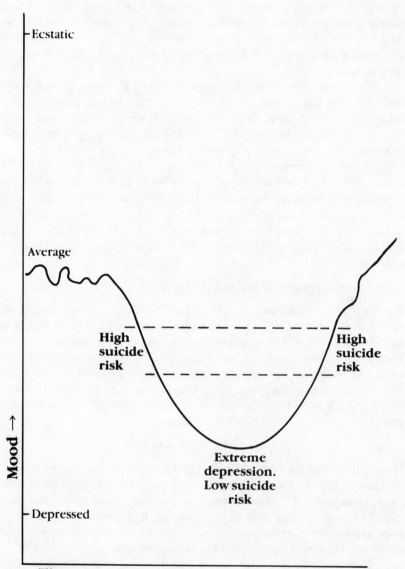

are considering?" For instance, the person may be considering suicide if s/he:

— has recently made out a will
— has recently bought a gun
— has shipped the kids off to a relative for the weekend
— has put the dog in a kennel
— has written several close, personal letters to old friends and relatives.

Remember, if suicide seems at all possible, *ASK!*

One thing to keep in mind is that at least part of the person does not want to die. He or she probably has not called you to say good-bye, but rather, he or she is reaching out, hoping that there is an alternative.

Step 2: Assessing Lethality

It is very important that you discover how close the person actually is to killing himself or herself. If the person has already taken pills or slashed wrists, tracing the call will take too long. Instead, do what you can to find out the person's location and then call the police or paramedics.

If the person has not actually harmed him/herself (and this is generally the case), you must find out two things: (1) what is currently going on in the person's life, and (2) how much thought has he or she given to suicide (i.e., does he or she have a plan, an easily available means, etc.). Try to find out if the person's life has recently undergone any major changes or if the person has had any particularly stressful experiences. For example, has there recently been a death of a close friend or relative? Is the person suffering from a painful physical illness? Has the person recently lost his or her job or is s/he under considerable financial stress? Has the person recently moved to a new place?

It is also useful to find out the person's "suicidal history." Is suicide something he or she frequently thinks about? Has the person attempted suicide before? This last question is very important. Repeated attempters have the highest suicide rate of all: eight or nine out of ten ultimately kill themselves.

Finally, it is very important to find out how real the act of suicide is for the person: How does he or she plan to kill himself or herself? Where are the pills? Where is the gun? Is he or she under the influence of drugs or alcohol? Is he or she alone? Try to get this information as quickly as possible. *But* it is important not to make the person feel as if he or she is getting the third degree. Continue to use your counseling skills: show accurate empathy; paraphrase accurately; reflect feelings.

Step 3: Getting Information and Reducing Lethality

It is usually not difficult to find out the first name of your client. However, other pieces of personal information may not come as easily. If possible, try to get the person's phone number. Explain to him or her that you are not sending out the police (assuming that the person has not harmed him/herself) but that you want the phone number for your own use, so that you can call back if you don't hear from him or her after an agreed-upon period of time.

It is important to determine if the person is alone or if there are others in his or her life who could be trusted. Is s/he seeing a therapist? Are there any close friends or relatives nearby? Try to determine what kind of support system exists for your client.

Finally, try to convince the person (again using counseling skills) to reduce the lethality of the situation—that is, to flush the pills down the toilet, unload the gun, or give the razor to a neighbor.

Step 4: Building Trust and Rapport

Before alternatives and solutions can be considered, you must allow the suicidal person to vent his or her pent-up feelings and thoughts. You might be the first human contact for the person in several days, so it is important to not rush him/her. Rather, use your counseling skills—ask open questions, paraphrase, work with feelings—to try to hear and understand what the person is saying. Validate his/her pain; recognize that his/her life might be rough. Show caring and concern; tell the counselee that you really are concerned that he or she might hurt himself or herself. This is no time to understate the person's feelings. It is important to paraphrase accurately. For example, if he or she says, "I'm so confused and scared, I want to end it all," don't just say, "So, things are a little rough right now." Remember, accurate empathy is very important.

If the person is crying uncontrollably, let him or her cry for a while. Reassure the person that it's okay to cry, that you won't hang up, that it's all right to get some of the feelings out. If the person can't stop crying and is feeling out of control, help him or her stop—be firm and supportive. Say "Take it easy, it's difficult for me to hear you. I can't understand you. Let's slow down for a minute." Be assertive, yet gentle. Continue to let the person talk about how he or she is feeling.

Step 5: Dealing with the Problem and Generating Alternatives

After the person has talked about his or her bad feelings for a while, it is important to turn the conversation gently toward more positive things and to appeal to the side of the person that wants to continue to live. First, offer the person support and encouragement by helping him or her reinterpret the situation in a positive manner—talk about his or her courage in calling and being willing to share such deep feelings with you. Then, try to get a handle on the situation: try to find out how long the person has been considering suicide and what precipitated the feelings of wanting to die. Talk about these thoughts as long as the person wishes, but try to stay with the situation as it exists here and now.

Next, discuss with the person the options or alternatives he or she might have. How has he or she handled similar situations in the past? What can he or she do to develop or build a support system? Who can he or she call for support and comfort? Discuss what he or she can do to change the current situation; find out what he or she is doing or can do to take care of himself or herself. Try to encourage the person to continue daily activities and to take things slowly, one step at a time.

Step 6: Terminating the Session

This is the most important part of suicide counseling: getting the person to make a no-suicide contract with you and convincing the person to obtain some kind of follow-up help.

The no-suicide contract is an explicit agreement between you and a suicidal person that he or she will not hurt himself or herself before speaking with you or another professional. Have the person actually say, "I will not kill myself without talking to you first." Then try to establish a time frame for the contract—have the person agree to call you back to check-in after a specific interval of time, such as 24 hours.* Sometimes it is necessary to get a contract for just an hour or two and then have the person call back.**

After making a no-suicide contract, refer the person to professional help. Ask the person to call you and tell you when s/he has made the contact. Reinforce the referral—encourage the person to complain (if things aren't going well) directly to the therapist.

Finally, if your support is not accepted and the person refuses to make a no-suicide contract, *don't hang up.* Buy time; talk some more. Go back to step 4 and move through the procedure again. If, as rarely happens, the person refuses all help and actually decides to kill himself or herself, you can try deterring the person with guilt by saying things like:

---

*If you were able to get the person's phone number and s/he doesn't call you after the agreed-upon time, you should not hesitate to call him/her.
**Drye, R., Goulding, R. and Goulding, M. "No-suicide Decisions: Patient Monitoring of Suicidal Risk." *Am. J. Psychiatry* 130 (1973): 2.

— You're copping out; you're taking the easy way out.

— How will your children feel knowing that Mommy (or Daddy) killed herself (or himself)? Your children will live a life of guilt and pain. Who will raise them?

— I know you could kill yourself. But give yourself one last chance. It's your *life!*

Let us warn you: don't use these obvious manipulations unless you are convinced'that there is no other way to get the person to save his or her life.

After dealing with a suicide call, even if the outcome is good, *you* might consider talking to another counselor or professional about your feelings. If you use the procedure outlined above, you will know that you've done everything you could to prevent a suicide. But remember, it is also important to take care of yourself; if you are feeling at all guilty, unsettled, manipulated, or anxious, talk to someone about it. Support groups for suicide counselors are very important. Don't let your feelings and thoughts about suicide end when you hang up the phone; share them with others.

Suicide Checklist*

Step 1.   Define the Problem. Remember, if at least a part of the person didn't want help, he/she wouldn't call.

A.   A suicide call is a "cry for help" from the part of the person that wants to live. This part is fighting other parts of the person that want to die, give up, avoid pain.

B.   Possible motives for suicide may vary.

1) Manipulation—the ultimate revenge

2) Anger—misdirected murder (particularly after abuse from a loved one)

3) Psychosis—distorted reality

4) Self-determination—"I'm not going to wait for painful death"

5) Trial by ordeal—"If I'm supposed to live, I'll just wake up"

6) Limited alternatives. Caller does not know how else to avoid his/her painful life and does not feel it possible to change his/her life.**

---

*Adapted from Evans, Joan and Boyd, Mike. "Suicidal Crisis." Riverside, CA: Helpline Volunteer Center, *n.d.*
**Note: If we view suicidal people as motivated by a lack of alternatives, we can best deal with all motives. Be careful not to let your personal prejudices enter into your work. ALL SUICIDE CALLS MUST BE CONSIDERED REAL. *See appendix B.

Step 2. Assess Lethality.
　　　A. Recent major changes and/or stresses in a person's life increase the likelihood of suicide.
　　　　1) Loss of loved one (death, divorce, separation)
　　　　2) Physical illness (particularly fatal)
　　　　3) Loss of job (fired, retirement)
　　　　4) Financial stress
　　　　5) Moved to new place (house, town, etc.)
　　　　6) No support systems: family, friends that listen
　　　　7) Hopelessness
　　　B. It is important to determine how much thought a person has given to a suicide attempt and whether his or her immediate environment contains specific tools of suicide.
　　　　1) Thinking about suicide—especially impulsively?
　　　　2) Attempted suicide previously?
　　　　3) Plan developed (giving away possesions, etc.)?
　　　　4) Means available (know where to get pills, gun, etc.)?
　　　　5) Intoxicated with drug or alcohol?
　　　　6) Alone and means immediately available?
　　　　7) Speed and reversibility of method?

Step 3. Get information in a natural way, in the course of the conversation, *not* in a forced way) and reduce lethality.
　　　A. Anyone else there?
　　　B. Therapist, relatives, friends in area they trust? (Support system.)
　　　C. Reduction of lethality (get rid of pills, gun, etc.).
　　　D. First name (particularly important with drug overdose)?
　　　E. Phone number?
　　　F. Full name?
　　　G. Address?

Step 4. Build trust and rapport, and encourage the caller to vent emotions.
　　　A. How to deal with:
　　　　1) *Yelling, screaming, ranting, raving*—Say in an assertive, supportive manner: "Take it easy. It's difficult for me to hear you. I can't understand you. Let's slow down now."
　　　　2) *Crying, sobbing*—Gently say, "I'm listening to you. It's okay. I won't go away. Go ahead and take some time to cry—get some of it out."
　　　　3) *Uncontrollable crying, loss of control*—Help him/her *stop* and get back his/her self-control. (See 4A1 above.)

4) *Anger*—The person is not angry at you! Don't take it personally: "I'm trying to listen but it's hard when you yell at me. I know you're angry, and you have a right to be, but I want to hear you and it is hard when you direct your anger at me."

B. How to:
1) Build rapport: Facilitate the venting of feelings. Hear and understand what the person is saying.
2) Validate: Recognize that the person's hurt and pain are real. "Yes, it *is* painful and rough . . . right now."
3) Clarify the state of depression: Ask the person directly if suicide is one of the alternatives that s/he is thinking about.

Step 5. Offer realistic hope, support, and encouragement.
A. Reinforce the person for having the courage to call.
B. Reinterpret the situation in a positive manner.
C. Reinterpret the caller's self-image as having worth. "To be in this much pain you must feel deeply. People who allow themselves to feel that deeply are very special, indeed!"

Step 6. Deal with the problem and generate alternatives.
A. What precipitated the feelings of wanting to kill yourself?
B. How long has the situation existed?
C. What kinds of things have you tried and/or thought of?
D. What does this situation or feeling mean?
E. How have you (your friends) handled similar situations in the past?
F. How can you build a support system?
1) Who can help you through this time? (People can't help if they don't know.)
2) If not family or friends—or a partial support from them—then how about a counselor, agency and/or self-help group? (AA, Suiciders Anonymous)
G. How can you change your situation and/or feeling now?

Step 7. Termination phase: Make a no-suicide contract and refer to professional help.
A. If support is accepted, develop a plan of action.
1) Contract: a promise not to harm self, and to remove suicidal means to a "safer place."
2) Appointment with therapist, agency, etc.
3) Calling a friend or relative to come spend the night.

4) A few days rest in the hospital (if necessary).

5) Contact the next day, after the plan has been going, to make sure that the person's support system has begun to form. At that time make it clear that you are glad that s/he is taking care of himself/herself and that you could help in this crisis. If necessary, the line is still available on a 24-hour basis.

B. If support is not accepted:

1) If the person has harmed himself/herself, CALL POLICE.

2) Buy time for the person. Keep talking.

C. If all supportive efforts fail (i.e., you have heard and understood what the person is trying to say, it has been established that you are interested and genuinely concerned, and you have taken the time to form a positive relationship), try to dissuade the person as supportively, positively, and truthfully as possible with these devices:

1) Suggest that the person is copping out—taking the easy way out.

2) Say, "Your children will be raised with guilt and pain. And who will raise them?"

3) Say, "You're not being fair to yourself. You could live in this world and experience some fun and happiness. Tomorrow usually feels better. Try it. You can kill yourself another time."

4) Existential reality: "You can kill yourself. BUT your life doesn't have to be absurd, unfair, painful. You're bright and sensitive, and have more strength and courage than you give yourself credit for. With some help, you can learn better how to deal with life."

Exercise 1. Test Your Suicide I.Q.

TRUE OR FALSE:

1. People who attempt suicide rarely talk about it.
2. Suicidal tendencies are not inherited.
3. People who attempt suicide never *really* want to die.
4. All people who attempt suicide are psychotic.
5. If a person seems calm after they talk about suicide, they are over the crisis.
6. More men than women complete suicide.
7. Most people leave notes of intent or cause.
8. Suicide is usually done for revenge against another person.

9. Once truly suicidal, people will be suicidal the rest of their lives.
10. All of the people in this room are capable of being suicidal if they
    are pushed far enough.

Exercise 2

Students should consider the following statements. Discussion could be
held in class or in small groups.
IF YOU WERE IN THESE SITUATIONS, WOULD YOU CONSIDER
ENDING YOUR LIFE?

1. Incurably ill, middle income, facing a long, painful death.
2. Just had all loved ones die in an automobile accident.
3. Broke up with spouse through divorce.
4. There seems to be no meaning to your life.

Exercise 3

If a videotaped sucide crisis call is available, instructor and class review
it, using assessment scheme suggested as an outline for viewing and discussion. Appendix B may be used if no tape is available.

REVIEW OF CHAPTER 4: CRISIS COUNSELING SKILLS

A. Crisis Counseling
    1. Crises are normal reactions to sudden changes or unanticipated,
    stressful events.
    2. In crisis, a person's usual coping behavior is strained or begins
    to break down.
    3. The counselor is active listener and collaborator, encouraging:
    —   assessment of situation, setting it in context
    —   evaluation of resources
    —   exploring/suggesting options and additional resources
    —   modeling a joint effort in organizing the problem and system-
        atically exploring possible responses or options.
    4. Follow-up provisions allow evaluating of interventions.
    5. Counselor is alert to untoward appearance of unusual anxiety, de-
    pression, or disorganization.

Answers to Exercise 1: 1:F. 2:T. 3:F. 4:F. 5:F. 6:T. 7:T. 8:F. 9:F. 10:T.

B. Depression
  1. Symptoms
     — Physical—changes in eating and sleeping patterns, fatigue, constipation, urinary frequency, no interest in sex, dizziness, headaches
     — Emotional—sadness, helplessness, hopelessness, crying, melancholia, occasionally anxiety
     — Cognitive—negative view of self, others, and the future; self-blame; guilt; pessimism
     — Behavioral—passiveness, lack of motivation, no initiation of activities, psychomotor retardation and lethargy
  2. Counseling
     — Focus on specific problems rather than generalized sadness.
     — Explore events that are "controllable" by the client.
     — Initiate small tasks, small steps the individual can actually take.
     — Initiate larger tasks by breaking them down into smaller subtasks.
     — Use behavioral contracting.

C. Suicide
  1. Define the problem—Is there a motive for suicide? Is suicide an option being considered?
  2. Assess lethality—Is a method easily available? What method? Has there been much "suicide planning"? Have there been recent losses or traumas in person's life? Does the person have a suicidal history?
  3. Get more information, reduce lethality—Name and phone number, support systems, remove weapon, pills, etc. from home.
  4. Build trust, help person vent emotions—validate client's negative feelings, reflect feelings, show accurate empathy.
  5. Offer realistic hope, support, and encouragement. Reinforce the caller, reinterpret the situation, and encourage feelings of self-worth.
  6. Deal with problem, generate alternatives—help client to realize that s/he does have alternatives.
  7. Terminate session—establish no-suicide contract, referral, and follow-up.

References

Avery, D., and G. Winokur. "Suicide, Attempted Suicides and Relapse Rates and Depression." *Archives of General Psychiatry* 38 (1978): 749.

Bruyn, H.B., and R.H. Seiden. "Student Suicide" *Journal of the American College Health Association* 14 (1965): 69–77.

Devries, A.G. "A potential suicide personality inventory." *Psychol. Rep.* 18 (1966): 731–8.

Dublin, L. *Suicide: A Sociological and Statistical Study.* New York: Ronald Press, 1963.

Friedman, Paul, ed. *On Suicide: With Particular Reference to Suicide among Young Students.* New York: International Universities Press, 1967.

Goodwin, D.W. "Alcohol in suicide and homocide." *Q.J. Stud. Alcohol.* 33 (1973): 33–64.

Hawton, K., et al. "Attempted suicide and Suicide among Oxford University Students." *British Journal of Psychiatry* 132 (1978):506–9.

Hendin, Herbert. *Age of Sensation.* New York: W.W. Norton & Co. Inc., 1975.

Hollinger, Paul. "Adolescent Suicide: An Epidemiological Study of Recent Trends." *American Journal of Psychiatry* 135 (1978):754–7.

Knight, James. "Suicide Among Students" in *Suicidal Behaviors,* H.L.P. Resnik (ed.), Boston: Little, Brown, 1968.

Mishara, Brian, et al. "The Frequency of Suicide Attempts." *American Journal of Psychiatry* 136 (1976): 516–20.

Motto, Jerome. "The Psychopathology of Suicide: A Clinical Model Approach." *American Journal of Psychiatry* 136 (1979): 516–20

Paffenbarger, R., and D. Asnas. "Chronic Disease in Former College Students." *American Journal of Public Health* 56 (1966): 1026–36.

Parnell, R.W. "Mortality and Prolonged Illness among Oxford Undergraduates." *Lancet* 1951, 731–3.

Rosenbaum, C.P., and J. Beebe. *Psychiatric Treatment: Crisis, Clinic, and Consultation.* New York: McGraw-Hill, 1975.

Rosen Krautz, A. "A Note on Adolescent Suicide." *Adolescence* 13 (1978): 208–14.

Seiden, Richard. "Campus Tragedy." *Journal of Abnormal Psychology* 71 (66): 389.

Wold, L. "Characteristics of 26,000 Suicide Prevention Center Patients." *Bull. of Suicidology* 6 (1970): 24–34.

———. "Suicide Among Youth." USPHS #1971.

Part II

SPECIAL PERSPECTIVES IN PEER COUNSELING

INTRODUCTION TO PART TWO

The following chapters present material aimed at assisting peer counselors who are working in special circumstances or with specific cultural and ethnic issues.

For example, students who work as resident staff in college dormitories are asked to perform a variety of tasks, among them counseling other students around academic and personal issues. Students involved in this specialized form of peer counseling often do not receive focused training or consultation to help them in this role. The chapter on the role of the resident advisor as a personal counselor is aimed at providing information and material to assist the student in developing skills in counseling and referral as a resident advisor.

The earlier section on interpretation reviewed the importance of belief systems and personal points of view. Cultural and ethnic issues involve the special belief systems of minority groups. The ways in which cultural points of view and ethnic traditions affect Blacks, Asians, and Chicanos often represent a puzzling dilemma to an Anglo counselor. In working with an individual with a different cultural background and world view, the Anglo counselor finds that the usual way of framing, thinking, and solving personal problems is hampered by a lack of instinctive understanding and empathy. These matters are addressed by the papers in the following section.

Chapter 5. Cultural and Ethnic Perspectives

5.

Cultural and Ethnic Perspectives

BLACK CULTURAL ATTRIBUTES AND THEIR IMPLICATIONS FOR COUNSELING BLACK CLIENTS

by Sam Edwards, Jr., M.S.W.

Culture exerts strong influences on the personality. Composed of the "values, attitudes, customs, beliefs, and habits that are shared by members of a society" (Parrillo, 1980), culture affects everything from our unconscious to our thinking to our behavior. It determines how we see the world and how we react to it. It helps us understand other people, choose our friends, and distinguish ourselves from members of other cultures. It also affects our patterns of interaction, choices of occupational goals, and definitions of success and of good and bad. It gives us directions for coping with and resolving personal problems. Comprising learned attributes that are parts of our personality, culture is a highly dynamic force.

This section focuses on some of the Black cultural attributes that may influence the counseling relationship and/or that may become activated in conjunction with the counseling situation. Selected cultural attitudes, values, and beliefs are discussed, along with their implications for the enhancement of counseling. Further, efforts are made to add to the counselor's cognitive and emotional understanding of Black counselees from an essentially cultural perspective. It is important that counselors combine sensitivity and empathy with the intellectual application of counseling techniques.

The Cultural Belief that Blacks Are a Strong People

Among the many facets in the Black culture is the belief that Blacks are a strong people. This may be a scar left by oppression: it may be rooted in the culture of slavery, wherein Blacks were valued for their physical labor and stamina. In the agrarian society of the South, Blacks comprised the bulk of the work force, were forced to function as if they were strong animals or powerful machines, and were expected to reproduce strong offspring.

Having basic psychological needs for some form of validation of their self-worth as human beings, Blacks probably began to concentrate on their physical stamina. It was an asset which whites and society needed in order to be successful, and Blacks probably idealized and identified themselves with it. One may speculate that their real or imagined physical abilities were sources of pride, inspiration, and comfort. That they were directly or indirectly rewarded for strength may have led to the idea that Blacks are a strong people and that being strong is good. Like any aspect of culture, it was probably transmitted from one generation to another.

As cultural beliefs often do, this concept lacks a specific definition, but it is shared and understood by many Blacks today. When carefully examined, it denotes several abstract qualities: (1) racial pride based on the achievement of survival through severe periods of oppression; (2) strength of emotional constitution to endure and persevere under untoward socio-economic pressures; (3) physical stamina; and (4) collective racial power to exert social influence.

In many variations, the belief is embedded in the Black culture. Black folklore is filled with tales of sexually prodigious Black men. Some of the blues songs are rich with statements pertaining to the sexual might of Blacks. Some of the poems speak about survival capacities and perseverance under adversity. John Henry and Jack Johnson, who are Black cultural heroes, are symbolic of the physical stamina and pride of Blacks.

In addition to its manifestations in various forms of Black art and folklore, this belief is evident in the daily interactions of Blacks. Ministers sometimes preach about Blacks as a strong people who have come through dark, trying times. In discussions among themselves, Blacks boast that they are stronger than white people; a favorite notion is that white people would have "cracked up" under the pressures that Blacks have had to bear. Many Blacks unhesitatingly expect that Black prizefighters and football players will perform better than white ones. The whites who are exceptional are often thought to have acquired their assets from Blacks. Writers may appeal to the belief in strength when they call on Blacks to take collective actions. For example, in the "Publisher's Statement" column of the December 1981 issue of *Essence,* Ed Lewis writes: "We are a people with an enormous reservoir of strength and ability to adapt to the most trying circumstances. Once again, that creative reservoir of strength is being tapped, that ability is being tested . . . . Most important, we must stand together."

Implications for Counseling

The notion that Blacks are a strong people may exert considerable influence in the counseling situation or on decisions about seeking counseling. It defines and inhibits the expression of "weaknesses." It defines and mandates manifestations of "strength." Most often, having personal problems and seeking counseling are perceived as significant weaknesses; being continuously able to withstand or to resolve problems is often interpreted as strength.

The belief discourages seeking or accepting help, and many Blacks who need counseling will avoid getting it. Rather, they are likely to conceal problems while attempting to resolve them alone. Many may strongly devalue and feel hostile toward and threatened by counseling services. They experience tremendous feelings of shame and of humiliation when faced with personal problems and diligently avoid seeking counseling.

However, some do obtain it. With them, the counselor may need to be alert to cultural patterns of behavior. Blacks may express, reveal, and conceal problems and feelings through familiar cultural patterns of behavior. Problems and emotions may be modeled after culturally-based images of strength: cool calmness ("Be cool, man"), controlled detachment, intimidating sullenness, postures of questioning the counselor's knowledge and understanding of Blacks, and threats of physical violence. While the counselor may see them as normal, some of these cultural patterns may constitute indications of problems, feelings related to the problems, or feelings about seeking help.

It is essential that the counselor be able to sense and appreciate the content of the cultural forms of responses. The failure to be aware of the counselee's feelings and problems may encourage the counselee to perceive the counselor as too weak to help him or her. Further, the counselor who fails to "see through" forms of cultural responses may find it harder to accept and to be empathic toward the Black counselee. Empathy and acceptance may be the factors that enable the counselee to accept help and to feel safe enough in the session to relinquish culturally based patterns of behavior that conceal or that constitute the problems.

It is also crucial that the counselor bear in mind that the belief that Blacks are a strong people is probably the parent of the idea that Blacks do not commit suicide. Some Blacks have the notion that suicide is a behavior of whites or of Blacks who have adopted the values of whites. However, the notion is incorrect.

Studies suggest that suicide is a serious problem among Blacks. Hendin (1969) observes that "in New York, suicide is twice as frequent among Negro men between twenty and thirty-five as it is among white men of the same age." He explains that suicide is actually more of a problem among Blacks of both sexes between the ages of twenty and thirty-five than it is among whites of the same ages. *The Crisis* (1981) reports that Chunn has found that "suicide has reached epidemic proportions among Blacks from ages fifteen to twenty-nine and is the leading cause of death today in that group." The Black researcher is further quoted as saying that there has been a "marked increase" in the number of Black suicides among both males and females over the past ten years. Chunn's data reveal that "the rate today for Blacks is 24 per 100,000 persons, compared with 15 per 100,000 in 1973, nine per 100,000 in 1940, 13 per 100,000 in 1932 and 1920."

Chunn identifies several factors that are linked to Black suicide. They include chronic unemployment, loss of personal relationships (largely through migration), alienation, lack of opportunity for advancement, and alcohol and drug abuse.

The counselor needs to be alert to the suicidal ideas and/or plans that Black counselees may have; he or she may need to inquire actively about such thoughts when the person asks for help with depression or with problems that are linked to Black suicide. Many Blacks perceive suicidal thoughts as expressions of weakness and are likely to conceal them.

Cultural Attitudes Against Self-Disclosure

Like the notion concerning the "strength" of Blacks, the cultural attitude against self-disclosure may exert prominent influences on the Black counselee's relationship with a counselor. A general disposition shared by some Blacks is that personal problems should not be discussed outside the family. This attitude may come to play at any time during counseling; but, like many attributes of culture, it is likely to become apparent in earlier sessions when the level of unfamiliarity is the greatest between the two participants.

It may be expressed in a host of forms, including guardedness, discussions on nonprivate matters, concealing secrets, silence, stubbornness, and feelings such as guilt and hostility. Avoiding situations in which the disclosure of personal matters is expected is one of the most common behaviors.

Some case examples will add further clarity. Ms. V is a thirty-three-year-old, lower-middle-class Black mother of three young children. She is married, is employed full-time with a flexible work schedule, and attends junior college. She seems to be extraordinarily ambitious and success-oriented. Her initial behavior and comments in the first counseling session were common to many Blacks. She was silent initially and was obviously hesitant to begin talking. Before discussing the problems for which she was seeking help, she explained that her mother had taught her to "never tell your business to strangers" and that "Black people have to be careful about who they talk to in this world." She commented that she felt "bad" about coming to talk to a counselor, adding that she just had to talk to someone who could help her. She observed that she felt as if she were "ready to blow up" because of marital, academic, and work pressures. Ms. V kept every other appointment and missed three of six before abruptly terminating. She seemed to have felt guilty about discussing personal matters with the stranger-counselor.

Ms. B manifested another variation of the anti-self-disclosure attitude. A twenty-one-year-old, middle-class Black senior majoring in pre-medicine at a highly prestigious university, she asked many questions. She asked if Black students who used the counseling services "spill their guts" to the counselor. She asked the Black counselor about his attitudes concerning Blacks "spilling their guts" in "these kind of places." The impression was that she was attempting to employ the counselor to attentuate the feelings of guilt she was experiencing about the prospect of confiding in the counselor.

When questioned by a counselor, some Blacks may have knee-jerk-like hostile reactions. Verbal responses may include statements such as, "That's none of your business," "That is personal," "You don't have anything to do with that," "You don't need to know that to help me," and "What do you want to know that for?" Of a forty-year-old Black patient who was hospitalized because of a suicide attempt, Hendin (1969) states, "The patient came close to losing his usual politeness when he warded off questions about his mother. 'How would I know? I mind my own business,' the patient defended." Hendin viewed this reaction as an indication of the patient's feelings that Hendin did not mind Hendin's business. While the anti-self-disclosure attitude constitutes and give rise to resistance, it is likely to be culturally based and culturally formed; its influences at times may be particularly evident.

Implications for Counseling

As a highly specialized helping method that works largely with the cognitive-intellectual realm of the personality, peer counseling depends heavily on the active cooperation of counselees. As with other forms of counseling, therefore, the process should be adapted to the individual needs of the Black counselees.

The counselor may consider several possibilities when observing the impact of the cultural anti-self-disclosure attitude on the counseling relationship. Perhaps first and foremost, the counselor should avoid interpreting a counselee's responses in a literal, concrete way; the counselor should see reticence and/or hostility as signals of anxieties and as styles of armor.

To react defensively is to give legitimacy to the counselee's need for the protection; it may also inhibit the counselee from resolving the feelings of guilt that may be generated by his or her violation of the cultural anti-self-disclosure attitude in the session.

Second, the counselor who feels a genuine acceptance of these attitudes as part of the counselee's personality may understandingly explain that the peer counseling process works best with the full cooperative participation of the counselee. Sometimes, depending on his or her judgment, the counselor may raise open-ended questions that encourage the Black counselee to talk without subtly making the counselee feel defensive. Sometimes it pays off to wait acceptingly until the person decides to disclose, but the counselor should rarely resort to simple silence. Some Blacks may perceive such a stance as a "put-down" and a needless show of superiority; the behavior of the counselor in the session is often observed and assigned meanings.

Cultural Attitudes of Distrustfulness

Closely paralleling the attitude of anti-self-disclosure is that of distrustfulness. A cultural trait of anticipatory expectations of danger and hurt, it is characterized by doubts regarding others' interest in and authenticity toward oneself. It also consists of vague thoughts concerning the potential deceptiveness of others, perceptions of anger in the environment, feelings of unsafeness, and vulnerabilities to humiliation. Grier and Cobbs (1968) portray the attitudes as a Black norm and see them as adaptive. The psychiatrists explain that, because of their many years of painful experiences, Blacks have developed "a suspiciousness of their environment which is necessary for survival. Black people, to a degree that approaches paranoia, must be ever alert to danger from their white fellow citizens. It is a cultural phenomenon peculiar to Black Americans."

Moore and Wagstaff (1974) conducted a study of Black educators in white colleges and obtained data that coincide with the observations of Grier and Cobbs. Of their findings, they write:

> So general is the feeling of alienation, discrimination, unfairness, anger, and frustration among Black educators, that those who did not share unpleasant experiences and felt they were being treated fairly in their jobs also felt the need to apologize for their lack of suspicion and feelings of satisfaction.

The cultural attitude of distrustfulness is widespread, seemingly transcending class. It is also dynamic. It tends to surface when Blacks are in unfamiliar situations such as white restaurants, white communities, and large institutions. It tends to subside once they feel at ease in the situation.

Implications for Counseling

In the office of the Black or white counselor, distrustfulness may be reflected in the counselee's reluctance to provide a phone number, home address, or other identification data. It may also be reflected in questions pertaining to confidentiality. Thus, it is often useful to explain with honesty the counseling agency's policies and practices regarding confidentiality; the counselor should attempt to be faithful to the policies.

The counselor may need to observe the signs of distrustfulness quite carefully. They may constitute as well as conceal serious disorders of paranoia, although they may be manifested as what appear to be legitimate concerns about the realities of racism and other kinds of racial injustices in America. The counselor should not immediately attempt to validate the manifested concerns; nor should he or she allow himself or herself to feel guilty. Counselors should observe these concerns empathetically. Distrustfulness is a dynamic attitude, and it tends to diminish once the individual is familiar with or has accurate information about the anxiety-evoking situation.

The persistence of suspicions, misinterpretations of activities in the environment, obviously erroneous ideas concerning abuses of confidentiality, and preoccupations with the dangers of whites may strongly suggest psychopathology (although the dividing line between real-life experiences and manifestations of psychopathology may be extraordinarily thin in Blacks). The peer counselor does not typically make formal diagnoses, but he or she is alert to the presence of problems that are best dealt with by other professionals. The counselor may attempt to refer the client to a psychotherapist after a few meetings if he or she senses that the client has an emotional problem that may interfere with solving problems through peer counseling.

Cultural Values Pertaining to Communication Skills

The desirability of "good" communication skills is an emotionally charged issue in the Black culture. Blacks have adopted a general standard of communication skills that are judged to be acceptable by the dominant culture. Using that concept as a basis for comparison, many Blacks often evaluate their own individual communication skills as bad and undesirable. These perceptions may stimulate considerable personal and group shame and other painful reactions.

Good communication skills are sometimes seen by Blacks as the sine qua non for self-approval and for authentic membership in the white world. The case of Mr. D is instructive, although it may not necessarily be typical. Almost in the middle of one of the many sentences he had difficulties verbalizing in the first counseling session, the forty-two-year-old

Black man stopped talking. With a sense of embarrassment, he said, "You see that I get this speech thing; I get mixed up. But I talk the way I am; I'm me—nobody else! I'm not suppose to talk like Sinatra or somebody like that. I'm different. Some people think you have to talk like white peoples to be somebody."

While complicated, the vignette seems to allude to many points. Mr. D has apparently observed the communication skills of the Black counselor and is feeling ashamed and defensive of his own. Further, he appears to see Sinatra as the embodiment of whites and of good communication—by which he judges himself. Also, through his preoccupation with and negative evaluation of his skills, he seemingly reveals a great sense of personal inferiority and of being in poor control of himself. One may speculate that he is saying in part that he would "be somebody" were he skilled in communicating verbally and were he white.

Shame, anger, and self and group devaluations are common responses for some Black people who are self-conscious about speaking. Because many Blacks associate verbal skills with intelligence and personal acceptability, they may "talk proper" and use pretentious words. They may apologize for "busting verbs" or for using words incorrectly. Some may avoid talking in situations in which they fear their skills will betray their intelligence.

Blacks' concept of good communication skills sometimes encourages particular patterns of interacting among Blacks. They are prone to feel embarrassed and critical of Black leaders who demonstrate unsatisfactory communication skills in public. They sometimes engage in verbal critiques of each other's manner of talking. "You can't even talk," "You ought to go somewhere and learn how to talk before you try to talk about me," and "You are trying to talk like the white people" are some of the expressions Blacks may exchange. Some parents impress on their children concepts of good speech. On the other hand, when a relative returns home in the South after a long stay on the East or West coasts, his or her "style" of talking is scrutinized by friends and relatives. The returnee may be thought to have changed if he or she has a modified way of talking. Simultaneously, Blacks may isolate or admire Blacks who are natural in the employment of "good" communication skills. Essentially, large numbers of Blacks are self-conscious about their communication skills and are prone to be ambivalent about "good" skills manifested by other Blacks.

Implications for Counseling

Blacks' values regarding communication skills suggest several implications for the counselor. One is that the counselor needs to be aware that some Black counselees may be feeling ashamed and humiliated by their communication skills while they are talking. The counselor ought to become familiar with the specific types of signs that point to counselees' emotions, although he or she may not work actively with these feelings. To humanize the relationship to a greater degree, the counselor may allow himself or herself to experience silent compassion freely toward the counselee. An awareness of the counselee's emotions is invaluable; it facilitates the development of links between the participants and it enhances the likelihood that the counseling will be effective.

Another implication is that the Black counselee is likely to scrutinize the counselor's communication skills and compare them to his or her own. Of importance is that the counselee may have a variety of reactions to this evaluation, all of which the counselor should make mental note of.

Another specific implication is that the counselor should maintain a natural style of communicating. He or she ought not to shift to more "polished" or "down-to-earth" skills. Interventions such as paraphrasing should reflect empathic listening and should be natural. Altering one's style may be seen by some Black counselees as a "put-down." Further, it is generally helpful to keep in mind that the counselor's manner of talking with a Black counselee will inevitably reflect the counselor's attitudes concerning the counselee (and concerning his/her own momentary senses of personal insecurities or securities).

Finally, there is the specific risk that the counselor may make value judgments about the Black counselees based on the communication skills of the counselee. Like the counselee, the counselor may associate verbal skills with degrees of intelligence and personal worth. The counselor needs to be aware of his or her own values in this area and to monitor their influence on any evaluations of the counselee's communication skills.

Cultural Values Pertaining to Education

The Black culture places great value on education. Like communication skills, a good education is seen as a passport into the world of professional, economic, and political power. Although it sometimes acquires the proportions of a cure-all remedy for the personal and social problems of Blacks, education is always considered an important qualification for self-determination. For example, in one of his weekly newspaper articles, "Racism: What Should You Do?," Dr. Charles Faulkner (1981) offers suggestions to Blacks for coping. Among other things, he suggests: "Get as much education as you can—be prepared for what is to come."

Blacks' strong embrace of this cultural value is reflected in many aspects of Black life. The importance of formal schooling is a recurring theme in Black publications. Many Black professional, social, political, and religious organizations have scholarship funds and/or education committees. Black ministers preach sermons about the values of education, and parents admonish their children to "get a good education." Graduation ceremonies are particularly important for many Blacks. Older Blacks sometimes apologize for their lack of an education, guiltily pointing to some of the obstacles that were in their way. Some of the Blacks who seek counseling impress upon the counselor the urgency of their need to get an education.

Implications for Counseling

Again it is the case that culturally esteemed achievements and standards may be very dynamic forces. They may be the sources of realistic and of unrealistic aspirations for Black counselees. Failure to attain such goals may prompt strivings for compensatory types of achievement, either deviant or socially sanctioned. Or failure to attain them may prompt defeatist attitudes, which are all too common among many Blacks.

Clearly, an education is an esteemed Black cultural value. Peer counselors should become familiar with this value, largely because it may contribute to states of low self-esteem and discouragement in many Blacks. It also lends itself easily to disguises of serious psychopathology.

Considerations Regarding Referring Blacks

Informal observations suggest that Black counselees are high-risk referral prospects, particularly after a counselee–counselor relationship has been established. Most Blacks terminate counseling when referred to another counselor. They strongly prefer the rapport that they have with the original counselor, Black or white. They resist referrals by offering a variety of obstacles—a lack of time, inconvenience, a scarcity of money, a lack of need for further help, doubts about the usefulness of counseling, the prospective counselor's lack of knowledge about them, and feelings of being pushed around. Some return to the original counselor later if the referral is executed, but most Blacks rarely follow through on a referral or successfully become attached to another therapist.

One may offer a number of general speculations concerning Blacks' tendency to terminate rather than accept referrals. In addition to being perceived as a personal abandonment by the counselor, the referral probably arouses fears of venturing into another unfamiliar setting. Many Blacks restrict themselves to familiar locations and people. At the same time, like counseling itself, the referral lacks cultural support and/or sanctions.

The counselor should therefore avoid referring the Black counselee to another counselor except when the problems of the counselee clearly indicate it. Should the counselor determine that a referral is warranted or required after a rapport has been established, he or she should in general avoid referring Blacks to group methods of counseling. The Black culture emphasizes individualistic attitudes, self-reliance, self-sufficiency, and autonomy. It opposes the resolution of personal problems in the context of groups, and many Blacks may perceive group counseling as "white folk's stuff." Such a referral might stimulate anxieties that discourage the person from seeking counseling altogether.

Summary

Comprising a variety of values, attitudes, beliefs, and habits, the Black culture exerts strong moral-like directives for behavior and perceptions. It rewards compliance with and punishes opposition to cultural rules and expectations, thus exerting a major influence on the personality of Blacks. This chapter has focused on the following aspects of that culture:

1. The belief that Blacks are a strong people.
2. Cultural strictures against self-disclosure.
3. Cultural attitudes of distrustfulness.
4. Cultural values pertaining to communication skills.
5. Cultural values pertaining to education.
6. Considerations regarding referring Blacks.

These factors inevitably affect the counseling relationship and Blacks' decisions to seek counseling. They also suggest possible sensitivities of the counselee and some bases of his or her painful feelings. To enhance the effectiveness of counseling and to enable the Black counselee to resolve feelings generated specifically by the culture, counselors must have an emotional and intellectual appreciation of Black culture and its influence. Success in the counseling process rests on the counselor's ability to combine empathy, acceptance, and understanding with the application of various counseling techniques.

References

The Crisis. "Suicide Taking Its Toll on Blacks." October 1981, p. 401.

Faulkner, Charles W. "Racism: What Should You Do?" *The Observer,* December 3–9, 1981, C-6.

Hendin, Herbert. *Black Suicide.* New York: Basic Books, 1969.

Moore, William, Jr., and Lonnie Wagstaff. *Black Education in White Colleges.* San Francisco: Jossey-Bass, 1974.

Parrillo, Vincent N. *Strangers to These Shores: Race and Ethnic Relations in the United States.* Boston: Houghton Mifflin, 1980.

COUNSELING CHICANOS: SOME CONSIDERATIONS

by Alejandro Martinez, Ph.D.

The goal of this section is to help counselors become aware of culture-specific aspects in the counseling process and in their particular counseling styles so that they can deal more skillfully with individuals of Mexican descent.*

Mental health professionals have identified several significant issues in intracultural counseling. These issues have been most succinctly summarized into four themes by Draguns (1976): (1) the etic–emic distinction, (2) relationship versus technique, (3) the mutuality of the client–counselor relationship, and (4) the autoplastic–alloplastic dilemma. It is hoped that counselors working with Chicanos will share and be sensitive to these concerns.

The Etic–Emic Distinction

The terms etic and emic represent two contrasting frames of reference for describing and analyzing behavior. An *etic* approach provides insight into the human universals of certain problems, while an *emic* approach clarifies the culturally unique elements of these problems. Recognizing the value of each of these orientations and understanding their complementarity is essential, because the concerns that Chicanos bring to a counseling situation are not necessarily uniquely Chicano problems. They often appear similar to or indistinguishable from those faced by any other individual (i.e., self-doubts, indecision about a career choice, interpersonal conflict, motivational problems, etc.). Interpreting these concerns solely in terms of their universal attributes may provide the Chicano counselee with an appropriate and well-intentioned intervention; however, it ignores the problem's cultural characteristics and significance.

For example, counseling that focuses on individuation issues of a young Chicano outside the context of family and familiar values is less effective than counseling that also explores the impact of the process of individuation on the relationhsip with the rest of his or her family. It is often the case that family is relatively more important to Chicanos, and thus of

---

*The word Chicano as used here refers to persons of Mexican descent. The reader should be aware, though, that this and other ethnic group labels (i.e., Mexican American, Latino, Mexicano, Hispanic, American of Mexican descent) can have ideological implications. It should not be assumed that its use here represents a consensus of the way that individuals of Mexican descent self-identify ethnically.

greater significance when dealing with the emergence of independence in young Chicanos.

Relationship versus Technique

A second consideration for counselors is the relative importance of relationship and technique. Despite their great variety in theoretical orientation and methods, counselor training programs in the United States are based on certain assumptions and values that reflect an American cultural viewpoint. The following chart* contrasts some of these assumptions and values with those that might prevail elsewhere.

The indiscriminant and uncritical use of counseling techniques that are rooted in the dominant culture lead to an unfulfilling undertaking for both the counselee and the counselor. Counselors must be prepared to adapt their techniques to the cultural background of the individual. When working with Chicanos, this might mean explicitly asking about language-related issues, nonverbal cues, and the different meanings that might be ascribed to various uses of personal space, eye contact, and conversational conventions.

When meeting an individual for the first time, a counselor may not hear the real problem right away. The Chicano client may want to chat first or may present a problem he or she considers to be socially acceptable. The counselor must be sensitive to the self-disclosure style of each individual and attempt to provide an opening where clients can feel comfortable discussing the issues that really concern them. This may be achieved with such questions as: How are things at home? How is school going? Are you finding enough time to be with friends? The counselor may also need to be relatively more active in the interaction, for aloofness may be interpreted as a lack of interest in the counselee's concerns.

In sum, the counselor must be able to engage in supportive communication that promotes the development of trust, support, and ease in disclosing concerns or problems.

The Mutuality of the Client–Counselor Relationship

The counseling interaction is a reciprocal process, affecting both the counselor and the counselee. By working with Chicanos, a counselor can learn a great deal about people of Mexican descent and their acculturation issues: ethnic identity; family roles and role expectations; family structure; gender identity issues; effects of poverty, racism, prejudice, and opportunities; attitudes toward the family, competition, marriage, sex, death,

---

*Reprinted from Horner et al., *Learning Across Cultures,* by permission of the publisher, the National Association for Foreign Student Affairs (Washington, DC: 1981; pp. 37–38).

American Assumption/ Value	Contrasting Assumption/ Value
1. People are isolable individuals.	1. People are integrally related with other people (in groups such as families).
2. Personal growth and change are valuable and desirable.	2. Conforming to time-tested ways of behavior is desirable.
3. Individuals have control over their life circumstances.	3. One's life circumstances are dictated by external (political, economic, social, natural) forces.
4. Personal problems are often soluble, through greater understanding of their origins and/or through remedial action.	4. Problems are fated to occur, and fate may or may not remove them.
5. "Professional" people can help other people solve their problems. a. People (counselors) can be genuinely interested in the welfare of strangers. b. People (counselors) can be dealt with as occupants of roles.	5. One's problems are beyond the control of other human beings. a. Only one's close friends and relatives can be trusted. b. Other people are dealt with as whole people.
6. Open discussion of one's problems can be beneficial.	6. It can be dangerous to reveal oneself to others.
7. Emotional disturbances have their roots in the individual's past.	7. Emotional disturbances have their roots in external forces or situations.
8. People are (more or less) equal.	8. There is a hierarchical ranking of people in society.
9. Males and females are (more or less) equal.	9. Males are superior.

Whites, Blacks, religion, etc.; and a host of other culturally diverse and interesting aspects. While this is a legitimate and valuable avenue for learning the "subjective culture" of Chicanos, counselors should not indulge their own curiosity at the expense of the counselee's efforts and time. The counselee's concerns and goals must be paramount in the counseling relationship.

The Autoplastic–Alloplastic Dilemma

Should counselors help people adapt themselves to troublesome circumstances, or should they help them to change those circumstances? This is the autoplastic–alloplastic dilemma, a fourth concern for counselors working with Chicanos.

Historically, counseling has encouraged *autoplastic* behavior by helping counselees accommodate themselves to their social settings and structure. It was not until the sixties, with the development of the Civil Rights movement, that this approach to human problems was seriously questioned. The community mental health movement offered exciting and innovative ways of approaching problems. Social situations were no longer assumed to be immutable, and institutional and broader social changes were sought.

For Chicanos, it was an extremely significant development. As a group, they have encountered major socio-political barriers to opportunities in education, employment, housing, cultural expression, and political participation. This new *alloplastic* orientation encouraged them to shape external realities to suit their needs.

The appropriateness of each approach continues to be debated. Counselors must examine their own values and attitudes about what constitutes an ethical intervention. What are the immediate and long-term political implications of either orientation? We walk a tightrope between helping Chicanos learn to act on other people, objects, and situations, and helping them be able to accommodate themselves to the existing situation. An example of this dilemma is presented by a Chicano student who begins to lose interest in school or becomes depressed and angry because he or she cannot find faculty who understand or even appreciate an academic interest in ethnically oriented topics. Does one help this person "see the reality" of the situation and adapt to what the school offers? Or does one work with this individual so that he or she changes the status quo? These tough questions must be confronted by all counselors working with Chicanos.

Counselor, Counselee, and Ethnicity

Who can best counsel Chicanos? Is the most appropriate counselor a bicultural-bilingual Chicano? A Chicano counselor who has assimilated the Anglo culture? A non-Chicano counselor?

There seem to be two predominant positions on the matter. One suggests that a counselor whose cultural background parallels that of the client can understand the client's personal experience and perspective much better than a counselor who has a different background. The shared experience may enhance rapport and promote the counselee's willingness to disclose material, and the common mode of communication may enhance the counseling process. It may help, too, if the counselee perceives the Chicano counselor as a potential change agent who is sensitive and responsive to the unique socio-cultural attributes of Chicanos. Working with a Chicano counselor may help change a counselee's perception that counseling is only for the white middle class or that the "status quo" has no interest in Chicanos being able to maintain ethnic identity and self-pride.

The other position suggests that some clients may prefer a counselor whose background differs from their own, particularly if they want to deal with material that would be embarrassing to share with individuals of the same ethnic background. For example, it may be easier for the counselee to talk about not feeling a strong affiliation to Chicano culture and values if he or she is seeing a non-Chicano counselor. Or, someone dealing with constant antagonism by the white majority may best be helped by "confronting" a white counselor with his or her feelings of anger, helplessness, and anxiety.

Both positions have some merit. Each offers important benefits, yet each has potentially negative aspects. In the white-counselor–Chicano-client dyad, there can be significant language barriers. White counselors tend to be English-speaking monolinguals, while some Chicanos speak only English, others speak only Spanish, and many speak both. There also tend to be significant dissimilarities in values; some are primarily due to differences in socio-economic class and others are due to cultural differences in self-disclosure styles, normative behaviors, family values, and customs, for instance). These differences can and often do contribute to mutual stereotyping or denial of cultural dissimilarities, resistance, transference, countertransference, misdirected diagnosis, patronization, and low expectations of success of counseling.

The barriers in the Chicano-counselor–Chicano-client dyad have received less attention but are equally important. A Chicano client may react with anger or jealousy when confronted by a Chicano counselor. The counselor may be perceived as being overly identified with an Anglo-controlled institution; he or she may be resented for breaking out of an oppressive environment; or he or she may be stereotyped as a super-Chicano. Another concern is that the Chicano counselor may deny identification with the Chicano counselee. On the other hand, the counselor may over-identify and make unjustified assumptions about shared feelings or inappropriate projections of self-image onto the client because the two are culturally similar.

Counseling the Chicano Student

How a Chicano student deals with higher education and its many intellectual, social, and personal challenges depends largely on the extent to which he or she identifies with either the Anglo culture or the Mexican/Mexican-American culture. Those who strongly identify with one culture or who have a strong dual identity will probably not experience major problems with their identity or self-concept, although they may still find themselves in situations where others pressure them to choose one cultural identity over the other. In contrast, those who are deliberately attempting to replace one set of cultural values with another or those who may not identify with either culture often experience particularly powerful and debilitating stress.

The more one knows about the cultural identity of a Chicano student, the more possible it becomes to successfully counsel that student. Counseling a bilingual student whose parents are immigrants from Mexico, who is a member of an extended Roman Catholic family, who prefers ethnic food, and who would rather be called Mexican is likely to be very different from counseling an English-speaking, non-Catholic Chicano from a nuclear family who has no preferences for the diet or clothing of his or her ethnic group and who would rather be called American.

Both of these students may present concerns about self-concept and ethnic identity, for example, yet the issues will probably be quite different. The first student may be concerned about the pressures of acculturation toward the American culture and is likely to be more sensitive to culture-specific pressures (such as obligations to parents). The other may be more concerned with external pressures to be Mexican or (as is the case with students who "rediscover" their ethnic heritage in college) the struggle to integrate something that has always been theirs and the accompanying feelings of mourning, sadness, anger, and excitement.

Certain stresses affect most Chicano students regardless of cultural preferences. Historically, Chicanos as a group have been subjected to prejudice and discrimination. They generally have lower personal and family incomes, have fewer years of education, are over-represented in low-paying occupations, are under-represented in higher education institutions, and are victims of what has been described as the cycle of poverty. The negative consequences for the Chicano community are a reduced quality of life and denied opportunities for advancement. For the individual, they may be an impaired self-image, defensive attitudes of denial, withdrawal, passivity, self-depreciation, dissimulation, and identification with the aggressor.

The cost of breaking new ground in academia is another source of stress. The historical under-representation of Chicanos in higher educational institutions tends to present unique challenges to the Chicano student's sense of individual, familial, community, and cultural identity and continuity. While an educational experience can provide many majority-culture students with a means to integrate themselves into the community and dominant society, for Chicanos it frequently represents a distinct break with family and community. The stresses of this transition are often intensified and further complicated by the dearth of role-model Chicanos who have achieved success through continued education or training. The Chicano student can see what she or he is "leaving" but does not know where the educational experience will lead.

A Chicano in higher education, therefore, faces many questions that, because of cultural background, are of particular significance.

— Will participation in higher education mean alienation from my family and community?

— How will my family and community perceive personal change that is being brought about by my educational experience?

— Will I be able to retain the capacity for intimacy with my family and community?

— What responsibility do I have toward my community and family?

— How much education should I strive for when my parents may have less than a grammar-school education?

— How will I deal with the pressure of giving my family its first real opportunity to escape the poverty cycle?

Chicanos in universities also have to address some difficult self-concept and interpersonal questions, such as how well they can maintain their ethnic identity within the university and still be able to participate fully in an Anglo-dominated educational experience, or why they were admitted into institutions that in the recent past rarely accepted Chicanos in any significant proportions. What is the personal significance of affirmative action in higher education to Chicanos? How do they deal with the insensitivity of the institution to Chicanos' needs? How do they deal with overt and covert prejudice and racism? How do they deal with genuine feelings of acceptance and concern by Anglo students, staff, and faculty? What kinds of relationships do they want and what types of relationships can they have with other Chicanos? How about with non-Chicanos? Whom can they date? Whom should they date? Should they only date other Chicanos? What does it mean when they date non-Chicanos?

Summary

When providing counseling services to Chicanos, counselors should be aware of at least six issues:

1. There are two basic levels of analysis in counseling: one provides insight into the human universal of certain problems, while the other clarifies their culturally particular elements. Both levels need to be considered when counseling Chicanos.

2. Despite their great variety in orientation and methods, counselor training theories in the United States share certain assumptions and values that reflect the viewpoint of the majority culture. Those counseling minority-culture clients must adapt technique to the cultural background of each individual. With Chicanos this means explicitly checking out language-related issues, nonverbal clues, and different meanings that may be ascribed to variations in the use of personal space, eye contact, and conversation conventions.

3. The counseling experience is a reciprocal learning process affecting both the counselor and the counselee. It is a particularly meaningful way to learn about Chicanos, yet a counselor should not indulge his or her curiosity at the expense of the counselee's effort and time.

4. Given the often oppressive situation of Chicanos, counselors must address the ethical and political issue of how much to help the counselee to adapt to a given reality and how much to encourage him or her to work at changing that situation.

5. Counselors must recognize the unique demands of intraethnic and interethnic counseling. Both of these counseling dyads offer important therapeutic benefits as well as potentially significant limitations. The counselee's needs will determine whether a Chicano or a non-Chicano counselor will be most appropriate and effective.

6. Counselors need to be sensitive to and aware of the sources of stress that most affect Chicano students (prejudice, discriminatory practices, socio-economic conditions, and the unique social and psychological demands on Chicanos in academic settings) and how these stresses may be mediated by cultural preferences or by degree of acculturation to the majority Anglo culture.

References

Atkinson, Donald R.; George Morton; and Derald Wing Sue. *Counseling American Minority.* Dubuque, IO: Wm. C. Brown Co., 1979.

Draguns, Juris G. "Counseling Across Cultures: Common Themes and Distinct Approaches." *Counseling Across Cultures.* eds. P. Pedersen, W. J. Lonner, and J.D. Draguns. Honolulu: The University Press of Hawaii, 1976.

Horner, David, and Kay Vandersluis, co-editors with A.A. Alexander, Bashey Husain, Clarke Clifford, and Dennis Peterson. "Cross-Culture Counseling." *Learning Across Cultures,* ed. G. Althen. Washington, DC: The National Association of Foreign Student Affairs, 1981. pp. 30–50.

Morales, Armando. "Distinguishing Psychodynamic Factors from Cultural Factors in the Treatment of Spanish-Speaking Patients." *Chicanos: Social and Psychological Perspectus,* eds. N. N. Wagner and M.J. Haug. Saint Louis: the C.V. Mosby Company, 1971. pp. 279–80.

Pedersen, P., W.J. Lonner, and J.D. Draguns. *Counseling Across Cultures.* Honolulu: University Press of Hawaii, 1976.

Rodriquez, Richard. "Going Home Again: The New American Scholarship Boy." *The American Scholar* 44 (1974–75): No. 1.

Ruiz, Rene A., and Amado M. Padilla. "Counseling Latinos." *Personnel and Guidance Journal* March, 1977: 401–8.

CULTURAL CONSIDERATIONS IN COUNSELING ASIAN AMERICANS

by Jane Pao and Franklin Matsumoto

This section is primarily concerned with counseling situations where the person counseled is an Asian American. It further examines some culture-related problems that Asians in America face. The term "Asian American" covers a diverse group of Asians that includes Chinese, Japanese, Koreans, Hawaiians, Filipinos, Samoans, Pacific Islanders, and Southeast Asians. Each of these ethnic groups possesses its own distinct characteristics and unique culture. In counseling Asian Americans, knowledge and familiarity with the historical, political, and cultural factors behind the Asian American identity is crucial for effective interaction.

In this article, when we speak of Asian Americans, we are referring primarily to Chinese and Japanese Americans, since these two groups are the largest and oldest Asian groups in the United States. However, the guidelines discussed here can be adapted to helping members of other Asian cultures. It is our hope that readers will develop an awareness and sensitivity to the Asian American and that this section will stimulate further discussion on the cultural issues.

Image of the Asian American

Despite a long history of racial discrimination, abuse, harassment, economic exploitation, and prejudice, Asian Americans have managed to function reasonably well in society. The public's image of Asian Americans has shifted from one of "Yellow Peril" to that of a successful "model minority". It is believed that Asian Americans have a large degree of upward educational, occupational, and economic mobility. They are perceived as hardworking, quiet, law-abiding, and nonthreatening—and academically, as good students. These images of success attained by some Asian Americans are perpetuated by visible signs of affluence, acculturation, and assimilation into the community. The question is raised whether Asian Americans today accept these stereotypes and conform to them—and if so, to what extent? How does this affect the Asian American self-concept and psychological well-being? In some instances, failure to adhere to these expectations may add to the discontent and frustrations of Asian Americans. For example, Asian Americans are expected to perform well academically. When students are unable to meet the demands of scholastic achievement, they are faced with the dual stress of failing personally as well as experiencing some degree of shame and disgrace for not living up to an expected image. In another sense, when an Asian student's behavior is contrary to the stereotype of the passive, industrious, quiet student in class, the comment made by a teacher may be "I didn't expect that from you".

These dilemmas and others are often not expressed because there is a tendency for Asian Americans to resolve personal conflicts and problems independently. It is not unusual to hear the statement, "I prefer to work out my own problems rather than burden others with them". Most Asian Americans are reluctant to seek outside help. They are more likely to seek assistance within their own family. Social and emotional problems of youth and the elderly—such as juvenile deliquency, poverty, and unemployment—are therefore well hidden from the public. It is not surprising, then, that many people believe Asian Americans experience few problems. This misconception, unfortunately, is reinforced by studies that consistently reveal low utilization of mental health facilities by Asians (Kitano, 1973; Sue and Kirk, 1975; Sue and McKinney, 1975).

One possible reason for this underutilization could be cultural factors (such as pride, shame, or disgrace of admitting to adjustment or emotional problems) inhibit self-referral. Those Asians who come forth often express their problems in the form of somatic complaints (Sue and Sue 1974); or, as Bourne (1975) observed, they tend to suffer "major adaptive failures or have conflicts of considerably greater magnitude than Caucasian students".

The existence of these myths and stereotypes makes it doubly important for peer counselors to keep in mind the beliefs of students seeking help. It is especially important to examine your own culture-bound values and assumptions when interacting with students who experience difficulties related to their cultural background.

Traditional Cultural Values

For generations, the family has been the nucleus of Asian culture. It is the primary institution from which is woven the social fabric of life for the individual members. The structure of the family has been patriarchal; sons are desirable over daughters because they can ensure the family line and provide support for the aged. Filial piety is of prime importance. Respect and obedience to elderly authority figures is expected. Children are conditioned to restrain their expression of feelings and emotions that might disrupt the family's balance and solidarity. To control the behavior of children, parents tend to instill guilt and shame as part of their disciplinary action. Members of a family are expected to behave appropriately and not engage in acts that will bring dishonor to the family. When conflicts and disagreements between children and parents occur, anxiety and guilt are aroused. To express feelings and emotions openly is difficult and often not encouraged. One is expected to exercise self-restraint, endure hardships, and not disclose weaknesses. However, this traditional family model is gradually changing, as younger generations identify with the Western practice of asserting independence, and attempt to modify the family tradition and structure.

The emphasis placed on filial piety and family responsibility can at times create internal stress for the individual, as illustrated below:

> As a senior in high school, N had plans to go to college when he graduated. But while he was in college, his father became seriously ill. Being the eldest son, N felt a responsibility to return home to help the family. He became depressed while caught between the family's desire for him to pursue uninterrupted schooling and his own feelings of filial obligation to help out at home.

The peer counselor in this case needs to be cognizant of, and empathetic about, the profound obligation N feels toward his family. It is necessary to understand the feelings of guilt and obligation that accompany the conflict. Exploration of feelings could be encouraged gently only if a working relationship of trust and rapport has been established.

Cultural Conflicts

The term "culture conflict" is broadly defined as the "personal discomfort or dilemma of individuals exposed to different cultures" (Sue and Kitano, 1973, p. 7). With the process of assimilation and acculturation, Asian values are challenged, and this causes various kinds of cultural conflict. Sue and Sue (1971) offer a conceptual model which provides a framework for understanding these conflicts. Three types of stereotypical characters are described: the traditionalist, the marginal person, and the Asian American.

The traditionalists are individuals who wish to hold strongly to their traditional Asian values. Conflict occurs when the individual finds it hard to maintain allegiance to the traditional family expectations. Examples can be seen in situations involving conflict between family obligation and desires for individual freedom and independence over career choice and interpersonal relationships. An Asian American student describes his feelings this way:

> It's important that my parents are happy with me. They want me to become a doctor and have financial security. All their lives, they have self-sacrificed and saved so that I could get a good education. In a way, I feel obliged to repay them for what they've done for me. You see, I was once a pre-med. Now, I'm more interested in art. I'm afraid to even let my parents know. They'd be so disappointed in me. I've let them down, but why can't I do my own thing?

Another Asian American student related the following:

> I went with a white boy for three years. I could tell you how bad it
> was for my family. The most important thing to me was my personal
> feelings for the boy. The way my folks were behaving implied what
> I was feeling was wrong. That was a big conflict. Being Japanese is
> just as important to me. Not that interracial dating threatened it at
> all. My parents kept saying that I could lose something.

The marginal persons—the second type of characters described by
Sue and Sue—want to reject the old family tradition. They deal with cultural conflicts by attempting to dissociate themselves from their Asian heritage to the extent of repudiating it and Asians. When they cannot identify
substantially with either culture, they are confronted with an identity crisis. This may express itself in low self-esteem, self-hatred, insecurity, isolation, and ambivalence. Examples of this behavior are often manifested in
dating attitudes and social relationships. The following vignette shows that
rejection and hostility toward oneself may be a transitional phase which
could turn into a positive experience.

> I remember when I was age fifteen, I was an anomaly at school. I
> didn't have any real dates. I used to pray to God to make me blond
> and blue-eyed. I hated myself and the way I was. When my prayers
> weren't answered, I knew I was left with two alternatives. One, I
> would be miserable for the rest of my life, wishing that I could be
> someone else I couldn't be. Or two, I could become a fighter for Asian
> American pride.

A new Asian American identity emerges as individuals strive to seek
a balance between the two cultures. To promote their ethnic pride, these
individuals have collectively sought to raise consciousness among other
Asians about (1) their Asian culture and (2) society's unfair treatment of
them as a minority group. Some have adopted a militant approach to express their views on racism and stereotypes. In extreme cases, individuals
may become so obsessed with oppression that they become bitter and
angry toward others who do not think or feel the way they do. There are
some who feel that if they express themselves as Asian Americans, it may
appear that they are engaging in "reverse discrimination." Perhaps this
new identity can best be generalized by a statement that Sommers (1960)
made about two individuals who were experiencing cultural conflict:

> They can now enjoy a new-found sense of belonging—a belonging
> with their own family and their (Asian) heritage, as well as belonging
> to the country of their birth and their Western culture. Through this

fusion of both cultures . . . they are gaining something unique and valuable for themselves and society that they could not have done previously by their torn allegiances. (p. 644)

The level of cultural conflict experienced obviously varies from one individual to another. The reactions described above depend largely on one's degree of ethnic identification and acceptance of one's own culture. The impact of cultural values on a person's identity certainly covers a much wider range of behaviors. For most individuals, having problems related to cultural conflicts does not necessarily indicate clinical maladjustment. As young people they may merely be coping with youth's search for identity. It should be acknowledged that such stress-points in life do place additional pressures on Asian Americans. Thus in dealing with the concerns of Asian Americans, it helps to be aware of and knowledgeable about the experiences that have shaped their behavior. Sensitivity to their level of ethnic identification, and to some Asian Americans who may have inhibitions about self-disclosure and reflection of feelings, is also important. It has been suggested that Asians prefer structured counseling situations as opposed to nondirective counseling approaches that deal with affect and reflections (Sue, & Kirk, 1973; Atkinson et al., 1978). Finally, peer counselors need to be continually alert to their own cultural and class-bound values and assumptions, so that they do not impose them on others.

Summary

In working with Asian Americans, it is helpful to:

— be knowledgeable about the Asian American experience—recognizing the overt racism and oppression encountered by Asians in settlement, and the subtle forms of racism that may still prevail.

— be tuned in to your own cultural values and assumptions about others.

— be aware of the level of ethnic identification the person brings into the counseling situation.

— be sensitive to the inhibitions some Asian Americans may have concerning self-disclosure and expression of feelings.

— be sensitive to some Asian Americans who may be more receptive to structured, direct approaches in interactions as opposed to ambiguous ones.

Exercises

The following are examples of problems that can occur in peer counseling. We hope these examples will generate future thought and discussion on counseling members of different cultures. In each case, ask yourself how you might handle the problem. As a peer counselor, what skills might you use to establish rapport and help the culturally different individual clarify his/her problems?

1. "I've been dating this Caucasian girl for some time and I want to spend more time with her, but my parents are giving me a hard time lately about using the family car, coming home late, etc. . . . They weren't like this before."
2. "My parents are very pleased that I'm pursuing a pre-med program. I'm doing fine with the science courses but I'm finding literature fascinating and more interesting. I've always been told to enter a practical field like science, engineering, or computer sciences—I'm afraid my parents will cut off the financial aid if I switch."
3. "I just couldn't believe my mother when she actually took the yearbook out and went through every single Asian's picture and asked me about them."
4. "I'm so different from the rest of the Asians here. In Hawaii, there's no such thing as discrimination, and I've never heard of the term 'Asian American' before. I don't see why there's such a big fuss about it."
5. "I wanted to get involved in Asian American activities, but my Caucasian friends told me that I was alienating them so I didn't get involved."

References

Atkinson, D. R., Maruyama, M., and Matsui, S. The effects of counselor race and counseling approach on Asian Americans' perceptions of counselor credibility and utility. *Journal of Counseling Psychology* 25 (1978): 76–83.

Bourne, Peter G. The Chinese student—acculturation and mental illness. *Psychiatry* 38 (1975): 269–277.

Kitano, Harry H. L. Japanese-American mental illness. In S. Sue and N. Wagner (eds.), *Asian Americans: Psychological Perspectives,* Palo Alto, CA: Science and Behavior Books, 1973.

Sommers, Vita S. Identity conflict and acculturation problems in Oriental Americans. *American Journal of Orthopsychiatry* 30 (1960): 637–44.

Sue, Derald W. Ethnic identity: The impact of two cultures on the psychological development of Asians in America. In S. Sue and N. Wagner (eds.), *Asian Americans: Psychological Perspectives,* Palo Alto, CA: Science and Behavior Books, 1973.

Sue,. Derald W. Cultural and historical perspectives in counseling Asian Americans. In Sue, Derald W., *Counseling the Culturally Different: Theory and Practice,* New York: John Wiley & Sons, 1981.

Sue, D. W. and Kirk, B. A. Differential characteristics of Japanese-American and Chinese-American college students. *Journal of Counseling Psychology* 20 (1973): 142–48.

Sue, D. W. and Kirk, B. A. Asian Americans: use of counseling and psychiatric services on a college campus. *Journal of Counseling Psychology* 22 (1975): 84–86.

Sue, D. W. and Sue, S. Chinese-American personality and mental health. *Amerasia Journal* 1 (1971): 36–49. Also in S. Sue and N. Wagner (eds.), *Asian Americans: Psychological Perspectives.* Palo Alto, CA: Science and Behavior Books, 1973.

Sue, S. and Sue, D. W. MMPI comparisons between Asian-American and Non-Asian students utilizing a student health psychiatric clinic. *Journal of Counseling Psychology* 21 (1974): 423–27.

Sue, Stanley and Kitano, Harry H. L. Asian Americans: a success story? *Journal of Social Issues* 29 (1973): 1–209.

Sue, S. and McKinney, H. Asian Americans in the community mental health care system. *American Journal of Orthopsychiatry* 45 (1974): 111–18.

Tachiki, A. et al. (eds.). *Roots: An Asian American Reader.* Los Angeles: UCLA AA Studies Center, 1971.

Watanabe, Colin. Self expression and the Asian American experience. *Personnel and Guidance Journal* 51 (1973): 390–96.

6.

Perspectives in Gay Peer Counseling
by Peter Nye

Gay counseling can involve both counseling people (not necessarily gay) about their gay feelings, and counseling gay people (but possibly about problems that have nothing to do with being gay). Since counseling gay people is much the same as counseling anyone else, not much needs to be said about it here—except that it is important to watch your assumptions. Don't assume that a lover is of the opposite sex. If the counselee is avoiding pronouns, do the same. Also, if the person discloses that s/he is gay, a nice resounding paraphrase of that fact can be supportive and not leave her or him guessing how you are reacting to the disclosure. Once this is done, however, the fact should not be treated with any more importance than the counselee gives it.

This chapter, then, will deal mostly with counseling people about their gay feelings, especially people who are just beginning to come to terms with them. With this kind of problem, as with all problems, all the usual rules of peer counseling apply. Here are some of the major ones that apply to gay counseling:

1. You don't have to have experienced the other person's problem (or, in this case, be of his or her orientation) to be of help.
2. On the other hand, if a problem or situation triggers a lot of emotional responses in you that interfere with your counseling, it is a good idea to tell the counselee right away and try to refer her/him to someone else.
3. It is of paramount importance for the counselee not only to explore feelings and become aware of them, but also ultimately to accept them. Gay people usually spend some part of their lives, often a very large part, feeling ashamed about their gay feelings and wishing they

didn't have them. Talking to someone about these feelings can be the first step in accepting these feelings, and thus accepting themselves. Of course, accepting the feelings is very different from deciding if, how, and when to act on the feelings.

4. The role of the counselor in this whole process is to (a) ask sensitive questions and (b) give support for the feelings by empathetic paraphrasing.

5. As a counselor, you should be especially aware of personal biases that might cause you to push (however subtly) for one alternative over another. For example, if a woman is having trouble relating to men and at the same time is feeling attracted to other women, it is important to be sensitive to which area she wants to work on, rather than which area you think will ultimately bear more fruit. Or, if a man is just beginning to deal with his gay feelings, pushing for him to accept them or to start acting on them might very well make him feel threatened and become even more afraid of the feelings.

Labels often need to be dealt with. What is "being a Lesbian" or "being gay" as opposed to "having gay feelings"? In fact, why do people have to be "gay" or "straight" or "bisexual" at all? Why can't they be whatever they are? Of course, this is something the counselee must decide for herself or himself.

It would be better if people could relate to whomever they wanted, however they wanted. Some people, especially those who have become open-minded before they have become aware of their gay feelings, can do so to some degree. But for most people, gay feelings were accompanied initially by feelings of guilt, self-hatred, and isolation. For these people, taking on the label of "gay" can be an effective means of validating their identity by saying that they're proud to be what society-at-large sneers at.

This label doesn't have to be a limiting declaration of people's exclusive affectional preference; rather, it can be an affirmation of that part of them that has the capacity to love other people. Also, declaring oneself to be gay, and even publicizing it, can help reduce one's feelings of isolation. Most gay people spend a long time not knowing how to find other gay people and feeling that they are the only ones who are "abnormal," despite the fact that there are usually gay people all around them, many thinking the same thing.

At the same time, it is important to deal with labels carefully in the counseling situation. Be sensitive to the severe negative associations that words like "Lesbian" and "gay" and "homosexual" can have in our culture. For example, "I've found myself being attracted to some of the men in my gym class" should not be paraphrased as "So you've been

having some gay feelings recently." Try to use the same terms the counselee uses.

If this issue of labeling is a problem for the counselee ("I'm attracted
to my roommate. Does that mean I'm gay?") ("I can't decide whether
I'm straight, bisexual, or gay."), some good questions are "What is your
definition of being gay?" "What are some of your images of what gay people are like?" "What is the worst thing that might happen?" You may find
that the question of labeling is dropped quickly in favor of a more specific
problem.

Near the end of the session, the counselee may decide that s/he
wants to make contact with some other gay people. At this point, gay counselors can be particularly helpful, because they can:

1. provide an initial meeting with a gay person that is "safer" than typical
    social situations such as parties and bars;
2. provide role models that can dispel some of the stereotypes the person
    might have about gay people;
3. IF the counselee specifically asks for it, provide information about the
    gay world, often drawing on their own experiences; and
4. provide knowledgeable information about the best way to meet other
    gay people.

Some people prefer to talk to a gay counselor right away, because
they can be sure of how their disclosure about their gayness will be received. On the other hand, some counselees prefer NOT to talk to a gay
counselor, either because actually meeting a gay person face-to-face is still
too threatening or because they are undecided about their primary orientation and think that a gay counselor may push them too far in one direction.

FEELINGS ASSOCIATED WITH GAY PROBLEMS

A cardinal rule of peer counseling which you have already encountered
is that FEELINGS ARE IMPORTANT. It applies especially when we are
counseling someone who has grown up with gay feelings that s/he has
been unable to express. Merely bringing these feelings to light, perhaps
through the use of a "best-possible" fantasy, and giving support through
paraphrasing, can help a lot. There are often associated feelings which are
buried along with the gay feelings. Some of them are:

1. **Isolation and alienation.** Most gay people grow up not knowing any
    gay people, or even that other gay people exist, since the gay people
    around them are not visible. They have the feeling that they alone

are different. This is why "coming out" in terms of finding a community of gay people to be with can be such a major event.

2. **Guilt and self-hatred.** The only gay role-models people have are usually extremely negative ones. They think not only that what they feel is wrong, but also that if they feel this way, they must be like the awful stereotypes they hear about.

3. **Fear and anxiety.** The fear of discovery can often dominate the life of a person "in the closet."

4. **Anger.** Anger may arise because of not wanting to be discovered; anger may be felt towards people making "fag" and "dyke" jokes; and in general, anger may be directed toward a world that is trying to make them into something they are not. This anger is often repressed and internalized as a survival mechanism.

"Coming out" is often accompanied by a great sense of relief because of the abatement of the first three of these feelings. A person's acceptance of his or her gay feelings is accompanied by a general self-acceptance and a building of confidence. This is compounded as s/he begins telling friends about himself or herself, and (usually) finds that they are much more accepting than s/he thought. (People's preconceptions about gay people usually change drastically when they find that someone close to them, whom they have always considered likeable and "normal," is gay.)

On the other hand, these feelings often continue to figure in problems the person encounters later. This is especially true since sometimes people must continue to hide their sexual identity from parents, spouses, or employers. The inability to express anger, in particular, can be a continuing problem in relationships.

GIVING INFORMATION AND SELF-DISCLOSURE

Part of peer counseling is giving information. This is not the same as giving advice; the information that is given is usually a result of the kind of counseling the counselor is doing (crisis line, contraception counseling, career counseling), rather than a result of common sense or the experience of the counselor. Good rules for giving information are:

1. Wait until the counselee specifically ASKS for it.
2. Use open questions to narrow down the field. "Tell me more about what kind of X you're looking for."
3. Give information TENTATIVELY. "Is that the kind of thing you're looking for?"
4. Wait for further questions from the counselee, rather than telling everything you know. This will help you to see if you are on the right track.

In gay counseling, often the counselee knows nothing about the gay world and other gay people, and is interested in finding out more. A straight or undeclared counselor can give what knowledge s/he has, and can be useful in dispelling myths. For this reason a section on common myths about gay people is included here. A bibliography is also included, both for counselors who are interested in knowing more, and for something to recommend to counselees.

An extension of this for gay counselors is called "self-disclosure." Sometimes the counselee is interested in the counselor's experiences as a means of learning about the gay world. It can also be a great source of comfort for people who have never met anyone gay before to find someone else who has gone through the same problems. In this case, a counselor's talking about his or her own experiences can be helpful, as long as the guidelines above are followed.

REFERRALS

There often comes a point where the person wants to take the next step in finding other gay people. At this point (and not before!), there are several options available:

1. Gay peer counselors or telephone lines. Talking to a gay peer counselor can provide a structured, nonthreatening first encounter with a gay person. Gay peer counselors are also likely to have the best information on ways to meet people, and are often willing to serve as a bridge into the gay community.
2. Gay organizations. There are often a number of ways to meet people through gay organizations or women's organizations. They are most prevalent on campuses and in large cities. Some national directories of organizations are mentioned in the bibliography at the end of this chapter.
3. Bars and coffee houses. These can be intimidating for a person just coming out, or sometimes they can be very friendly places. Often, they are the only alternative available.

The person may be interested also in longer-term therapy. If your peer counseling work calls for many occasions to refer people, it's a good idea to start building a list of counselors you can trust to send people to. While you're doing this, find out their ideas about homosexuality, and try to sense if they will be supportive of gay people's feelings.

In general, it is more important to find a good therapist than to find a gay therapist; however, all things being equal, it is less risky to send someone to a gay therapist. Many straight therapists have caused considerable damage to gay people because of their attitude toward homosexuality.

MYTHS ABOUT GAY PEOPLE

Another important part of a gay person's growth is finding out that the negative stereotypes and myths s/he has grown up with aren't true. Here are some of the myths, and the realities.

1. Gay men are effeminate (limp wrists, lisping, high voices) and Lesbians are masculine (short hair, built like bulls, ride motorcycles).

     Although this is true for some gay people, for the vast majority it isn't true; they come in all shapes and sizes, and it is impossible to tell them apart from their straight counterparts. The usual reaction to someone coming out is surprise ("I never would have guessed . . .").

     On the other hand, one of the things gay people often like about being gay is that it gives them more freedom to express and acquire positive traits usually associated with the other sex in addition to the ones that are traditionally ascribed to their own sex. For women, this means that they can be independent, strong, analytical, mechanical, "successful." For men, it means they can be supportive, "in touch" with their emotions, creative, spontaneous, sensitive to beauty.

2. Women become Lesbians because they can't get a man, or because they have had bad experiences with men, or because they haven't found the right man.

     The current opinion is that a person's potential for experiencing love and sexual attraction is set at a relatively early age, and is not (and cannot be) changed by subsequent conditioning. Thus, women's attraction for other women appears in spite of other experiences they might have. On the other hand, it is not an uncommon experience for women to feel that, although they may have had enjoyable and close love relationships with men, they find relationships with women more productive. In this case, the word "gay" does not represent an exclusive sexual orientation so much as an affirmation of their capacity for love for people of their own sex, and their bonds with other women in a more general sense. The term "woman-identified woman" is sometimes used to emphasize the positive effect that women can have on each other.

3. In gay couples, one person usually plays the male role and one person the female role.

     Again, while this is sometimes true, most gay people seek equality in relationships, and enjoy freedom from conventional strictly-defined sex roles.

4. Gay teachers seduce children.

   Gay people are generally not any more interested in sex with children than straight people are. Nearly all of the sexual assaults on children by teachers are perpetrated by straight men.

5. Having gay teachers will cause a child to become gay.

   People rarely become gay simply through contact with other gay people. Most gay people are aware of gay feelings long before encountering other gay people. And children who have gay parents show the same spectrum of sexual preference as other children.

6. People are either gay or straight.

   Studies have shown that the vast majority of people have had some experience with both orientations. In Kinsey's famous study conducted in 1948, he found that only 38% of white American adult males were exclusively heterosexual, and that 12% were predominantly homosexual.

   Furthermore, a person's sexual orientation can change during his or her lifetime. Many people don't become aware of gay feelings until much later in life, when they are married and have children. And sometimes people who are gay for most of their early life start broadening their perspectives as they grow older.

7. Gay people are doomed to be unhappy.

   Recent studies have shown that gay people are about as happy as straight people, although they sometimes appear to have a somewhat more unhappy time growing up.

8. Homosexuality is a disease.

   Freud believed that homosexuality represented arrested development and was caused by a harsh, cold, distant, or absent father, and a seductive, close-binding mother. This theory is now pretty well discredited. In fact, the whole problem of how sexuality and sexual orientation develop is still unsolved.

   Although some therapists still believe homosexuality should be classified as a disease, the prevalent view is now coming to be that since a person can be happy and well-adjusted and still be gay, treatment should be centered on the person's problem with his sexual orientation, sometimes called "homophobia," or fear of homosexuality, rather than the orientation itself.

9. Homosexuality can be cured.

   Most gay people at one time or another actively try to be "straight," to make their gay feelings go away and to fall in love with members of the opposite sex. They often seek help, either through God or through therapy. Their attempts are notably unsuccessful. While a therapist can sometimes help someone who is truly bisexual with the obstacles in the way of his or her relating to the opposite sex, the forms of therapy that are aimed toward repressing someone's gay feelings don't usually work. And in fact, most therapists find the suppression of feelings to be the opposite of what they are trying to accomplish. Therapy that seeks to make people comfortable and accepting of their feelings tends to be much more successful.

10. Homosexuality is a sign of a decadent culture.
     There is evidence of homosexuality throughout history. There is also evidence of its acceptance in many other cultures. One study found that it had an established place in about 65 percent of the cultures studied. In some cultures there are special roles created for gay people. In others, there is a certain age during people's life, or a period during each year, in which homosexuality is common.

11. Homosexuality is a sin.
     There is a wide spectrum of opinion on this question. Part of this disagreement is no doubt caused by the fact that there are a large number of gay men in the clergy. The spectrum of opinion is gradually shifting with the times, but there are still very few denominations that will, for instance, ordain openly gay ministers.

12. All that gay people are interested in is sex.
     Most gay people have the same needs for closeness and the same interest in finding long-term relationships as straight people.

13. Gay people who talk about their orientation in public are publicizing what is usually kept private.
     In reality, gay people often have to hide that which most people talk about freely. They have to lie or be evasive when people ask about their love life; they have to watch out for showing signs of affection in public which would be normal and accepted for a heterosexual couple; and they have to pretend not to be offended when encountering faggot or dyke jokes. As I mentioned earlier, having to hide these things can cause damage, both in terms of what it does to people's self-image, and in terms of the way it isolates them, not only from other gay people, but from friends and relatives with whom they can't discuss one of the most important parts of their lives.

References

Clark, Don. *Loving Someone Gay.* Millbrae, CA: Celestial Arts, 1977.
>One of the most useful books for gay people coming to terms with themselves, as well as for family and friends of gays. Written by a gay clinical psycologist who works primarily with gay people.

Silverstein, Charles. *A Family Matter: A Parent's Guide to Homosexuality.* New York: McGraw-Hill, 1978.
>Shows, through case histories, different ways that families have of handling the revelation by a daughter or son that they are gay. A good book for parents of gays.

National Gay Task Force. *Our Right to Love: A Lesbian Resource Book,* ed. Ginny Vita. Englewood Cliffs, NJ: Prentiss-Hall, 1978.
>Compiled by the women of the National Gay Task Force, this voluminous book is a wealth of information and ideas "for Lesbians, students, teachers, parents, families, legislators, counselors, and movement organizers." Includes large bibliography and national directory of organizations.

Betty Berzon and Robert Leighton. eds. *Positively Gay,* Millbrae, CA: Celestial Arts, 1979.
>A compilation of essays on subjects of vital concern to today's Lesbians and gay men who are in search of new information, ideas, and guidance for positive growth.

Adair, Nancy, and Casey Adair. *Word is Out.* San Francisco: New Glide and Dell, 1978.
>This contains interviews with a cross section of gay people, and is especially interesting in the diversity it reveals. The movie on which it was based, made for PBS, is excellent, and is available in a three-hour and a one-hour version.

Brown, Howard. *Familiar Faces, Hidden Lives.* New York: Harcourt Brace Jovanovich, 1976.
>The story of a number of different gay men in America.

Martin, Del, and Phyllis Lyon. *Lesbian/Woman.* San Francisco: Glide, 1972
>This landmark book is candid and intimate and has something valuable to say about almost every aspect of being a Lesbian.

Abbot, Sidney, and Barbara Love. *Sappho was a Right-On Woman: A Liberated View of Lesbianism.* Brancliff Manor, NY: Stein and Day, 1972.
>An excellent book about lesbians by lesbians. It skillfully combines lively personal examples with social and political

analyses of lesbianism and recent historical perspectives of the lesbian movement.

Sisley, Emily L., and Bertha Harris. *The Joy of Lesbian Sex.* New York: Simon and Schuster, 1977.

Silverstein, Charles, and Edmund White. *The Joy of Gay Sex.* New York: Simon and Schuster, 1977.

>These books provide an excellent introduction to the variety of gay love and sex, as well as surrounding issues.

Weinberg, George. *Society and the Healthy Homosexual.* New York: St. Martin, 1972.

>An authoritative treatment of the issue of homosexuality from a sociological and psychiatric point of view.

Bell, Alan, and Martin Weinberg. *Homosexualities.* New York: Simon and Schuster, 1978.

>Presents the results of an ambitious survey of gay women and men. Also contains a bibliography of scientific publications about homosexuality.

Gearhart, Sally, and William Johnson. *Loving Women/Loving Men: Gay Liberation and the Church.* San Francisco: Glide, 1974.

>A collection of essays written by an ordained gay minister and a lesbian feminist theologian.

Len Richmond and Gary Noguera, eds. *The New Gay Liberation Book.* Palo Alto, CA: Ramparts Press, 1979.

>A collection of essays on different aspects of being gay by noted authors.

Brown, Rita Mae. *Rubyfruit Jungle.* New York: Bantam Books, 1977.

>A semi-autobiographical story about growing up poor and lesbian in Florida. It's a moving and powerful book, and also tremendously funny.

Warren, Patricia Nell. *The Front Runner.* New York: Bantam, 1975.

>A classic love story about two men.

Hobson, Laura Z. *Consenting Adult.* Boston, MA: Warren, Gorham & Lamont, 1976.

>A story about the struggles of a mother and her son with coming to terms with the fact that he is gay. A sympathetic and accurate portrayal of both sides.

Hauser, Marianne. *The Talking Room.* New York: Fiction Collective, 1976.

>The story of a lesbian mother, seen through the eyes of her thirteen-year-old daughter.

Kantrowitz, Arnie. *Under the Rainbow: Growing up Gay.* New York: Pocket Books, 1977.

>An autobiography of one of the leaders of the Gay Liberation Movement, showing all his processes of "growing up," even well into adulthood.

7.

Resident Advisors and Peer Counseling
by Alice Supton and Matthew Wolf

Probably the single largest group of peer counselors on a college campus is resident advisors working in dormitories and other forms of student housing. Unfortunately, "RAs" often receive minimal training in peer counseling skills. The purpose of this chapter, then, is to explore those issues and problems that are particularly common in student residences and to provide the RA with a framework for dealing with such problems.

One of the things that Resident Advisors (RAs) do is "counseling." We can broadly define counseling as a process of assisting someone in using resources they already have, or directing that person to other resources they can use to reach their desired goal. It includes simply giving people information or advice, helping them sort out alternatives with the information already available to them, steering them to some resource which might be an appropriate aid in solving problems they face, and so forth.

Much of the success in counseling lies in knowing the resources available to both you and the person you are counseling. A knowledge of the bureaucratic, academic, and personal resources available will be helpful to you in many situations. The act of counseling helps define any problem for both the counselor and the counselee. It also helps sort out alternatives and define resources needed in solving the problem.

Although RAs are not trained counselors, they are in position to be

---

This chapter is reprinted in part from "The RA's Role in Counseling," a training booklet for Stanford University's residence staff, written by Alice Supton and the staff of Stanford's Counseling and Psychological Services. An earlier version of the incidents on pp. 155 *et seq.* was written by Matt Wolfe and Vince D'Andrea and distributed at Stanford as "How to be There When You're There."

very effective helpers for students with problems. Because they share the same residence, RAs will know the individual students, and most residents will feel comfortable talking with RAs.

SHOWING YOU CARE

To be helpful counselors to students in their house, RAs need to be accessible and approachable. RAs should be visible around the residences, present at mealtimes, and available in their rooms (perhaps with their doors open) a fair amount of time. The way RAs organize their rooms and interact with students on a day-to-day basis can either invite or discourage students' visits.

Being approachable also means showing interest in and concern for others. By sitting at dinner with a student who doesn't seem to have many friends, the RA communicates concern, presents the student with an opportunity to talk, and establishes the basis for future contacts.

RAs should be alert to how students in the house are feeling. Although the RA has a large role in recognizing and helping residents cope with problems, RAs also share students' joys and successes. RAs can show interest in and compliment students when they have performed well, contributed to dorm life, and otherwise acted in a constructive way.

RAs should also be sensitive to students' moods and watchful for signs of unhappiness or stress. Because they live in the dorm, RAs will notice changes in students' normal living patterns. Usually, students who haven't been eating or sleeping properly and who don't appear to be taking care of themselves in other ways are sending out messages that all is not well and that they need help. When RAs find themselves remarking on a students changed habits of appearance, they should report their observations to the Senior Resident Advisor* and talk with the student. As in this example, when roommates or other students report that a resident is upset or anxious, RAs should follow up by talking with that resident.

> One Friday night a student came to me and told me about a woman who was knocking back straight shots of vodka on the patio. She told the student to go away and he came to me. I did not know the woman.
>
> I went out onto the patio and sat down next to her. I asked her if she wanted to talk and she said that it didn't matter because nobody cared. I told her that I cared and that I approached her because I cared. I took her hand in mine and she thanked me for my concern.

---

*The title used to refer to senior staff in residences varies widely amoung campuses. We are using "Senior RA" to describe the person most responsible for administering the residential program and maintaining the residents' quality of life.

She said that she wanted to talk with me about the problem the next day and she stayed on the patio.

I went inside and got a close friend of hers to go outside and get the drinking woman inside and to bed. I saw her the next day. She thanked me for my concern and related the difficulties of an interpersonal relationship. She had good reason to be upset.

I handled the situation in a good way. I let the woman know verbally *and* nonverbally that I was concerned. I called upon her existing social supports to get her to stop drinking and go to bed. I gave her the freedom to refuse my help. I followed up on the incident as I had promised I would; from my actions she learned to trust me.

Students really appreciate it when an RA notices how they are feeling. Just knowing that the RA is aware of a problem and cares can be helpful to a student facing a difficult time.

Around Thanksgiving one woman in our dorm was upset with the approaching anniversary of her mother's death. I talked to her about her feelings, directed her to sources of professional counseling, suggested various plans of activity for the Thanksgiving weekend. She survived the holiday well, and we've talked about family problems several times. She seemed to benefit from knowing there was someone near who knew how she was feeling but kept things confidential. Also, we have developed a friendship beyond her family problems.

Often, opening up to the RA can enable the student to talk to others.

This quarter I've kind of taken two guys in my hall under my wing. Both of them have been programmed to be the "macho male" and never talk to anyone about any problems or thoughts going on in their heads. By some long talks and just spending time together they've opened up to me and I feel really good about it because I think it's really healthy for them. The last couple of weeks one of them has started opening up with someone else in the dorm and it really excites me to see him talking to people in this way when he never had before.

Some RAs have found that talking to a student away from the dorm has given the person some perspective on the problem.

One woman in our house was feeling maladjusted, insecure, homesick, and lonely. Her roommate, on the other hand, was feeling just the opposite (which made the woman feel even worse). After one unforgettable 3 A.M. scene in my room—replete with tears and general hysteria—I took her out for lunch . . . (and) we just had a heart-to-heart talk. As it turned out, she concluded that her expectations of herself were too high and unrealistic and that she would be happier if she relaxed more and studied less. While her formula might have been dangerous for others, I'm pleased to report a happy ending—she's more at home and she even scored a 4.0! I think taking her off-campus was good because we had more privacy, and being physically removed from the scene of her anxieties afforded her a special and well-needed objectivity. All I had to do is listen, be sincerely sympathetic and promise support. This was a rewarding experience.

WHAT IS THE PROBLEM?

Students may come to the RA with a clear idea of what is bothering them. A student may think she's pregnant. Some may have failed a midterm in calculus. A resident may be upset because a family member is sick. A student may be fighting with a roommate over the volume of the stereo. A dorm romance may break up and leave the couple uncertain about how to relate to one another. A student may be considering taking a leave of absence from school.

Each year RAs in houses with freshmen report that first-year students often think that someone somehow made a mistake in deciding to admit them. Everyone else appears incredibly smart, athletic, attractive, talented. They feel themselves somehow at the bottom of the heap whereas in high school they were valedictorians, class presidents, yearbook editors. Lowered self-esteem and worries about whether they'll make it in college are feelings common to new students.

Upperclass students are concerned about what will happen to them after they graduate. Often, in addition to worries about career or graduate school, students experience feelings of anxiety related to becoming independent from their families and striking out on their own. Friendships and romantic relationships are the source of many counseling concerns, as are feelings of loneliness and alienation.

Sometimes students aren't exactly sure what is bothering them. They may have general feelings of anxiety, depression, or ennui. This "depressed-for-no-particular-reason" syndrome, as one RA described it, might show up as poor appetite, failure to go to class, or lack of interest in house activities. RAs can encourage students who seem depressed to talk about how they are feeling. When students are distressed because they feel depressed and don't know why, it is particularly important to free them from the need to provide explanations—for themselves or for the RA—of why they feel the way they do. By showing concern and by listening, RAs can help depressed students air their feelings, which is the first step in helping them get in touch with what is troubling them. Homesickness, death, or divorce of parents, unexpressed anger, and unresolved questions of identity often occasion feelings of depression among college-age students.

It is useful for RAs to be familiar with the problems that appear most frequently, but as this RA points out, each problem is different and unique.

> I try not to label any one-to-one interaction with students as "my counseling them" on roommate or emotional/romantic problems or whatever. I try not to categorize other peoples' problems because I can then avoid treating a person as "just another homesick freshman" and my listening skills improve so that I can pick out the key, personal details. Nonetheless, I have spent a great deal of time counseling students about their academic needs/goals/expectations; helping with many types of male/female communication problems, pointing out personal biases and personal strengths; smoothing roommate situations; encouraging a workable balance between home and college. More than anything else, I want people to know that it is *not* wrong or a great failing to admit personal defeat or confusion . . . we are only human.

WHOSE PROBLEM IS IT?

Regularly, students come to RAs wanting to switch roommates. They complain that the roommate is a slob. They protest the roommate's sexual activity in the room. They say the person is inconsiderate and selfish. Often they want the RA to tell the roomate to behave differently—to clean up the room, to entertain elsewhere, to stop playing the stereo at 10 P.M. RAs may need to examine who has or "owns" the problem and to help the complaining student do the same. Is it the offending roommate or the complaining student?

When the RA asks the student, "Have you spoken with your roommate about this?" the answer is often "no." The student is afraid that the roommate will be angry or resentful. Students often need help being assertive. RAs can encourage students to tell their roommates how they feel about certain behaviors. RAs can give students practice in voicing their complaints by role-playing a discussion between the student and the roommate.

It is often helpful for the RA to encourage the student to verbalize his or her ideas of the worst possible reactions from the roommate. An effective technique is first to have the student play the role of the person he or she must confront, then to reverse roles so that the student plays himself or herself and the RA takes the part of the roommate. This kind of practice can allay anxieties about the real-life encounter. By helping students practice assertive behavior, RAs enable them to solve their immediate problems and to gain confidence in their ability to handle future problems on their own.

RAs often find that roommates can settle things between themselves without the RA becoming an actor in their conflict.

> A student came to talk about her roommate who spent all of her time with a boyfriend in the room the two women shared. The student would often leave her room angry, unable to study or sleep. My perception of the situation was that both women were extremely nice and liked each other a great deal. Yet the arrangement of the roommate and her boyfriend was creating tension. I had to convince the student of her right to use her room too. The student didn't want to intrude on her roommate's relationship. I also convinced the student that she had done nothing to resolve the situation; the roommate didn't know the student was uncomfortable and beginning to resent her. What I suggested to the woman was that she have a talk with the roommate, for I felt the problem would escalate as the year progressed. My evaluation of the result was this: (1) The student saw herself as being part of the room. She had a *responsibility* as well as a right to correct the situation. (2) The roommate became aware of the woman's feelings and the initial conversation has helped the women become closer and enjoy each other more. (3) The roommates have a satisfactory living arrangement without any harsh feelings. I was right, the roommate didn't know the woman was upset and wasn't intentionally hogging the room. (4) I think the situation showed the woman she doesn't have to avoid conflict and that her feelings are important. (5) The problem was solved before it became too difficult.

When the RA does get involved in a roommate dispute it is often in the role of diplomatic negotiator. Usually RAs should not take sides. Rather, they should provide encouragement to the roommates and help them hear each other and agree on some compromise solution to their differences. RAs have sometimes learned the hard way that, if they are going to have a role in resolving a roommate or other dorm conflict, they need to make sure they have heard from everyone affected by the problem. They cannot rely simply on what one roommate reported. In roommate switches, for example, it is essential to speak to all four parties, not just the two roommates desiring the switch.

If attempts to deal with roommate conflicts or other problems meet with limited success, RAs may want to involve the Senior RA. In fact, it is a good idea to keep the Senior RA informed of problems, even if they seem to have been resolved.

One woman in my dorm was not getting along with her roommate. She couldn't bring herself to talk to her roommate and express what was bothering her. She wanted me to tell her roommate not to sleep with her boyfriend while she was there, to turn off the light when she was trying to sleep, etc. Most of her complaints seemed legitimate, but I told her that I would only mediate between her and her roommate to encourage some interaction. She had to face her difficulties and try to solve them. Well, she tried to talk to her roommate, who flew off the handle and reacted with verbal abuse. This happened repeatedly. I made some attempts to talk to the roommate, but was either ignored or verbally insulted. I talked to the Senior RA who agreed to talk to the roommate. I set up an appiontment—they talked. A roommate switch was made.

Although the results may seem a disaster, I think we all learned quite a bit. I learned when I couldn't handle a situation alone. The roommates found how necessary it is to communicate with others to prevent misunderstanding from growing to overwhelming proportions.

Sometimes, no matter how skilled the RA or the Senior RA is in negotiating, the conflict cannot be easily resolved. As in the example above, one of the persons involved may be unwilling to cooperate with the problem-solving process. Or the problem may not have "an answer." A student who is grieving over the death of a parent cannot be offered a "remedy" for those feelings. RAs need not feel helpless at times like these, however. RAs can help the troubled person by noticing how they feel, by expressing concern, and by offering to spend time together. One very important way the RA can communicate support and caring is through good listening skills. RAs can also direct students to campus offices with professional staffs trained to deal with students' problems.

LISTENING AND REFERRAL SKILLS

RAs need two basic kinds of skills in their counseling role:

1. **LISTENING SKILLS.** RAs who listen effectively help students express their thoughts and feelings. Helpful listeners do not offer advice or assume responsibility for solving students' problems. They help students clarify the problem and identify appropriate responses to it.
2. **REFERRAL SKILLS.** RAs need to know appropriate campus resources to which counseling problems can be referred and how to make an effective referral. RAs can assist the student to follow through on the recommendation and, when necessary, can take an active role in setting up a meeting between the student and the appropriate office or service.

Most of you already possess an intuitive ability to listen well, to indicate to others that you are attentive and responsive to what they are saying, and to offer your advice and opinions only when it is appropriate to do so. Even though you may possess instinctively or have learned the following skills, we think it helpful to review here some of the components of good listening. As you read, please remember that we are not urging the acquisition of mechanical and artificial techniques. On the contrary, we are convinced that these skills, adapted to and interwoven with your own personal style, will lead to more natural and more effective counseling experiences for you and the students.

IDENTIFYING ALTERNATIVE SOLUTIONS

RAs can use open questions to help students identify and evaluate possible solutions to their dilemmas. "What have you tried?" "How did that work?" "What are you planning to do?" "What would you like to happen now?" are helpful questions to ask. By asking a student to focus on coping strategies, an RA expresses confidence in the student's ability to solve his or her own problem.

We all like to come up with our own solutions to problems. Although RAs might think they have perfect remedies in mind, they have to decide if and when it is appropriate to offer suggestions or to direct students to resources. No matter how apt the advice of an RA may be, students will be getting a message that the RA thinks they can't handle the problem themselves. What RAs want to do is help students take responsibility for their own problems and gain confidence in their ability to work out their own solutions. So, before offering suggestions, RAs need to find out what the person has tried and how the coping strategies have worked. By assessing why a problem-solving approach was or was not successful, students are often able to arrive at effective solutions on their own.

After the person has talked about what has been tried and how the various attempted solutions have worked, the RA may think it appropriate to offer suggestions. If so, the RA can say gently, "Well, I have some ideas that may or may not work." or "There are some people I might suggest you talk to." If students are responsive, the RA can help them anticipate how they will act on these suggestions or approach the resources. By helping students to create a "game plan." RAs enable students both to do something to better the troubling situation and to act on their own behalf. If students seem hesitant to pursue their own or the RA's suggestions, the RA may say, "You seem apprehensive about this. What feels uncomfortable to you?" By enabling students to explore their fears ahead of time, RAs help reduce students' anxiety about acting to solve their own problems.

PUTTING PERSONAL VALUES ASIDE

Inevitably, in counseling situations some alternatives a student considers to resolve the problem will conflict with an RA's personal values. You might or might not approve of abortion. You might be an advocate or an opponent of gay rights. You might have strong, definite religious beliefs. Your role as an RA is to help students clarify their opinions, beliefs, and values. You should try to be conscious of situations in which your own moral viewpoint may influence your interaction with a student, and be honest about your feelings. For example, you might feel strongly that abortion is not an acceptable way to deal with an unwanted pregnancy and therefore you might say, "I want you to know that my upbringing influences me a great deal in responding to your problem. I can suggest another person to talk to about what you want to do. What I can do is help you know what all your options are. The choice is yours."

Sometimes you may be asked and it may be appropriate to tell a student what you would be inclined to do in a particular situation. When you can, try to turn the question around so the student is deciding which course of action seems right. What you might do probably isn't relevant to the student's choice. The student needs to decide which alternative is best for him or her.

MAKING THE TECHNIQUES YOUR OWN

RAs who are effective listeners are relaxed and open and natural in their counseling style. They practice the traits of good listening in their own personal way. Knowing a repertoire of possible responses enables the RA to choose the most appropriate way of handling a situation. But each RA will need to fit the techniques to his or her own personality and to the situation. After a while, techniques don't feel foreign or awkward. Try out the skills in various situations and find what feels comfortable to you. Your counseling effectiveness will be enhanced by personalizing the techniques and integrating the skills with your own style of relating to others.

MAKING REFERRALS

RAs should be able to judge when a student's question or problem needs to be referred elsewhere, should know the appropriate offices to which referrals can be made, and should be able to make referrals in ways that help students assume responsibility for solving their own problems.

RAs will be able to handle many student questions and problems. Even the most well-meaning RA, however, may not be able and cannot be expected to cope with certain kinds of questions or problems. The questions may require a degree of sophisticated knowledge or understanding beyond the scope of the RA's experience. The problems may indicate a need for counseling help beyond what the RA can offer, or serious emotional or behavioral disturbance requiring professional attention. RAs need to know the limits of their own experience and competence. Though they are not trained counselors, RAs are in a crucial position to help students. With encouragement and assistance, the student can be guided to the resource best equipped to provide help.

How the RA makes a referral may influence whether the student acts on the suggestion. "The Information Center on the third floor of the administration building is the place to check whether or not you've completed the distribution requirements. The office is open the whole day, except for the lunch hour." Here the RA told the student the name, location, and hours, and identified that office as the place to secure information on the student's particular question. The RA enabled the student to find an answer to the question and did not do it for the student.

Most students are able to act on a referral without the RA's involvement. Sometimes, however, students will not follow up on an RA's referral. Often reminders and encouragement still don't help the student to act. In situations where students are hesitant or afraid to follow up on a referral, RAs can help students think through plans for approaching the offices. The RA might invite the student to the RA's room and say, "Why don't you call now. I have the office number here. Let's rehearse what you'll say and then you can call on my phone." Learning how to ask for information, help, and advice is part of the process of assuming responsibility for solving one's problems. When necessary, however, the RA can offer to set up the first appointment and accompany the student to it.

It is often the case that just setting up an appointment may make a student feel better about the problem. Sometimes following up on a referral is the first positive step the student is making toward dealing with the problem.

Most often, the RA will not feel any need to contact the office to which the student has been referred. It may happen, however, especially in counseling situations, that the RA wants to provide some background to the person who will be seeing the student. The RA will have to decide whether or not to tell the student or ask for the student's okay to make the call.

RAs should check back to see that the student followed through on the referral and to make sure that the referral was appropriate and helpful: "How did it go? Did you get into the study skills class you talked about?"

REFERRALS TO COUNSELING OR OTHER PSYCHOLOGICAL SERVICES

It is important that you, as an RA, trust your own feelings both in handling situations yourself and in referring students to help. It is also important to judge the situation for itself, and not to make things more complicated or more tense than they need to be. Because these are developmental years, all students experience periods of stress, moments of anxiety, feelings of inadequacy, and times of depression. If RAs understand this, they can avoid interpreting as personal crises what may in fact be predictable and normal ups and downs experienced by most students in the university setting.

While RAs need to avoid turning psychological molehills into mountains, they also need to be realistic about their own role. RAs sometimes think they should be able to manage situations that are really too much for them. Many student problems such as roommate conflicts, feelings of loneliness, and anxiety at exam time can be handled well by the RA. There are some counseling problems, however, which RAs not only can't but shouldn't even try to handle on their own. Severe eating disorders, prolonged depression, violent or self-destructive behavior are examples of counseling problems that require professional treatment. Realizing that some matters require professional attention should help you avoid any feelings of inadequacy in referring matters to the health service or counseling center.

If you decide that a student needs counseling help beyond that which you can provide, you can share those feelings with the student. "I am really concerned about how depressed you've been feeling all quarter. I appreciate the way you've confided in me but I don't feel I'm giving you all the help you need. I think it would be a good idea for you to speak with a professional counselor—somebody who has more experience than I do in helping people who are in the doldrums and can't seem to get out."

Many students may regard referrals to professional counselors in a different light than they would referrals to other university staff. Despite the fact that in our society all kinds of people seek professional counseling for all kinds of problems, for many people a stigma is still attached to the idea of psychological and psychiatric help. Some students think they must be "sick" or "emotionally unbalanced" to seek professional help. They need assurance from the RA that such help is available and appropriate to students seeking help with a wide range of concerns.

FOLLOW-UP ON CASES REFERRED TO COUNSELING

Because each case is unique and because counseling personnel take individual approaches, and also because residence staffs are different, it is difficult to predict exactly what will happen when situations do involve professional staff. However, it is important for residence staff to know something of what to expect when professional assistance is requested.

When a problem is referred to counseling staff members, they will assume responsibility for the situation if it is appropriate to do so. Their professional judgment and their assessment of the situation will determine what is done in a particular case. They may decide to continue to involve the RAs and Senior RA or they may choose to take the matter entirely out of the hands of the residence staff. They may ask RAs to describe the student's history in the dorm and the interactions the student has had with house residents and the RA staff. A counselor may solicit information and then determine a course of action without consultation with the resident staff, or the counselor may consult the residence staff about what he or she intends to do.

Once a client/counselor relationship is established between a student and a counselor staff member, the communication between them is privileged and confidential. The staff member cannot reveal to members of the residence staff any information about a client's mental state, even when that information might be helpful to the staff or useful in dealing with other residents. However, the staff member, without revealing specific details of the patient's condition, can give general advice about how residence staff can be of assistance.

When possible, the counselor may report back to the residence staff about the disposition of the case. Sometimes, due to the pressures involved in taking immediate action as well as other demands on the counselor's time, RAs may not hear a report of the outcome of a case as soon as they would like. If that is the case and the RAs are concerned and upset about how the situation is being handled, then they are encouraged to follow up themselves.

RAs have expressed frustration and resentment over feelings of being left out once the matter has been referred to a professional person. It is understandable that, having spent a great deal of time dealing with a particular situation, the RAs would like to see the matter through. Often RAs have invested a great deal of their own emotional energy trying to support a troubled student and to assist other residents affected by that student's behavior. They have probably also expended a large amount of time as a staff discussing the situation and providing emotional support to the staff members dealing most closely with the problem. Naturally, it is hard to be so involved, as a staff member and as a caring individual, and then suddenly to feel that you are out of the picture. Knowing that this happens may help you prepare for what may be feelings of frustration and resentment once the matter is out of your hands.

After the crisis has passed, it is a good idea to review what happened and to identify what the staff learned from the experience that might be applied in other counseling situations. That process can increase RAs' ability to respond effectively to other counseling problems.

Exercises

The vignettes or "critical incidents" presented here are intended to suggest the need for learning about resources and cooperating with fellow staff members in using these resources. It is our hope that reading and discussing these incidents will achieve the following goals.

1. Expose staff members to the range of problems which may occur, so that there will be few or no surprises.
2. Provide opportunity for discussion of problem-solving alternatives based on what others have done in the past.
3. Teach staff members some helpful responses through discussion, group problem-solving, and peer feedback.
4. Open avenues of communication within the house staffs.
5. Suggest the possibility of consultation with the staffs of student services, including the dean's office, health service, counseling and psychological services, etc.

How to Use This Section

In our experience, the incidents presented here are fairly typical of the kinds of problems you may expect to encounter. The resident fellow or senior house associate can serve as a discussion leader for one or more incidents, exploring the group's knowledge of the range of resources and approaches to solving a particular problem. Experience tells us that the best way to learn about what is available is to work with a particular student who has a particular problem and then to find out what can be done about it. Unfortunately, many staff members don't learn the necessary information until after they have handled a problem. *It is our hope, then, that house staffs will use these incidents in small group discussions as a dry run for working with real-life problems in the residences.* In this way, the RA can broaden his or her knowledge of the kinds of resources available to students.

In using the incidents, we encourage you to be creative in teaching each other how to perform in your roles as staff members. In working with the incidents, you may find it helpful to use techniques other than simple discussion, such as role playing in pairs of "students" and "RAs," or using other methods of simulating the real-life situation. Sharing information and approaches *constructively* also gives staff members a way of structuring part of their time together while focusing on common and often problematic areas of concern.

We have provided a sketch of the background for each of the incidents presented, including characteristics of the student involved, the situation in which the problem was presented, and the important issues involved in solving the problem. In solving the problems presented here, you may wish to ask the following questions:

1. What are the important issues of the problem presented? (Be certain
    to consider the effects of an individual's behavior in a dorm situation.)
2. What are some helpful responses? Why?
3. What responses would be least helpful? Why?
4. Are there any appropriate student services to which you could refer
    the student if need be?
5. How would you follow up to determine whether or not your help
    was effective?

At the end of this section, we have provided a brief account of what
the RAs actually did in each situation. After discussion try to decide
whether or not the RA involved took a constructive course of action, realizing also that some problems do not present easy solutions.

Incidents

1. You are a woman staff member in a co-ed, all-freshman dorm. A
    freshman male comes to your room, wanting to talk, in the middle
    of fall quarter. He says that he was very "experienced" sexually in
    high school, but can't seem to find a girlfriend in the dorm. He an-
    nounces somewhat arrogantly that he wants to get "back into the
    swing" of things and that he has been "noticing" you around for
    some time now. He then states that you are a most "likely candidate"
    for him.
    What do you say? How do you feel? How might he respond to what
    you say? Why?
2. You are a male staff member in an all-freshman dorm. You gradually
    become aware that a male student on your floor is not getting along
    well with people in the dorm. Although the student is vaguely aware
    that something is wrong, he is not aware that his bearing and manner
    are offensive to nearly everyone in the dorm. Consequently, he has
    made no close friends and people avoid him because he frequently
    acts inappropriately in social situations. You and others are uncom-
    fortable with him but he seems insensitive to these signals from other
    people.
    How do you talk to him about his "problem" without putting him
    down? How could you help him to improve his relationships, even
    though he might not be aware that they need improvement? How
    would you feel about talking to this person about how other people
    see him?
3. You are a woman RA on an all-women's floor in an upperclass coed
    dormitory. You first learn of two roommates having problems when
    roommate A tells you early in fall quarter that "something is wrong
    with my roommate—she is very quiet." Roommate A, who now has

acquired a boyfriend and is having academic problems, returns in winter quarter with the same story. The conflict grows and you next hear of it when roommate A goes to the infirmary and refuses to return to the dorm until roommate B leaves her room. In the meantime, roommate B has developed an eating problem, seems depressed, and is losing weight. You soon discover that no one is willing to room with A.

How would you intervene? Whom would you talk to? Who could help you in determining a course of action?

4. You are an RA in a coed dorm and learn that a junior male has been selling large quantities of drugs for quite some time. Lots of strange people are coming to the dorm and the student is beginning to have some regrets about selling. You have not talked to the student directly, but know of the situation from other students who have bought drugs from him.

    What would you do?

5. As a woman RA in an all-freshman dorm, you are approached repeatedly by freshman women who are having to adjust to intense academic and intellectual pressures in the university. In particular a freshman woman talks to you several times about her feelings of inadequacy in getting into intellectual conversations in groups, particularly with men. She is considering leaving school because of her feelings.

    How would you approach the problem? What are her needs in this situation?

6. A freshman student comes to you worried and upset after receiving a notice of academic probation. She is considering dropping out of school because she fears she may flunk out. You have noticed that the student has irregular sleeping habits and other students tell you that she has poor study habits. She also lacks confidence in her ability to succeed academically.

    How do you help her to stay in school?

7. As a female RA, you are continually plagued by complaints of wronged parties in love affairs between RAs and other students, or stories of one seeking (and failing to achieve) a relationship with another, all of which point out the difficulties of relationships between staff members and students. In one incident, you are informed by a freshman woman that a male RA in your house is searching for the perfect lover among the freshman women and repeatedly throwing over the rejects. After finding the perfect freshman mate, the male RA withdraws from involvement with the rest of the dorm students.

    What can you do to help the women who have been rejected? How would you approach the RA about his behavior?

8. Roommate A knocks on your door at 2 AM on Saturday night and tells you that he is very concerned about B who is tripping on LSD and seems to be having trouble with it. A informs you that B has had upsets before while tripping, but none so serious as this one. How do you handle it?

9. You and other staff members gradually become aware that a certain male staff member, X, is not performing his job up to par. He is rarely in the dorm, and you suspect that he is exploiting some students in personal relationships. You understand through rumors that he may be having problems in a personal relationship outside the dorm.

    How do you confront the very sensitive issue of inappropriate or incompetent actions on the part of another RA?

10. On the first day of fall quarter, you receive a phone call from the infirmary informing you that a male student on your corridor, M, was found passed out drunk the night before, and is now in the infirmary. You are asked to visit him and provide company. You see him several times during the next few weeks and gradually realize that drinking is a serious problem for him.

    What can you do?

11. A sophomore woman on your corridor, Q, begins acting in a bizarre manner. She laughs inappropriately, and runs through hallways bumping into walls and shrieking. By the third week of fall quarter her roommate indicates that Q has stopped attending classes. "Q" comes to your room, talking with you repeatedly for several hours at a time, insisting that people are watching her, and because people keep staring at her in class, she can no longer go to class. Finding that she has a disease resembling hemophilia, you refer her to the health center, but she refuses to continue going there after two visits, claiming that the doctors "know too much about her." You arrive at the dorm one evening to discover that Q has taken a bottle of aspirins and may be in serious danger from stomach bleeding. How do you respond? Whom do you call?

12. You are an RA in an all-male, freshman dorm. Two roommates, both of them black students, begin to have trouble getting along because of differences in lifestyle. You learn of their conflict as each comes to you individually, complaining of the other's actions. They argue quite frequently over petty issues and soon request that they be allowed to change rooms. Because it is house policy in freshman dorms to switch roommates only as a last resort, and because there are interracial tensions in the dorm, you encourage the two to try to communicate and offer sensible advice on how to get along with the conflict. However, it continues, to the point where some action must be taken.

    What do you do?

13. You are a male RA in a coed freshman dorm. Many of the men in your dorm are, for various reasons, concerned about their inability to establish good relationships with the women in the dormitory. L, one of the males, who is a somewhat immature student, gradually becomes known for his aggressiveness in "hustling" women. He is ridiculed by the other dorm members, and as the quarter progresses, he gets more and more lonely and isolated from the rest of the dorm. What can you do?

14. A sophomore woman, W, comes to your room and tells you that she is seriously considering dropping out of school. As you talk, you discover that she feels out of place, that she does not really "belong" on campus. She has been unable to decide upon a major, has received only mediocre grades in recent quarters, and doesn't really know why she is in college at all. Furthermore, she is not very satisfied socially, she has made only a few friends, and does not really feel comfortable with the people in the dorm.
What do you do?

15. A freshman male, B, comes to your room late one night in a panic, explaining that he has an important exam the following morning, but he is too anxious to study for it. You talk and discover that he has had this problem before and on several occasions his mind has "gone blank" during exams, even though he had adequately prepared for them. He also mentions that his study habits have deteriorated greatly in the last few weeks in that he puts off work until the last minute and then attempts to "cram" before exams.
How can you help him for tonight? What can you suggest for the future?

Note: The following incidents are presented without responses so that you and your staff can discuss them without the benefit of prior knowledge.

16. V, a roommate of L, informs you that he thinks L is a homosexual and is extremely uncomfortable living with him. A few days later, L comes to you and states that he is worried about "sexual matters." How do you respond to each student? Would you refer L to someone?

17. You notice that C, a female student on your floor, has been spending a great deal of time in her room, and has been frequently missing meals and classes. C's roommate tells you that C seems very distracted and withdrawn, but won't talk about what is bothering her. C's roommate finally requests a roommate change because of C's behavior. What can you do to help?

18. You become aware that there is growing friction between the black students and white students in your house. The students tend to congregate in color-exclusive groups in the lounge. A white student

comes to you to complain that he can no longer live with his two black roommates because of subtle pressures he feels from them. How can you ease the situation? Who could help you?

19. A freshman woman tells you that she thinks that she may be pregnant and doesn't know how it could have happened. How do you respond to her?

20. A senior comes to you, telling you that he has been rejected by all of the 15 medical schools to which he applied and is now very confused about his future. How can you help him to sort it out?

Responses to Incidents

1. The RA responded by telling him that she was flattered, but it wouldn't work, because of her position as a staff member in the dorm, among other reasons. Because his ego is involved, he feels rejected and there are awkward feelings between the two for the rest of the year. He eventually finds a partner to "satisfy his needs."

2. The staff met to discuss the student and enlisted the advice of persons trained in counseling. One of the staff members approached him and asked general questions about how he was doing in school, how he was feeling, etc. The discussion then focused on how he felt about his lack of friends. The staff member confronted him with his perception that the student was unhappy and perhaps lonely. The staff member suggested he might be able to talk to someone at the peer counseling center in order to learn how to relate to others more effectively. The student's "problem" continued and found no solution during the year because of his unwillingness to seek help.

3. The RA consulted with other staff members and they decided to hold a floor meeting. Several roommate switches were made after a long meeting in which many feelings were aired. A was referred to a psychiatrist and eventually decided to leave school temporarily. B also sought professional help and decided to leave school.

4. The RA approached the dealer and advised him on the possible consequences of his behavior, including legal repercussions, potential harm to drug users, the possibility of thefts in the dorm, etc.

5. The female RA tried to get the student to focus on her strengths and to understand that she couldn't compete equally well in all situations. She also assured her that upperclassmen weren't perfect either and that she (the RA) also had some of the same feelings.

6. The RA took these steps to help the student:
1) Clarified the meaning of "probation" (which was not so serious, as it turned out) and explained the alternatives to the student. Pointed out that she was not the only one on probation.

2) Suggested "easy" courses to help bolster her grade-point average.
3) Referred student to a learning assistance center in order to improve study habits.

7. The RA discussed the issues with the Senior RA and then decided to talk to some of the women who had been rejected, in order to help them understand what was going on. The female RA and the Senior RA both discussed their concerns with the male RA about not performing his job adequately.

8. The RA talked to the tripping student, carefully avoiding making judgments about B's drug-taking behavior. The student and the staff member decided to go to the peer counseling center, where they talked with a peer drug counselor. After a few hours, B calmed down and decided to go to the night at the infirmary. The RA visited B the next day and B decided to seek professional help in working through some of his personal concerns.

9. Two RAs discussed the matter and decided to discuss the issue with the Senior RA. The three called a staff meeting (which the RA in question failed to attend) and discussed the problem. The person who knew X the best, Y, approached him and discussed the concerns of the other staff members. X and Y conferred with the Senior RA and X admitted that he was having personal difficulties. X decided to withdraw from the staff at the end of the quarter.

10. The RA slowly developed a relationship with M over the course of the year by eating with him and paying attention to him frequently. The RA was able to gain his trust by not pressuring him to talk, and M began to talk about his drinking problem. It turned out that most of his friends also drank heavily, and the RA was able to introduce M to a new group of friends who did not drink so heavily. By the year's end M was doing a lot better and had reduced his drinking.

11. The RA had been in touch with the woman's roommate and with the Senior RA for several weeks with regard to Q's behavior. Taking a bottle of aspirin was tantamount to an act of suicide for Q, because she had a bleeding problem. The RA acted quickly to get medical attention for Q, but made certain that the incident was not disruptive to the other members of the floor. Eventually, this case involved the Dean of Student Affairs office and both the medical and psychological units of the health service. The RA regrets that he did not respond sooner by pressing the woman to get professional help or to contact her parents.

12. The RA eventually had to make a roommate exchange, but before doing so, consulted with the Senior RA and the associate dean and his staff because of the various tensions present in the dorm. Making a satisfactory roommate exchange required much time and effort in

meeting with the students involved in order to find a compatible combination.

13. The RA approached L to talk over the situation. In this and subsequent discussions, he learned that L was not the only male in the dorm who had bad feelings about the lack of relationships with women in the dorm. Many freshman males in this dorm had, like L, decided to eliminate themselves from such relationships. Withdrawing from the "competition" for women in the dorm and harboring resentments about their failure to have relationships, several of the men felt the same as L, but were not as demonstrative of their feelings. After several talks with the RA, L was able to relax more in the dorm and to participate in dorm life more actively.

14. After getting to know W through several more discussions, the RA discovered that W was under a great deal of pressure from her parents to stay in school, even though she preferred to take some time off. The RA suggested that W might wish to see a counselor at Counseling and Psychological Services to help work through her dilemma. W eventually decided to take some time off and work, and later returned to school with a better idea of what she wanted to do.

15. The RA encouraged the student to go to sleep, miss the exam, and then go talk to the instructor afterwards, explaining his problem and requesting a make-up assignment. B was also referred to the Learning Assistance Center, where he worked on developing better study skills and habits. LAC referred him to the counseling center where he was able to reduce his acute test-anxiety.

A FINAL WORD

To be helpful to students in their houses, RAs need to take care of themselves. Try to make time for yourself, see your friends, and maintain a balance between your RA responsibilities and the rest of your life. When you think it would be helpful, talk over your feelings about the job with friends, other RAs, or your senior RA. By attending to your own needs, you can maintain a healthy perspective on yourself as an RA and on students' problems.

Appendix A

Suggested Peer Counseling Curriculum

A good peer counselor training program should rely primarily on experiential learning through role-playing and other exercises, supplemented with didactically presented material and group discussion. We recommend that listening and counseling skills be presented slowly in a one-step-at-a-time fashion. Subsequent sessions can be used to integrate skills. Videotape training is invaluable.

We have found it most appropriate to schedule two class sessions each week. The first is a two-hour session in which the "skill of the week" is introduced, good and bad role-play models are presented and discussed, and, if time allows, students have a chance to practice the skill. In the second session, students meet in groups of four or five with an experienced counselor for ninety minutes. More intensive practicing is combined with critical feedback from the counselor/trainer.

The material in this book is actually best presented in two ten-week courses. In the first course, called "Introduction to Peer Counseling and Basic Attending Skills" the following syllabus is recommended:

Week 1:   Introduction, non-verbal attending skills

Week 2:   Open questions

Week 3:   Paraphrasing

Week 4:   Working with feelings

Week 5:   Summarization

Week 6:   Integration of all skills learned so far, loose ends, etc.

Week 7:   Decision-making and problem solving

Week 8:   Crisis Counseling

Week 9:   Depression

Week 10: Suicide

A second ten-week "Advanced Peer Counseling" course can also be offered. For it, we recommend the following curriculum:

Week 1: Review of listening skills

Week 2: Counseling skills overview, differences between counseling and therapy, role and responsibility of peer counselors

Week 3: Contracts

Week 4: Confrontation

Week 5: Interpretation

Week 6: Gay counseling

Week 7: Ethnic perspectives

Week 8–10: Special topics appropriate to the counseling center at which students will be counseling (e.g., advanced suicide-counseling skills for hotline volunteers, contraceptive information for birth control counselors, vocational guidance information for career counselors, information about draft laws for draft and consciencious-objector counselors, information about campus resourses for residential advisors, etc.).

The above syllabus is the one we use for training peer counselors to work in a general college campus drop-in and telephone counseling service. Your particular program may require you to modify this sequence of events. Obviously, you should tailor the training your peer counselors receive to the goals of your program. Determine what kinds of activities peer counselors in your program will be engaged in and then design your program accordingly. For example, counselors in a strictly academic advising role probably only need one ten-week training course that covers the five basic listening skills plus information about careers and programs. Suicide, crisis, and depression do not need to be presented at all. Generally, if suicide and crisis are not concerns of your counseling program, you can replace weeks 8 to 10 in the introductory course with the material from weeks 8 to 10 in the advanced class.

Appendix B

A Suicide Hotline Call

Don:	Hello, Counseling Center.
Pete:	Hi.
Don:	Hello, who's this?
Pete:	My name is Pete.
Don:	Hi Pete, I'm Don.
Pete:	Hi. My name's Pete, and I think I'm going to kill myself.
Don:	What's going on, Pete?
Pete:	What's going on is that I've just got a lot of shit going on in my life, and I'm going to kill myself. I've got a gun right here.
Don:	Uh huh.
Pete:	And I called you. You're supposed to be able to do something about it, right?
Don:	Yeah. The first thing I'd like to do about it Pete, is to talk to you—try to find out a little more about what's going on.
Pete:	I don't want to talk! I want some help!
Don:	Uh, sometimes it . . .
Pete:	I've been talking all my life, and it hasn't done me any good. I need some help!
Don:	I'm here to help you, Pete, and I really want to do that. Sometimes it does help if you can let somebody know exactly what's going on. I'll try to see if, together, we can work out a plan or something that can improve things for you.
Pete:	What's going on is that I've got this gun here, and it's a .22, and it's loaded, and I got my finger on the trigger. That's what's going on.
Don:	Okay. Could I ask where you are, Pete?
Pete:	I'm sitting in my apartment.
Don:	Are you alone, or is anyone else . . .

Pete:	Yeah, I live alone.
Don:	You live alone.
Pete:	Downtown, in a crummy little apartment.
Don:	What's the address, Pete?
Pete:	Don't . . . Never mind what the address is. Hey! Are you tracing this?
Don:	No, I'm not, Pete.
Pete:	How do I know you are not tracing this call? If I think you're tracing, I'm going to hang up on you.
Don:	Yeah, well, what I can tell you, Pete, is that I am not tracing it, and more generally, I can tell you that I am really going to be honest with you in this call. That's one of the things that I can do, to give you straight answers and straight talk. And I won't lie to you, Pete. I promise, and I am not tracing this call. I couldn't trace the call even if I wanted to. We don't have that capability.
Pete:	Okay, well, you better not be.
Don:	I'd really like to know a little bit about what's going on, Pete. It would help me to think about suggestions I could make.
Pete:	Yeah, well, what's going on is my life is just a mess. That's why I am sitting here with this goddamn gun.
Don:	Yes. Has something happened recently, Pete, that's really brought it to a head?
Pete:	Yeah. I lost my job.
Don:	I see.
Pete:	And my old lady just split.
Don:	Uh huh. When did she leave?
Pete:	About three days ago. I've been up since then. I haven't been eating. I'm so wired, I can't get to sleep.
Don:	When was the last time you ate, Pete?
Pete:	I don't know. I don't know. Two days ago, maybe?
Don:	Uh huh. It's really got you really upset, huh?
Pete:	Yeah. I'm really upset, and, you know, I don't see any options. That's why I'm sitting here with this gun. I've just had it, you know?
Don:	Have you ever tried suicide before?
Pete:	Yeah. Yeah.
Don:	When was that?
Pete:	About two years ago.
Don:	And what did you do then?
Pete:	Well, I'd applied to go to grad school, 'cause I'd been working for about six years, and I just didn't dig that at all, and so I was trying to get into school, and I applied, and I couldn't get in.
Don:	Uh huh. And what happened?
Pete:	I took a bunch of pills.

Don:	Uh huh.
Pete:	My old lady came home and found me.
Don:	I see. How did you feel after that whole episode about trying to kill yourself and not doing it?
Pete:	I felt pretty stupid, I guess. Stupid and embarrassed. I mean like, you know, that's why I've got a gun now. I mean, the pills, you know, like they obviously don't work very well. There's a long time span. Somebody can find you. With this gun, though, you know, like any minute it could be all over. Like, while you're talking to me right now, I could blow my brains out.
Don:	Yeah. That's really true.
Pete:	I just want to make sure you know that.
Don:	Yeah, I do. I do know that. And, I know that it's up to you—that you can make that decision, and I want you to know that I really hope that you'll talk to me and that you won't pull that trigger.
Pete:	Well, I don't have anybody else to talk to. That's why I have to rely on you.
Don:	Sometimes we have to start somewhere, and I'm glad that you called, and I'm glad that you're talking to me, and I really want to try help you to think about other things that you can do.
Pete:	Like what?
Don:	Well, I'm wondering if there is anyone else that you've thought about talking to? Anyone else that you're in contact with?
Pete:	Well, my parents live back East. I moved out here, you know, from Massachusetts, went to college, and then I got a job. And so, I guess—I don't know. I don't have many friends. I guess I'm sort of isolated. You know, like I was sitting here and thinking, wow, who could I call that I could really tell this to, and there wasn't anybody.
Don:	So, you really did want to tell this to somebody, huh?
Pete:	Yeah, I don't know. I guess I feel like I do and I don't. I don't know. You know, things are just going around and around in my head. Like, I have these flashes where I just say the hell with it, I'm going to do it, you know. And then, I back off from it a little. I don't know, it's just sort of going up and down, and up and down, and up and down.
Don:	What are you saying to yourself in those times when you're backing off a little? What's the argument there? What kind of thoughts do you have there?
Pete:	Well, I guess I hope maybe I can get back with my old lady. I don't know. I don't know. But she's been putting up with me for like four or five years, and she just finally got disgusted.
Don:	Is this the first time that you two have split?
Pete:	Well, no. When I tried the other time, a couple of years ago, she split too.

Don: Uh huh.

Pete: But I convinced her to come back. I don't know. I just—I don't know.

Don: What did she say this time when she left, Pete?

Pete: She said—see, I drink, too. I mean, that's another problem I've got. She said she couldn't handle my getting drunk all the time. Ah, she couldn't handle—she says I'm depressed all the time, which is true. I mean, what can I say? It's true. I am. It's true.

Don: Yeah.

Pete: And, she just couldn't handle it anymore. She felt like I was too much of a downer for her. You know, I agree with her. I mean, you know, maybe—I'm too much of a downer for everybody.

Don: So where does that relationship stand now? She left three days ago.

Pete: She left, and I haven't heard from her. You know, she hasn't called. I guess she just got fed up. I don't know; she's probably staying with friends or something.

Don: You don't know where she is?

Pete: No. She hasn't called. I think—you know, she's through with all this.

Don: Are there any. . . . Do you have any relatives other than your parents? Anybody closer?

Pete: Relatives? No. All of my relatives live back East, pretty much.

Don: How would you like things to be, in terms of . . . when you get back together with—what is your wife's name?

Pete: Faye.

Don: Faye. When you got back together after the last time you attempted, what kinds of things were you . . . did you have in mind that you wanted to see happen? What kinds of things were you working toward?

Pete: With her, you mean?

Don: With that relationship, or in general.

Pete: I don't know. I'd like, I'd like, you know. I don't know. I just want to feel good. You know what I mean.

Don: Yeah, yeah, I do.

Pete: And, I wasn't feeling good. I wasn't feeling good in my job, you know, like I just feel my job is just a mess! It's boring work, and I don't like the people there, and it's a real shitty place to work, and I don't have much in common with those people.

Don: So, there wasn't really much incentive to stay there anyway, huh?

Pete: No, no. I sort of got myself fired, almost. That's like . . .

Don: Yeah, you really figured you could do better for yourself, huh?

Pete: I just couldn't handle the pressure anymore. Like, I just always felt there was a lot of pressure on me. Pressure being around

	people. Being around people is pressure for me, for one thing. That's probably why I don't have many friends.

Don: Yeah.

Pete: And I have been trying to work on that, and trying to work with my old lady, and it just doesn't work out, and that's why I am sitting here with this gun.

Don: How are you feeling talking to me? What kinds of feelings do you have about me?

Pete: I don't know. I feel like I don't know if you know what I'm talking about.

Don: Uh huh. I think I do, at least part of it. I can't feel the feelings that you're feeling. I know that you're frustrated, and you're feeling like you don't have any options open to you. I can't feel it as intensely as you're feeling it, but I do understand some of the issues. I certainly understand the thing about wanting to have people to talk to. I'm the same way. That's real important to me, and that's a really tough area.

Pete: Yeah, but why is it so hard for me? I mean, I see other people around. They don't have trouble. They make relationships. They have friends, you know? And, that's just so hard for me.

Don: Do you think that being married . . .

Pete: Okay, we're not married. We're just living together.

Don: I see.

Pete: Are you married?

Don: No, I'm not.

Pete: Okay. Well, have you ever thought about committing suicide? I mean, how do you get off sitting here talking to people?

Don: Uh, I have thought about suicide, and that's maybe one of the reasons why I thought about doing this. Not that I was above people who would think about that, but rather I'd had some sense that that was a place I was at once, too, and that a lot of the feelings are feelings that come up again. I think we all go through that from time to time. I think the difference, Pete, between me and you is that right now in my life I do have a little more support, maybe—you know, some things and some people that I can turn to. And so, when something like what's happened to you comes along, I've got a little more strength. And you just happen to be at a time when you got caught off-guard, you know, with nothing to fall back on. I really think that that's the main reason we think about suicide.

Pete: Yeah, but it's been like that all my life. I mean, it's not like my life's real hunky-dory, and then I went into a bad period and got caught off-guard. It's like, you know, it's been like this all my life. And, I'm getting tired of it!

Don: What . . .

Pete: You know, like, what can I do, man? What can I change? How
          can I get people to—how can I feel comfortable with people?
Don: Well, one thing you could look at is the job. You know, you
          could think about what it was about that last job that you didn't
          like and think about maybe trying to get in an area where you
          are more comfortable, 'cause that can be a real way of getting
          in touch with people, too. You know, if you are comfortable on
          your job, you are more open with the people that you're meet-
          ing on your job.
Pete: Okay. It wasn't so much that it was a bad job, it's just that being
          around people made me nervous, you know? Like, somebody
          would come into my office to talk to me, and I'd get nervous,
          you know? It wasn't that a different job would put me around
          people, and then things would be okay. It's being around people
          that's the problem.
Don: Well, I feel like I'm beginning to know you a lot better. I don't
          know how you are feeling about talking to me, but it seems to
          me there are some things that we can work with here.
Pete: I don't have any answers yet from you. What I need is answers.
Don: Pete, are you holding the gun?
Pete: Yeah, I've got it in my hand.
Don: I'm wondering, just while you're talking to me, if you could put
          the gun down. Just because, if you are going to die . . .
Pete: How about if I put it in my mouth instead?
Don: Uh uh. I really don't want you to do that, Pete. My sense is that
          you're wanting to talk to me, and even though you're frustrated
          because I'm not giving you all the answers that you want, you
          do want some answers, you do want to work on this thing.
Pete: Well, what can I do? Tell me something I can do.
Don: Well, in terms of your discomfort with other people, there are
          some ways to work on that. Have you ever tried any sort of coun-
          seling? Have you ever gone to a professional who has some
          background in interpersonal relationships, and talked it out with
          them?
Pete: Yeah, you know when I tried with the pills, I got hauled off to
          the emergency room and I was in the County Mental Health
          crap for awhile, but, you know, those guys are jerks. I know
          more than they do. I mean, you know, they just want to get you
          out so they can take care of rape cases, or whatever. You know?
          I mean, people in real emergencies.
Don: There are some counseling agencies in the area here that aren't
          part of that system—that are much smaller and more personal.
Pete: Yeah, well, how much do they cost?
Don: They are not expensive, Pete.

Pete: A small fortune?

Don: No, really, they are not expensive. There is a family service
        agency in town which is a small organization that has a lot of
        branches, and it's well known and well established, but it's a
        much more personal thing. The first visit is five dollars, and
        thereafter, they set up a sliding scale based on your ability to
        pay. It's not that expensive, and I'm thinking that maybe just
        getting started with something like that might make a big differ-
        ence. It wouldn't necessarily be a long-term thing, but just to
        have a sense that you are doing something. You know, because
        right now, with Faye leaving, and you losing the job, both, you
        are really kind of at a standstill. That's the way it seems to me.
        There's not much going on.

Pete: Well, I sure the hell don't know where to go next or what to
        do next. You know how hard it is to get jobs around here?

Don: Yeah, I do.

Pete: You know, like getting a job, you know . . .

Don: Have you ever heard of New Ways to Work?

Pete: Yeah.

Don: It's a place in town, and again . . .

Pete: Yeah, but I've known lots of . . .

Don: It's not a big bureaucratic kind of thing.

Pete: Okay. I know that I can be able to get a job. I mean, I've known
        people who have gone down there. I mean, they've got all these
        high-falootin' ideas about job-sharing and stuff, but when it
        comes to the nitty-gritty of getting you a job, you know, they
        can't do it.

Don: Well, I think there are two things going on here, Pete. I think,
        you know, there are practical decisions that you have to make
        about the job. You're going to be making some decisions about
        where to go with your relationship with Faye. You know, I real-
        ize that we haven't really even talked about that, but you are
        going to have to kind of do some things in those areas. But there
        are also your feelings, and I really think that if we could begin
        working on some of these things, even before it's all worked
        out and resolved, before you have a job, for instance, it can feel
        better for you. It can feel like you are at least headed some-
        where, and I think that makes a difference. Maybe you feel a
        little bit of that just in talking to me. I don't know; I hope so.

Pete: Well, at least you are willing to talk to me. I mean, you know,
        most people, if I said I had a gun in my mouth, they'd freak out.

Don: Yeah, well, I'll be honest with you. That's scary for me.

Pete: Well, okay, I'm glad to hear that, 'cause that tells me a little bit
        about, you know . . .

Don: But, you know, I don't know. . . . There's not too much I can
        do about that, to tell you the truth. If you are going to shoot
        yourself, you are going to shoot yourself. I can't stop you. So,
        maybe the best thing I can do is not to try to wrestle with you
        about that but try to help you with what's behind it.

Pete: Yeah. I guess, you know, the major thing is Faye leaving. I can
        go through a lot of shit, you know, with her around, but, like
        she's pretty much my only social contact. And, with her gone,
        that's just like somebody just kicked out the last piling under-
        neath me.

Don: Yeah, that's really rough—especially just three days ago. You
        must still be right in the middle of all those feelings.

Pete: Yeah, I'm just . . . yeah, sure I'm guess I'm in shock. The feelings
        are hard, I guess. I guess I'm not feeling a lot of feelings. I'm
        feeling angry.

Don: Uh huh. Angry at whom?

Pete: Angry at her. Angry at my job. Angry at myself. Just angry at
        the world. Angry because I've been trying so long, and it hasn't
        worked. I'm just—I don't know. I'm angry now, and it will prob-
        ably turn into depression, which is my normal state.

Don: Yeah. I'm hoping that if we kind of stay with it, we talk about
        it a little more now and line up something, you know, that you
        can stay with—that if you are dealing with it and doing some-
        thing about it, that you won't fall into that depression. Some-
        times depression is hardest if you're just wallowing in it, you
        know? And, I know that it's rough with . . .

Pete: Wallowing! You think I'm wallowing?

Don: No, I don't. I don't think you're wallowing. I mean, I think you
        picked up the phone and called me. I've talked to people that—I
        see people that aren't really asking for help, that aren't looking
        for specific things to do like you're are. They have just given
        up, and I think that really feeds the depression. What I'd like
        to suggest, for one thing, is that maybe you could come in and
        we could sit down and talk about it face-to-face. I'd really like
        to meet you, and sometimes that can be a more effective thing.

Pete: No, I don't know about coming in. I mean, like, this is all anony-
        mous. You are not tracing the call, or anything?

Don: That's right. All I know is your first name, right now. You know,
        I just think that that would be a little more personal thing, and,
        you know, we've got a lot of materials here that we could look
        through, thinking about what to do. But just in terms of just your
        feelings, I think it might be helpful to be able to talk to someone
        face-to-face. Maybe if you're not sure about the counseling, that
        would be a good first step.

Pete: Well, I think I'd probably feel better talking to you than going
         into some counseling agency and saying, well, I just decided to
         kill myself.

Don: Yeah, yeah, that's—I know that's hard. I think that one of the
         things that's maybe a little different about this counseling cen-
         ter, too, is that, you know, we're not professionals. I am not
         a professional, Pete. I'm a volunteer, and I feel like I've got
         some pretty good training, but I don't feel like you are a client
         or, you know, somebody that's . . . that I'm any better than
         you. It would be more just kind of two guys talking. And yet,
         I have some experience in terms of what's in the community
         and also talked to some people that have been in similar posi-
         tions, and maybe I could be helpful. I'd really like you to do
         that if you'd be willing, and my schedule's real flexible. We
         could set that up almost anytime.

Pete: Yeah, I don't know. You know, like I've been sitting here and
         talking to you, and you know, I could, you know, I could make
         one more try, but I don't know. It just feels . . . I feel real tired.
         Just tired.

Don: I understand that.

Pete: Tired of feeling.

Don: How about this, Pete? How about if we at least make an agree-
         ment that you won't use that gun tonight, and that I'll give you
         a call in the morning, and then we'll see then how you are feel-
         ing and whether you'd like to come in then. You know, one
         night, Pete. It's your life.

Pete: Okay. I mean, it's what, 11:30 now, you know. And I've been
         . . . like I've been up for two days, and you know, I'm pretty
         wired up, and there's a lot of funny things going in and out of
         my head. You know I'd like to be able to get some sleep.

Don: You know, I think that would probably help a lot. You know,
         you've got so many things going on, Pete. You've lost a job,
         and Faye left, and you are upset about that, and now on top of
         that you're tired, and you haven't eaten for two days.

Pete: Yeah, every time I eat I just puke it back up.

Don: Yeah.

Pete: You know, and . . .

Don: You know, I really—this may sound funny, but you know, on
         one level, I really believe that you have a right to kill yourself
         . . .

Pete: Damn true.

Don: Yeah, well, I do believe that, but I'd like to see you make that
         decision when you're—I'd like to see that be, you know, sort
         of a carefully considered decision. You know? Like, something

you decide about when you're a little more together. You are
upset now, and you're tired.

Pete: I'm never going to be together! Words, words, words! You're
just giving me a lot of words!

Don: Well, you said you'd like to get a night's sleep to see how you'd
feel after that.

Pete: But I feel like I've gotta make this decision tonight. I mean, it's
gotta be tonight, or—like waiting a day, that—no, it's gotta be
tonight.

Don: How are you feeling about killing yourself right now, Pete?

Pete: I don't know. I go up and down on it.

Don: Okay. What about right now?

Pete: Yeah, right now, I feel like, you know, I feel like . . . you're
saying all these things, and that's all real nice, but I, you know,
I mean, like this has been going on for a long time.

Don: Yeah. I think we need to start somewhere, Pete. Uh, and I really
believe that it doesn't have to go on like this.

Pete: Wait a minute. When you say "we"—if I come in and talk to
you tomorrow, say like I talk to you for an hour, and that's it.
So, big deal, you know. Where does the "we" end up?

Don: Well, I feel like I have a relationship with you, Pete. I really do.
I mean, you have told me a hell of a lot, you know, in a short
period of time. I really feel involved. I really feel like I am in
this thing, and, ah . . .

Pete: Well, you are. You'll probably feel pretty bad if I blow my brains
out right now.

Don: Yeah. Yeah, I will. I'll have some strong feelings about that. But
I think one of the things that you can do that maybe you haven't
done before, and one of the things you have already begun to
do by just calling and being willing to talk to me, is, you know,
to reach out to another person—to let contact with another person be part of working out the problem. You know, not just talking about places in town to go. We're talking about you and me.

Pete: Yeah, but that's what's so hard! Like, if I let you into my life,
you know? If I come and see you tomorrow, and say, okay, yeah,
I'm going to trust this guy. What's going to happen? Are you
just going to split like everybody else? I mean, you know,
that's—you know, it's real hard for me to trust people. It's really
hard for me. You know, this is hard to do right here.

Don: Yeah, I understand that.

Pete: I guess I'm asking are you going to leave me? "Say, well, nice
talking to you today. I'm going home and having dinner."

Don: Well, I can tell you that I am not going to say that tomorrow.
I can tell you that I really am interested in you, and I feel like

we can work on this thing together over a period of time. I really feel that, and I also think that, you know, you're having the experience of reaching out a little bit to me and opening up a little bit with me will make it a little bit easier the next time with somebody else, too. I'm not saying I'm going to solve all your problems. You know, we both know that that's bullshit. But, I think you'll be in a better place to do that again and again, and that's why when I said I know that's its hard reaching out to people, that's what I mean. You know, it's a rough thing for all of us to do, but it gets a little easier, I think, each time. You get a little more strength each time.

Pete: Yeah. I guess I just don't want to be hurt. I guess I feel like I could really get hurt.

Don: Well, you are talking about killing yourself. I think there would be more in it for you talking to me tomorrow than dying. I really—that's my feeling.

Pete: I guess what I'm saying is it almost is less pain to kill myself than to go through the other pain, the pain of maybe getting hurt, hurt by somebody.

Don: Well, I understand that. I mean, I know what you mean. You know, in a sense that's what . . . we all make that decision or take that risk in dealing with people every day, you know? You put yourself on the line a little bit with someone. You take a little bit of risk, and I can understand that at some point you might not be willing to do that anymore, and I honestly believe that you are not at that point, Pete. I think in talking to you today, I'm hearing that you're not at that point. You are talking to me.

Pete: I don't know. Maybe I'm not, maybe I am. I'm just mixed up—feeling real mixed up.

Don: Yeah. How about this, Pete? How about if you hang up now, and we make an agreement that you won't shoot yourself in the next hour, and I'll give you a call back in an hour. You know, give you a chance to think about it a little bit, or take a shower, or do what ever you want to do. Kind of get away from it a little bit, and then I'll give you a call back, and we'll see where you're at.

Pete: Okay, for an hour. All right.

Don: You know? And, uh . . .

Pete: But, if I start feeling real bad I can call you back, right?

Don: Yeah, I'll be right here, because, I know you're real upset tonight, and it seems like every hour it might change a little bit, so, let's see where it is in an hour. Can you tell me what your phone number is, Pete?

Pete: No deal. No deal. I don't want any cops out here.

Don: Pete, I promise I won't send the cops.

Pete: What do you want to know my phone number for? I'm going to call you.

Don: Well, to be honest with you, that's a selfish thing. You know, if I hang up, and I don't have your number, I might not ever hear from you again, and that'd be real rough for me.

Pete: Yeah, but if I give you my number, I am going to lose control. I mean, I don't know what could happen. I don't know. You might send the police out here.

Don: Okay. Pete, I'm telling you I am not going to send the police, and I'll tell you why I am not going to send the police. I think, if I send the police, that anger that you are feeling is just going to get worse.

Pete: That's damn straight. I'm going to take a bunch of them with me if you send any cops out here.

Don: Yeah, I believe that you might do that. I certainly believe that you might shoot yourself if I did that. You know, the feelings that I talked about that I have, they are really there, and I really do care about you and I care about you staying alive, and I'm not going to do that. I also am just not going to lie to you for that reason. But, I'm asking you to . . .

Pete: What do you want my number for? If I'm going to call you, what do you want my number for?

Don: I told you. I want it for my peace of mind, so that I know that I can get in touch with you. I mean, hell, you can shoot yourself the minute you hang up, you know. If you wanted to, you could do that. The reason I'm not—and I'll be honest with you about another thing, Pete. If I thought you were just about to do that, I would be thinking about trying to get somebody out there to help you, you know. Because, your life is really important to me, but what I'm feeling about this conversation is that we are making a little bit of progress, and that you would be willing to back off a little bit, take an hour, and talk to me again. I believe that you'd be willing to do that.

Pete: What'd you say your name was again?

Don: I'm Don.

Pete: Okay. Okay. All right, I'll give you the number, but don't send anybody out here.

Don: I promise I won't send anyone, Pete. Okay, what's your phone number?

Pete: Okay. 321-5261.

Don: Okay, Pete.

Pete: Okay. Well, what am I supposed to do now?

Don: Well, I just thought maybe a little bit of time by yourself might be good, too. I mean, we can keep talking if you want to. I can try to get a little more specific about some things.

Pete: I'm getting kind of tired. Maybe I'll just try to lie down and get some rest a little. My body just feels like I've been through the mill.

Don: Yeah. Maybe you could go to sleep.

Pete: Yeah, I think I'll do that.

Don: Pete, I'm really glad that you called me, and in a way I feel good about talking to you.

Pete: You feel good about talking to me?

Don: I mean, I know it's a lot of rough stuff that you're going through, but I really feel good about your being willing to open up about it with me and I feel like maybe we can work on it. And, you know, maybe some good can come out of this.

Pete: I hope so. 'Cause it's sure time for things to turn around. They have been going the wrong way for a long time.

Don: Yeah. Okay, well let's hang up now, and I'll give you a call back in an hour.

Pete: Okay, what time is that going to be? What time is it? I've even lost track of time.

Don: It will be quarter to one.

Pete: Okay. And if, okay, if I don't—if you ring for a minute, I might be in the other room sleeping, so it may take me a couple of minutes to get to the phone.

Don: Okay. I'd just as soon—you know, on the one hand, I'd like you to get some sleep, but as you say, things are going up and down tonight. I'll check with you that one time, and if you are asleep, then we don't have to talk. You can go right back. Okay?

Pete: Okay.

Don: But, I would like to talk to you again tonight.

Pete: Okay. Goodbye, Don.

Don: Talk to you soon. Bye.

Bibliography

CROSS-CULTURAL COUNSELING

Archer, James and Turner, Alvin L. A black peer counseling program. *J College Student Personnel.* 17(2) (Mar 1976):155.

Banks, G. The effects of race on one-to-one helping interviews. *Social Service Review* 45 (1971):137–46.

———. The effects of empathy training on staff members of a community based vocational development program for black students. *J Negro Education* 45(3) (1976):306–11.

Banks, G.; Berenson, R.; and Carkhuff, R. The effects of counselor race and training upon counseling process with negro clients in initial interview. *J Clinical Psych* 23 (1967):70–72.

Bryson, S., and Cody, J. Relationship of race level of understanding between counselor and client. *J Counseling Psych* 20(6) (1973):495–98.

Buck, Mildred R. Peer counseling from a black perspective. *J Black Psych* 3(2) (Feb 1977):107–13.

Carkhuff, R. *The Development of Human Resources.* San Francisco: Holt, Rinehart and Winston, 1971.

———. The differential effects of counselor race and social class upon patient depth of self-exploration and in an initial clinical interview. *J Consulting Psych* 31 (1976):632–34.

———. The effects of human relations training upon relations between races and generations. *J Counseling Psych* 1969.

———. Principles of social action in training for new careers in human services. *J Counseling Psych* 18(2) (1971):147–51.

Christensen, Carole P. Effects of dissimilarity in initial interviews: an experimental evaluation of cross-cultural training. *Dissertation Abstracts International* 41(8-A) (Feb 1981):3485.

Cutchins, Fred L. The effects of leader race and second-order training in a peer led systematic program on level of interpersonal functioning and self-concept of adolescents. *Dissertation Abstracts International* 37(8-A) (Feb 1977):4859–60.

Edgerton, R. B. and Karno, M. Mexican-american bilingualism and the perception of mental illness. *Arch Genl Psych* 24 (1971):186–90.

Fischer, E. and Turner, J. Orientations to seeking professional help: development and research utility of an attitude scale. *J Consulting & Clin Psych* 35 (1970):79–90.

Kane, Jacqueline A. Peer counseling: an experience. *J Non-White Concerns in Personnel & Guidance* 7(2) (Jan 1979):59–61.

Karno, M. and Edgerton, R. B. Perception of mental illness in a mexican-american community. *Arch Genl Psych* 20 (196):233–38.

Lemons, Robert L. The effects of passive listening and direct training in listening upon the reading and listening skills of a group of black fourth graders. *Dissertation Abstracts International* 36(1-A) (Jul 1975):43–44.

Settles, Carl E. The effects of two training modes on lay and professional therapy with black adolescent males. *Dissertation Abstracts International* 37(5-A) (Nov 1976):2704.

Sue, S. Training of "third world" students to function as counselors. *J Counseling Psych* 20(1) (1973):73–78.

Sue and Sue. Chinese american personalities and mental health. *Amerasian J* 1 (1971):36–49.

———. Ethnic minorities: resistance to being researched. *Professional Psych* 3 (1972):11–17.

Tucker, Anita F. Empathy training for undergraduate college students in a cross-cultural milieu: a cognitive-developmental curriculum intervention through psychological education. *Dissertation Abstracts International* 38(10-A) (Apr 1978):6030.

Vassiliou and Vassiliou. Subjective culture and psychotherapy. *Am J Psychother* 27(1) (Jan 1973):42–51.

Vontress, C. E. Cultural barriers in the counseling relationship. *Personnel and Guid J* 48 (1969):504–7.

———. Racial differences: impediments to rapport. *J Counseling Psych* 18 (1971):7–13.

Wolkon, Moriwaki, and Williams. Race and social class as factors in the orientation toward psychotherapy. *J Counseling Psych* 20(4) (1973):312–16.

Yamamoto, James, and Palley. Cultural problems in psychiatric therapy. *Arch Genl Psych* 19 (1968):45–49.

Yamamoto, J; James, Q. C.; and Bloombaum, M. Racial factors in patient selection. *Am J Psychiatry* 124 (1967):84–90.

MULTI-MEDIA REFERENCES

Bailey, K. G.; Deardorff, P.; and Nay, W. R. Students play therapist: relative effects of role playing, videotape feedback, and modeling in a simulated interview. *J Consulting & Clin Psych* 45(2) (Apr 1977):257–66.

Berger, M. (ed). *Videotape Techniques in Psychiatric Training and Treatment.* New York: Brunner-Mazel, 1970.

Boylston, W. H. and Tuma, J. Training of mental health professionals through the use of the "bug in the ear." *Am J Psychiatry* 129(1) (July 1972):92–95.

Briggs, L. J.; Campeau, P. L.; Gagne, R. M.; and May, M. A. *Instructional Media: A Procedure for the Design of Multi-Media Instruction.* Pittsburgh: American Institutes for Research, 1967.

Brown, J.; Lewis; and Harcleroad, R. *AV Instruction: Media and Methods.* New York: McGraw-Hill, 1969.

Cassata, D. M.; Conroe, R. M.; and Clements, P. W. A program for enhancing medical interviewing using videotape feedback in the family practice residency. *J Fam Pract* 4(4) (Apr 1977):673–77.

Chodoff, P. Supervision of psychotherapy with videotape: pros and cons. *Am J Psychiatry* 128(7) (Jan 1972):810–23.

Christian, P. L. and Smith, L. S. Using videotapes to teach interviewing skills. *Nurse Educ* 6(4) (Jul–Aug 1981):12–14.

Edling, J. V. Educational objectives and educational media. *Audiovisual Comm Review* 18:177–94.

Eisenberg, S. and Delaney, D. J. Using video simulation of counseling for training counselors. *J Counseling* 17 (1970):15–19.

Elbert, W. E. Video Feedback and sensitivity. *Disseration Abstracts International* 30:233A.

Fisher, T. L. Prediction of counselor facilitation. *Disseration Abstracts International* 31:147A.

Forrest, R. et al. Through the viewing tube: videocassette psychiatry. *Am J Psychiatry* 131(1) (Jan 1974).

Geertsma, R. H. and Reivich, R. S. Repetitive self-observation by videotape playback. *J Nerv and Ment Disease* 148(4) (1965):29–41.

George, Gary O.; Hosford, Ray E.; and Moss, C. Scott. Using videotape programs for training inmates in peer counseling techniques. *Teaching of Psych* 5(4) (Dec 1978):205–207.

Gerlach, V. S. and Ely, D. P. *Teaching and Media in a Systematic Approach.* Englewood Cliffs, NJ: Prentice Hall, 1971.

Gillingham, P. R.; Griffiths, R. D.; and Care, D. Direct assessment of social behavior from videotape recordings. *Brit J Soc Clin Psych* 16(2) (Jun 1977):181–87.

Goodman, Jane. Videotape evaluation of a paraprofessional peer counselor training program. *Dissertation Abstracts International* 39(3-A) (Sep 1978):1339.

Griffin, G. Audiovisual counseling scale. *Personnel & Guid J* 46 (1968):690–93.

Griffiths, R. D. and Gillingham, P. The influence of videotape feedback on the self-assessments of psychiatric patients. *Brit J Psychiatry* 133 (Aug 1978):156–61.

Guy, W.; Ragheb, M.; and Wilson, W. H. Utility of videotape in establishing interrater reliability. *Psychopharm Bull* 16(3) (Jul 1980):71–74.

Hartson, D. J. Videotape replay and recall in group work. *J Counseling Psych* 1973.

Hettinga, Peter. The impact of videotaped interview playback with instructional feedback on social work student self-perceived interviewing competence and self-esteem. *Dissertation Abstracts International* 39(6-A) (Dec 1978):3844.

Higgins, W.; Ivey, A.; et al. Media therapy: a programmed approach to teaching behavior skills. *J Counseling Psych* 17 (1970):20–26.

Hunt, D. D. "Bug-in-the-ear" technique for teaching interview skills. *J Med Educ* 55(11) (Nov 1980):964–66.

Hunt, D. D.; Dagadakis, C. S.; Ward, N. G.; and Ries, R. Live versus videotaped interviews. *J Med Educ* 56(11) (Nov. 1981):916–18.

Ivey, A. Media therapy: educational change planning for psychiatric patients. *J Counseling Psych* 20(4) (1973):338–43.

Lamb, D. and Nagy, D. The use of videotaped interviews as a training technique for paraprofessional counselors in residence halls. *J College Stud Pers* 14 (1973):89.

Lamberd, W. G. and Adamson, J. D. A study of self-image experience in student psychotherapists. *J Nerv Ment Dis* 155(3) (Sep 1972):1984–91.

Levine, N. R. Improving student understanding and management of patients through role-playing and videotaping. *Am J Optom Physiol Opt* 53(2) (Feb 1976):95–99.

Mayadas, N. and O'Brien, D. E. The use of videotape in the laboratory training of social work students. *TV in Psychiatry Newsletter* 6(2) (May 1974).

McCue, A. E. Multi-media approach to group counseling with preadolescent girls. *J Sch Health* 50(3) (Mar 198):156–59.

McLuhan, M. *Understanding Media: The Extension of Man.* New York: McGraw-Hill, 1966.

Miller, P. and Tupin, J. Multimedia teaching of introductory psychiatry. *Am J Psychiatry* 128(10) (Apr 72):1219–23.

Moore, G.; Gernall, E.; and West, M. Television as a therapeutic tool. *Arch Genl Psych* 12 (1965):217.

Moreland, R. Video programmed instruction in elementary psychotherapy and related clinical skills. *Dissertation Abstracts International* Univ. Films no. 1-71-25430.

O'Brien, Donald E. An investigation of the effects of videotape feedback in the training of interviewers. *Dissertation Abstracts International* 37(8-A) (Feb 1977):5361.

Paredes, A. et al. Behavioral changes as a function of repeated self-observation: a controlled study of self-image experience. *J Nerv and Ment Dis* 3 (1969):287–99.

Pederson, D. M. and Williams, B. Effect of the interpersonal gain upon intra and interpersonal concepts, personality characteristics, and interpersonal relationships. *Psych Reports* 22(1) (1968):166–68.

Russel, M. L. and Insull, W. Jr. Evaluation and training of medication adherence counselors in a clinical trial: application of a skill inventory to videorecorded interviews. *Controlled Clin Trials* 2(2) (Jun 1981):133–48.

Ryan, C. Video aids in practicum supervision. *Counselor Educ and Supervision* 8(2) (1969):125–28.

Smith, O. P. Changes in self-actualization with videotape. *Dissertation Abstracts International* 315 (1970):3280A.

Suess, J. F. Teaching psychodiagnosis and observation by self-instructional programmed videotapes. *J Med Educ* 48(7) (July 1973):676–83.

Sutnick, M. R. and Carroll, J. G. Using patient simulators to teach clinical interviewing skills. *J Am Diet Assoc* 78(6) (Jun 1981):614–16.

Tardiff, K. A videotape technique for measuring clinical skills: three years of experience. *J Med Educ* 56(3) (Mar 1981):187–91.

Taubman, Stanley B. Videotape confrontation for in-service training of social service workers: an experimental study. *Dissertation Abstracts International* 38(10-A) (Apr 1978):6324.

Thompson, Anthony J. A study of the effect of having a trainee co-counsel with a live model during a microcounseling practice session. *Dissertation Abstracts International* 37(10-A) (Apr 1977):6285.

Toler, Hayward C. The relative effectiveness of programmed instruction, cued-videotape modeling, and behavioral feedback on the acquisition and use of interview skills. *Dissertation Abstracts International* 36(9-A) (Mar 1976):5960–61.

Veatch, D. J. A videotape series for teaching job interviewing skills. *Am Ann Deaf* 125(6) (Sep 1980):747–50.

Waltz and Johnson. Counselors look at themselves on videotape. *J Counseling Psych* 1963:232–36.

Waters, Thomas J. Further comparison of videotape and face-to-face interviewing. *Perceptual & Motor Skills* 41(3) (Dec 1975): 743–46.

Watter, W.; Edder, P; et al. Psychotherapy supervision: a videotape technique. *Can Psych Assoc J* 16(4) (Aug 1971):367–68.

PEER COUNSELING

Aldridge, Ernest E. and Ivey, Allen E. The microcounseling paradigm in the instruction of junior high school students in attending behavior. *Can Counselor* 9(2) (Apr 1975):138–44.

Alwin, G. If you need love, come to us: an overview of a peer counseling program in a senior high school. *J Sch Health* 44(8) (Oct 1974):463–64.

Avery, A. W. Communication skills training for paraprofessional helpers. *Am J Community Psych* 6(6) (Dec 1978):583–91.

Ayal, Haviva and Bekerman, Rivka. Peer counseling: a means of actualizing adolescents' helping potential. *Brit J Guid & Counseling* 6(2) (Jul 1978):204–14.

Baldwin, B. A. Moving from drugs to sex: new directions for youth-oriented peer counseling. *J Am Coll Health Assoc* 27(2) (Oct 1978):75–78.

Baldwin, B. A. and Staub, R. E. Peers as human sexuality outreach educators in the campus community. *J Am Coll Health Assoc* 24(5) (Jun 1976):290–93.

Bauer, J. The hotline and its training problems for adolescent listeners. *Adolescence* 10(37) (Spr 1975):63–69.

Bernard, Harold S.; Roach, Allen M.; and Resnick, Harvey. Training bartenders as helpers on a college campus. *Personnel & Guid J* 60(2) (Oct 1981):119–21.

Bry, Brenna H.; Marshall, Judith S.; et al. A pilot course for the training of peer counselors for educationally disadvantaged students. *Teaching of Psych* 2(2) (Apr 1976):51–55.

Buck, Mildred R. Peer counseling in an urban high school setting. *J Sch Psych* 15(4) (Win 1977):362–66.

Butler, Cynthia. Peer mediated social skills training with withdrawn children. *Dissertation Abstracts International* 39(12-B) (Jun 1979):6111.

Callahan, Maureen A. An evaluation of selection and training variables with peer high school students and faculty using personal mastery counseling. *Dissertation Abstracts International* 39(7-A) (Jan 1979):4053–54.

Cooker, Philip G. and Cherchia, Peter J. Effects of communication skill training on high school students' ability to function as peer group facilitators. *J Counseling Psych* 23(5) (Sep 1976):464–67.

Copeland, Elaine J. Training advanced-educational-opportunity program students as peer-group counselors for freshman students. *J Non-White Concerns in Personnel & Guid* 7(2) (Jan 1979):62–66.

Corn, Roger. Aiding adjustment to physical limitation: a peer counselor training program. *Catalog of Selected Documents in Psychology* 9(9) (Feb 1979):ms. 1811.

Dalali, Isobel D.; Charuvastra, V.; and Schlesinger, J. Training of paraprofessionals: some caveats. *J Drug Educ* 6(2) (1976):105–112.

Davis, A. K.; Weener, J. M.; and Shute, R. E. Positive peer influence: school-based prevention. *Health-Educ* (Wash.) 8(4) (Jul–Aug 1977):20–22.

DeVol, T. I. Does level of professional training make a difference in crisis intervention counseling? *J Community Health* 2(1) (Fall 1976):31–35.

Dixon, M. C. and Burns, J. The training of telephone crisis intervention volunteers. *Am J Community Psych* 3(2) (Jun 1975):145–50.

Donahue, Michael J. Peer counseling for police officers: a program for skill development and personal growth. *Dissertation Abstracts International* 38(4-A) (Oct 1977):1992–93.

Dooley, D. Assessing nonprofessional mental health workers with the GAIT: an evaluation of peer ratings. *Am J Community Psych* 3(2) (Jun 1975):99–110.

Dorosin, D.; D'Andrea, V.; and Jacks, R. A peer counselor training program: rationale, curriculum, and evaluation: an initial report. *J Am Coll Health Assoc.* 25(4) (Apr 1977):259–62.

Edwards, Susan S. Student helpers: a multilevel facilitation program. *Elem Sch Guid & Counseling* 11(1) (Oct 1976):53–58.

Emmert, Barbara A. An analysis of the effectiveness of large group peer-helper training with pre- and early adolescents in the middle school. *Dissertation Abstracts International* 38(8-A) (Feb 1978):4581.

Enright, M. F. and Parsons, B. V. Training crisis intervention specialists and peer group counselors as therapeutic agents in the gay community. *Community Ment Health J* 12(4) (Win 1976):383–91.

Forbes, William D. Effects of microcounseling training on junior high school students' knowledge, attitudes, and behavior related to interpersonal conflict reduction. *Dissertation Abstracts International* 39(5-A) (Nov 1978):2752.

Glaser, Kristin. Women's self-help groups as an alternative to therapy. *Psychotherapy: Theory, Research & Practice* 13(1) (Spr 1976):77–81.

Goade, Gary J. A high school peer counseling program: training and effects. *Dissertation Abstracts International* 40(12-A, pt. 1) (Jun 1980):6151.

Goldin, J. Roger. Therapy as education: the effect of a peer counseling program upon the personal growth of student counselors: I and II. *Dissertation Abstracts International* 38(9-A) (Mar 1978):5248.

Guggenheim, F. G. and O'Hara, S. Peer counseling in a general hospital. *Am J Psychiatry* 133(10) (Oct 1976):1197–99.

Gumaer, Jim. Training peer facilitators. *Elem Sch Guid & Counseling* 11(1) (Oct 1976):27–36.

Hirsch, S. A critique of volunteer-staffed suicide prevention centers. *Can J Psychiatry* 26(6) (Oct 1981):406–10.

Hodge, Elaine A. Supervision of empathy training: programmed vs. individual and peer vs. professional. *Dissertation Abstracts International* 37(7-A) (Jan 1977):4134.

Hoffman, Libby R. Peers as group counseling models. *Elem Sch Guid & Counseling* 11(1) (Oct 1976):37–44.

Jacobs, Edward; Masson, Robert; and Vass, Molly. Peer helpers: an easy way to get started. *Elem Sch Guid & Counseling* 11(1) (Oct 1976):68–71.

Jennings, Stephen G. Effects of peer academic advising and study skills training on the intellectual disposition and study orientation of college freshmen. *Dissertation Abstracts International* 37(7-A) (Jan 1977):4135.

Kane, Jacqueline A. Peer counseling: an experience. *J Non-White Concerns in Personnel & Guid* 7(2) (Jan 1979):59–61.

Keat, Donald B. Training as multimodal treatment for peers. *Elem Sch Guid & Counseling* 11(1) (Oct 1976):7–13.

Klein, Nancy H. Learning in peer-led parenting groups with implications for higher education. *Dissertation Abstracts International* 41(6-A) (Dec 1980):2468.

Lawrence, J. C. Gay peer counseling. *J Psychiatric Nurs* 15(6) (Jun 1977):33–37.

London, Marion. A study of the attrition–retention of counselors trained in a peer counselor training program for women. *Dissertation Abstracts International* 39(9-A) (Mar 1979):5328–29.

McCann, Barbara G. Peer counseling: an approach to psychological education. *Elem Sch Guid & Counseling* 9(3) (Mar 1975):180–87.

McKay, S. R. A peer group counseling model in nursing education. *J Nurs Educ* 19(3) (Mar 1980):4–10.

McWilliams, S. A. Effects of reciprocal peer counseling on college student personality development. *J Am Coll Health Assoc* 27(4) (Feb 1979):210–13.

Margolis, C. G.; Edwards, D. W.; et al. Brief hotline training: an effort to examine impact on volunteers. *Am J Community Psych* 3(1) (Mar 1975):59–67.

Mastroianni, Michael and Dinkmeyer, Don. Developing an interest in others through peer facilitation. *Elem Sch Guid & Counseling* 14(3) (Feb 1980):214–21.

Miyashiro, Clifford M. Evaluation of lay telephone counselors: assessment of offered therapeutic conditions and their relationship to simulated callers' evaluations and self-exploration. *Dissertation Abstracts International* 36(10-B) (Apr 1976):5271–72.

Motto, J. A. Starting a therapy group in a suicide prevention and crisis center. *Suicide Life Threat Behav* 9(1) (Spr 1979):47–56.

Paur, Roman M. An assessment of an intensive forty-hour counselor skills-building program entitled "counselor training: short-term client systems for paraprofessional volunteer trainees." *Dissertation Abstracts International* 37(2-A) (Aug 1976):891–92.

Pepe, E. A.; Hodel, C. G.; and Bosshart, D. A. Use of peers to teach interviewing and clinical problem-solving. *J Med Educ* 55(9) (Sep 1980):800.

Perkins, Robert J. Effects of peer counselor assertiveness training groups on levels of assertiveness and self-actualization. *Dissertation Abstracts International* 40(5-B) (Nov 1979):2338–39.

Persons, Marilyn K. An indepth analysis of the development and evaluation of a peer counseling training program. *Dissertation Abstracts International* 37(2-B) (Aug 1976):982.

Restad, Raymond O. A training model for self-help, using peer counseling, with college-age students who have a chronic health problem: diabetes. *Dissertation Abstracts International* 39(11-A) (May 1979):6551.

Reutlinger, Ellen F. The effectiveness of lay helpers in working-class parent-training programs. *Dissertation Abstracts International* 37(4-A) (Oct 1976):1996–97.

Roberts, James P. An investigation of select personality dimensions of peer group counseling leaders in a junior high school setting. *Dissertation Abstracts International* 40(3-A) (Sep 1979):1367–68.

Roberts, Wesley K. and Hart, Betty K. Techniques for training paraprofessionals in rape-crisis counseling procedures. *Catalog of Selected Documents in Psychology* 6 (May 1976):46–47.

Ross, Bob and McKay, H. Bryan. Adolescent therapists. *Can Ment Health* 24(2) (Jun 1976):15–17.

Ruhf, Lawrence L. A training program in peer-oriented drug and crisis counseling: design, implementation, evaluation. *Dissertation Abstracts International* 38(4-A) (Oct 1977):1904.

Skuja, A.; Battenberg, B.; et al. The impact of paraprofessional alcoholism counselor training. *Int J Addict* 15(6) (1980):931–38.

Snodgrass, Gregory. A comparison of student paraprofessionals and professional counselor trainees in career counseling with university undergraduate students. *Dissertation Abstracts International* 38(11-A) (May 1978):6548.

Spiro, J. H.; Roenneburg, M; and Maly, B. J. Teaching doctors to treat doctors: medical peer counseling. *J Med Educ* 53(12) (Dec 1978):997.

Terrell, Thomas C. The effects of microtraining in attending behavior on response behavior and attending behavior of paraprofessional orientation leaders. *Dissertation Abstracts International* 37(7-A) (Jan 1977):4149.

Tuff, Richard J. A comparison of the effects of a counseling skills training group and a treatment group with peer-counselor trainees. *Dissertation Abstracts International* 38(4-B) (Oct 1977):1910.

Uhlemann, M. R.; Hearn, M. T.; and Evans, D. R. Programmed learning in the microtraining paradigm with hotline workers. *Am J Community Psych* 8(5) (Oct 1980):603–12.

Walker, Michael S. The effects of preferred versus assigned associates and peer versus instructor feedback on acquisition of a counseling strategy. *Dissertation Abstracts International* 39(11-A) (May 1979):6553.

Waring, M. L. The effects on alcoholism training on the knowledge, attitudes, and drinking behavior of college students in the human services. *Int J Addict* 13(5) (1978):849–54.

Weise, Richard. Diary of a peer facilitator program. *Elem Sch Guid & Counseling* 11(1) (Oct 1976):63–66.

Winters, R. Arthur and Malione, Anthony. High school students as mental health workers: the everett experience. *School Counselor* 23(1) (Sep 1975):43–44.

Zapka, J. M. and Mazur, R. M. Peer sex education training and evaluation. *Am J Public Health* 67(5) (May 1977):450–54.

Zwibelman, Barry B. and Hinrichsen, James J. Effects of training on peer counseling responses to human sexuality problems. *J Counseling Psych* 24(4) (Jul 1977):359–64.

RESIDENT ASSISTANTS

Banta, T. Selecting student orientation assistants: a comparison of approaches. *J College Stud Personnel* (July 1969):240–43.

Banta, T. and McCormick, J. Using the leaderless group discussion technique for the selection of residence hall counselors. *J Natl Assoc Women Deans & Counselors* 33 (Fall 1969):30–33.

Biehn, J. Community as counselor. *Personnel and Guid J* 50(9) (May 1972):730–34.

Biggs, D. A. Selecting residence counselors: job viewpoints and interpersonal attitudes. *J College Stud Personnel* 12(2) (Mar 1971):111–15.

————. Student evaluation of residence hall counselors. *J Educ Research* 65 (Mar 1972):305–08.

Carrenti, R. and Tuttle, C. An apprenticeship program for resident assistants. *NASPA,* Oct 1972, 132–37.

Casse, R. M. and Peckwood, W. T. New format for resident advisor workshop. *J College Stud Personnel* 12 (1971):371.

Comeau, Louise H. The effect of teaching counseling skills and concepts to women college student advisors. *Dissertation Abstracts International* 38(4-B) (Oct 1977):1948.

Cook, T. A technique for describing role of resident advisor: innovations in counseling. Report of Commission VII, Counseling. American College Personnel Association, 1971, pp. 43–44.

Coughlin, David D. Differential rehabilitation training models, self-disclosure and the acquisition of basic helping skills by resident advisors. *Dissertation Abstracts International* 36(10-A) (Apr 1976):6544–45.

Dendy, R. F. A model for the training of undergraduate resident hall assistants and paraprofessional counselors using videotape. *Dissertation Abstracts International* Univ. M-films no. 72-8676.

Duncan, James P. Student evaluation of residence hall counselors. *Detroit Convention Abstracts* (Washington, DC), 1968, p. 232.

————. Construction of a forced-choice rating scale for student evaluation of residence hall counselors. Student Housing Research and Information, 1965.

Duncan, James P. and Southam, M. C. (eds.). Resident advisor training programs. Report of Commission III, American College Personnel Assoc., 1969, p. 65.

Fisher, I. S. Personality and training to develop small group productivity skills and interpersonal competence. *Dissertation Abstracts International* 31 (1970):1617A.

Fullerton, B. A. The development of measures of residence hall counselor effectiveness. Ph.D. dissertation (1966). Penn State Unive. Microfilms 27:11:3613A.

Gagliardo, Ettore S. A determination of the relationship between Kohlberg's moral development training and hall advisors' effectiveness. *Dissertation Abstracts International* 39(8-A) (Feb 1979):4691.

Gimmestad, M. J. A multi-impact short term program for training counselors in perceptual sensitivity (empathy). Ph.D. dissertation (1971). Univ. of Minn. microfilms 32:175A.

Gonyea, G. G. and Warman, R. E. Differential perceptions of the student dormitory counselor's role. *Personnel and Guid J* 41(4) (Dec 1962):350–55.

Graff, R. W. and Bradshaw, H. E. Relationships of measure of self-actualization to dormitory assistants' effectiveness. *J Counseling Psych* 17(6) (Nov 1970):502–05.

Greenleaf, Elizabeth A. (ed.). *Undergraduate Students as Members of the Residence Hall Staff.* Washington, DC: National Assoc. of Women Deans and Counselors, 1967.

Hoyt, D. and Davidson, A. Evaluating residence hall advisors. *J College Stud Personnel* 8 (1967):251–56.

Jones, F. and Najera, G. A. The helping network: reactions and actions stimulated by students' acute mental illness in a university community. *J Am Coll Health Assoc.* 24(4) (Apr 1976):198–202.

Kirby, P. T. An evaluation of a residence hall personnel training program. Ph.D. dissertation (1971). U. S. International University microfilms 32:1879A.

Levin, Miriam K. Instrument development with subsequent measurement of resident advisor attitudes. *Dissertation Abstracts International* 38(6-B) (Dec 1977):2868.

Mesanic, R. W. An experimental investigation into the training of empathic skills in groups of resident assistants. Ph.D. dissertation (1971). State University of New York at Albany microfilms 32:4958A.

Mitchell, K. M. Effects of short term training on residence hall assistants. *Counselor Educ & Supervision* 10 (1971):310–18.

Moates, F. K. Some effects of human relations training on facilitative communication and self-actualization of resident assistants at the University of Georgia. Ph.D. dissertation (1970). University of Georgia microfilms 31:5773A.

Morgan, J. D. et al. Training the residence hall advisor: a workshop on expectations. *J College Stud Personnel* 13 (Jan 1972):76–77.

Mulozzi, A. and Spees, E. R. Factors in selecting residence hall fellows. *J Nat Assoc Women Deans and Counselors* 34 (1971):185–89.

Murphy, R. O. and Ortenzi, A. Use of standardized measurements in the selection of residence hall staff. *J College Stud Personnel* 7 (1966):360–63.

Nair, D. A. and Sonder, O. L. Sociodrama in the selection and training of male student residence hall advisors. *NASPA J* 7 (Oct 1969):81–85.

Newton, M. and Krauss, H. The health engenderingness of resident assistants and related student achievement and adjustments. *J College Stud Personnel* 14(4) (July 1973):321–25.

Nickerson, D. L. and Harrington, J. T. *The College Student as Counselor:*

A Guide to Residence Hall Counseling. Moravia, NY: Chronicle Guidance Publications, 1968.

Peiulio, R. S. 1970 freshman perceptions of staff members. *Dissertation Abstracts International* 31:3101A.

Perkins, S. R. and Atkinson, D. R. Effect of selected techniques for training resident assistants in human relations skills. *J Counseling Psych* 20 (Jan 1973):84–90.

Powell, J. R. and Phyler, S. A. *The Personnel Assistant in College Residence Halls.* Boston: Houghton Mifflin, 1969.

Richards, V. F. Advising staff training use of case studies and role playing. Proceedings of the Nineteenth Annual Conference. Seattle: Association of College and University Housing Officers, 1967, pp. 182–92.

Scharf, K. R. Training of resident assistants and peer group members in the communication interpersonal process skills of empathic understanding of student feeling and student depth of self-exploration. Ph.D. dissertation (1971). Michigan State University.

Schroeder, R. and Dowd, E. Selection, function and assessment of residence hall counselors. *Personnel and Guid J* 47 (1968):151–56.

Sheeder, W. B. Role playing as a method of selecting dormitory counselors. *J College Stud Personnel* 4 (Mar 1963):154–58.

Stormer, J. E. Y. Critical factors of more helping and less helping behavior of paraprofessionals in the residence hall setting. Ph.D. dissertation (1972). University of Florida microfilms 33:3310A.

Thayer, L.; Peterson, V.; et al. Development of critical incidents videotape. *J Counseling Psych* 19(3) (1972):188–91.

Turner, H. M. An in-service training program for dormitory counselors: the development and evaluation of a problem-centered in-service training program for nonprofessional dormitory counselors. Ed.D. dissertation (1960). New York University microfilms 21:10:2995A.

Whitney, Karen K. Short-term interview behaviors training for residence hall counselors and its effect on their in-residence activity and interview performance. *Dissertation Abstracts International* 37(3-A) (Sep 1976):1417.

Wyrick, T. J. A study of resident assistant effectiveness as measured by the Duncan Resident Hall Counselor Evaluation Scale, the Truax Scales and grade-point average. Ph.D. dissertation (1969). University of Arkansas.

Wyrick, T. J. and Mitchell, K. M. Relationship between accurate empathy, warmth and genuineness and perceived resident assistant effectiveness. *Discussion Papers,* Arkansas Rehab. Research and Training Center, University of Arkansas, 1969, p. 12.

THEORY

Alaghband, Setila. A model in-service microcounseling training program
for Iranian counselors, using television and videotape technologies. *Dissertation Abstracts International* 40(4-1) (Oct
1979):1821–22.

Allbee, Robert B. A comparison of the effects of two variations of a microcounseling paradigm on the development of human relations
skills of students in a community college setting. *Dissertation
Abstracts International* 37(12-A, pt. 1) (Jun 1977):7538.

Arnold, Bill R. Effectiveness of microcounseling as a supervisory model
for teaching interviewing skills. *Dissertation Abstracts International* 37(6-A) (Dec 1976):3506.

Ayal, Haviva, and Rivka Berkerman. Peer counseling: a means of actualising adolescents' helping potential. *Brit J Guid & Counseling*
6(2) (Jul 1978):204–14.

Baldwin, B. A. Moving from drugs to sex: new directions for
youth-oriented peer counseling. *J Am Coll Health Assoc* 27(2)
(Oct 1978):75–78.

Bandura, A. Psychotherapy as a learning process. *Psych Bulletin* 58
(1961):143–59.

Belle, Robert L. The effects of microcounseling on attending behavior of
counseling trainees. *Dissertation Abstracts International* 37(5-A)
(Nov 1976):2626.

Benjamin, A. *The Helping Interview.* Boston: Houghton Mifflin, 1969.

Buck, Mildred R. Peer counseling in an urban high school setting. *J School
Psych* 15(4) (Winter 1977):362–66.

Burwick, Ray O. The development and administration of paraprofessional
counseling and education workshops utilizing biblical principles. *Dissertation Abstracts International* 41(8-A) (Feb
1981):3339.

Bush, Bobby R. The effects of videotape preinterviewing orientation on
the placement interview of selected college seniors. *Dissertation
Abstracts International* 38(7-A) (Jan 1978):3951.

Carkhuff, R., and G. Berenson. *Beyond Counseling and Therapy.* New York:
Holt, Rinehart and Winston, 1967.

Carkhuff, R. Critical variables in effective counselor training. *J Counselor
Psych* 16 (1969):238–45.

———. Helper communication as a function of helpee affect and content.
J Counseling Psych 16 (1969):126–31.

———. Towards a comprehensive model of facilitative interpersonal process. *J Counseling Psych* 14 (1967):67–72.

Carkhuff, R., and C. B. Truax. Training in counseling and psychotherapy:

an evaluation of an integrated didactic and experiential approach. In B. Guerney (ed.), *Psychotherapeutic Agents: New Roles for Nonprofessionals, Parents, and Teachers.* New York: Holt, Rinehart and Winston, 1969.

Charonko, John J. The effects of microcounseling and monitor modeling upon the acquisition of group leadership skills. *Dissertation Abstracts International* 40(3-A) (Sep 1979):1274.

Cristiani, Therese S. Counseling skills and the child care worker: a research-based training program. *Child Care Quarterly* 7(1) (Spr 1978):87–97.

Dorosin, D., V. D'Andrea and R. Jacks. A peer counseling training program: rationale, curriculum, and evaluation: an initial report. *J Am Coll Health Assoc* 25(4) (Apr 1977):259–62.

Duncan, Jack A. Ethical considerations in peer group work. *Elem School Guid & Counseling* 11(1) (Oct 1976):59–61.

Eichenfield, Gregg A. The effects of self-disclosure on training paraprofessionals. *Dissertation Abstracts International* 40(7-B) (Jan 1980):3389.

Evans, David R., Max R. Uhlemann and Margaret T. Hearn. Microcounseling and sensitivity training with hotline workers. *J Community Psych* 6(2) (Apr 1978):139–46.

Forbes, William D. Effects of microcounseling training on junior high school students' knowledge, attitudes, and behavior related to interpersonal conflict reduction. *Dissertation Abstracts International* 39(5-A) (Nov 1978):2752.

Ford, Julian D. Research on training counselors and clinicians. *Review of Educ Research* 49(1) (Win 1979):87–130.

Fyffe, Anne E. and Tian P. Oei. Influence of modeling and feedback provided by the supervisors in a microskills training program for beginning counselors. *J Clinical Psych* 35(3) (Jul 1979):651–56.

Gagliardo, Ettore S. A determination of the relationship between Kohlberg's moral development training and hall advisors' effectiveness. *Dissertation Abstracts International* 39 (8-A) (Feb 1979):4691.

Garland, Diana R. The effects of active listening skills training upon interaction behavior, perceptual accuracy, and marital adjustment of couples participating in a marriage enrichment program. *Dissertation Abstracts International* 40(7-B) (Jan 1980):3481.

Geary, Edward A. A construct validity study of developmental empathy in counselor skills training programs. *Dissertation Abstracts International* 40(3-B) (Sep 1979):1365.

Gluckstern, Norma, Allen Ivey and Douglas Forsyth. Patterns of acquisition and differential retention of helping skills and their effect on client verbal behavior. *Canadian Counselor* 13(1) (Oct 1978):37–39.

Goade, Gary J. A high school peer counseling program: training and effects. *Dissertation Abstracts International* 40(12-A, pt. 1) (Jun 1980):6151.

Goldin, J. Roger. Therapy as education: the effect of a peer counseling program upon the personal growth of student counselors: I and II. *Dissertation Abstracts International* 38(9-A) (Mar 1978):5248.

Gomes, Schwartz B. and J. M. Schwartz. Psychotherapy process variables distinguishing the "inherently helpful" person from the professional psychotherapist. *J Consult Clin Psychol* 46(1) (Feb 1978):196–97.

Goodman, Jane. Videotape evaluation of a paraprofessional peer counselor training program. *Dissertation Abstracts International* 39(3-A) (Sep 1978):1339.

Hayman, Marilyn J. The influence of supervisor feedback in the microcounseling format. *Dissertation Abstracts International* 39(10-A) (Apr 1979):5950.

Hirsch, S. A critique of volunteer-staffed suicide prevention centres. *Can J Psychiatry* 26(6) (Oct 1981):406–10.

Hodge, Elaine A.; Paul A. Payne; and Daniel D. Wheeler. Approaches to empathy training: programmed methods versus individual supervision and professional versus peer supervisors. *J Counseling Psych* 25(5) (Sep 1978):449–53.

Hoffman, Libby R. Peers as group counseling models. *Elem School Guid & Counseling* 11(1) (Oct 1976):37–44.

Hutter, M. J. et al. Interviewing skills: a comprehensive approach to teaching and evaluation. *J Med Educ* 52(4) (Apr 1977):328–33.

Ivey, A. Demystifying the group process: adapting microcounseling procedures to counseling in groups. *Educ Tech* 13(2) (1973):27–31.

———. *Microcounseling: Innovations in Interviewing Training.* Springfield, IL: Charles C. Thomas, 1971.

Ivey, Allen E., and Jerry Authier. *Microcounseling: Innovations in Interviewing, Counseling, Psychotherapy and Psychoeducation,* second edition. Springfield, IL: Charles C. Thomas, 1978.

Ivey, A. et al. Microcounseling and attending behavior. *J Counseling Psych* 18 (1969):268–72.

Jacobs, Edward; Robert Masson; and Molly Vass. Peer helpers: an easy way to get started. *Elem School Guid & Counseling* 11(a) (Oct 1976):68–71.

Janoka, Caroline H. Twelve, twenty-four, and thirty-six hours of Carkhuff empathy training with federally incarcerated youth offenders. *Disseration Abstracts International* 38(11-A) (May 1978):6536.

Janoka, Caroline, and Albert Scheckenbach. Empathy training with inmates and staff utilizing the Carkhuff model. *Corrective & Social Psychiatry & J of Behavior Technology, Methods & Therapy* 24(1) (1978):6–12.

Jennings, Stephen G. Effects of peer academic advising and study skills training on the intellectual disposition and study orientation of college freshmen. *Dissertation Abstracts International* 37(7-A) (Jan 1977):4135.

Kane, Jacqueline A. Peer counseling: an experience. *J Nonwhite Concerns in Personnel & Guid* 7(2) (Jan 1979):59–61.

Klas, L. D. The counselling proficiency scale: the progressive development of a scale for the evaluation of specific counselling interview competencies. *Canadian Counsellor* 12(3) (Apr 1978):171–76.

Kramer, Judith A.; Julian Rappaport; and Edward Seidman. Contribution of personal characteristics and interview training to the effectiveness of college student mental health workers. *J Counseling Psych* 26(4) (Jul 1979):344–51.

Krumboltz, J., and C. Thoresen. *Behavioral Counseling.* New York: Holt, Rinehart and Winston, 1969.

Levene, Robert I. The effects of microcounseling/personal-growth groups and microcounseling-only groups on the self-actualization of community college students. *Dissertation Abstracts International* 41(6-A) (Dec 1980):2455.

London, Marion. A study of the attrition-retention of counselors trained in a peer counselor training program for women. *Dissertation Abstracts International* 39(9-A) (Mar 1979):5328–29.

Long, B. E.; C. M. Harris; and P. S. Byrne. A method of teaching counselling. *Med-Educ* 10(3) (May 1976):198–204.

McCarthy, Kay R. Microcounseling: its use with an older adult population and its relationship to internal control. *Dissertation Abstracts International* 39(3-A) (Sep 1978):1346.

McWilliams, S. A. Effects of reciprocal peer counseling on college student personality development. *J Am Coll Health Assoc* 27(4) (Feb 1979):210–13.

Mass, Irene E. The effect of paraprofessional training on the self-esteem of the trainees. *Dissertation Abstracts International* 37(12-B, pt. 1) (Jun 1977):6306–07.

May, Ronald J. The impact of interpersonal process recall upon medical students as a function of social values: ten case studies. *Dissertation Abstracts International* 41(9-A) (Mar 1981):3885–86.

Meade, Charles J. Human relations training and interpersonal process recall: an empirical investigation. *Dissertation Abstracts International* 39(8-B) (Feb 1979):4044.

Middleton, James G. A study of the relationship between listening skills and effectiveness of counselors in training. *Dissertation Abstracts International* 38(2-A) (Aug 1977):635–36.

Neimeyer, Robert A., and William D. MacInnes. Assessing paraprofessional competence with the suicide intervention response inventory. *J Counseling Psych* 28(2) (Mar 1981):206–09.

O'Toole, William M. Effects of practice in training interviewing skills. *Disseration Abstracts International* 38(10-A) (Apr 1978):5929.

Parish, Kathy L. Coping with critical client behaviors through IPR, modeling, and stress inoculation supervision. *Dissertation Abstracts International* 41(8-B) (Feb 1981):3193.

Pereira, Gabrielle J. Teaching empathy through skill-building versus interpersonal anxiety-reduction methods: a comparison of microcounseling and intersonal process recall. *Dissertation Abstracts International* 39(3-A) (Sep 1978):1348.

Peters, George A.; L. Sherilyn Cormier; and William H. Cormier. Effects of modeling, rehearsal, feedback, and remediation on acquisition of a counseling strategy. *J Counseling Psych* 25(3) (May 1978):231–37.

Powers, Paul C. An exploratory study of the Powers-Deevy model for training paraprofessional psychological counselors. *Disseration Abstracts International* 40(5-A) (Nov 1979):2486.

Richardson, Barbara J. The role of cognition in microcounseling. *Dissertation Abstracts International* 40(108-B) (Apr 1980):5016.

Rioch, M. J. Changing concepts in the training of therapists. *J Consulting Psych* 30 (1966):290–92.

Roach, William L. A comparative study of two models of communication skills training. *Dissertation Abstracts International* 37(9-A) (Mar 1977):5711.

Roberts, James P. An investigation of select personality dimensions of peer group counseling leaders in a junior high school setting. *Dissertation Abstracts International* 40(3-A) (Sep 1979):1367–68.

Rogers, C. R. The interpersonal relationship: the core of guidance. *Harvard Educ Review* 32 (1962):416–29.

———. The necessary and sufficient conditions of therapeutic personality change. *J Consulting Psych* 22 (1957):95–103.

———. What we know about psychotherapy. In *On Becoming a Person.* New York: Houghton-Mifflin, 1961.

Sage, Robert E. A comparison between two different approaches to teaching counseling skills: a modified human relations training model vs. a traditional approach. *Dissertation Abstracts International* 37(8-A) (Feb 1977):4872–73.

Scroggins, William F. An evaluation of a microcounseling model for use in the training in interpersonal communications of paraprofessional counselors. *Dissertation Abstracts International* 39(4-A) (Oct 1978):2071.

Settles, Carl E. The effects of two training modes on lay and professional therapy with black adolescent males. *Dissertation Abstracts International* 37(5-A) (Nov 1976):2704.

Snodgrass, Gregory. A comparison of student paraprofessionals and professional counselor trainees in career counseling with university undergraduate students. *Dissertation Abstracts International* 38(11-A) (May 1978):6548.

Teevan, Katherine G., and Harris Gabel. Evaluation of modeling, role-playing and lecture-discussion training techniques for college student mental health professionals. *J Counseling Psych* 25(2) (Mar 1978):169–71.

Thompson, A. Michael, and Donald H. Blocher. Co-counseling supervision in microcounseling. *J Counseling Psych* 26(5) (Sep 1979):413–18.

Thompson, Anthony J. A study of the effect of having a trainee co-counsel with a live model during a microcounseling practice session. *Dissertation Abstracts International* 37(10-A) (Apr 1977):6285.

Thoresen, C. E.; R. E. Hosford; and J. Krumboltz. Determining effective models for counseling clients of varying competencies. *J Counseling Psych* 17 (1970):369–75.

Toff, Margaret. A research note on a program for paraprofessional counseling skills. *J Community Psych* 5(4) (Oct 1977):347–49.

Tomory, Robert E. The use of the interpersonal process recall (IPR) model videotape and stimulus film techniques in short-term counseling and psychotherapy. *Disseration Abstracts International* 40(4-A) (Oct 1979):1975–76.

Truax, C. B., and R. Karhuff. For better or for worse: the process of psychotherapeutic personality change. In *Recent Advances in the Study of Behavior Change.* Montreal: McGill University Press, 1963.

Tucker, Anita F. Empathy training for undergraduate college students in a cross-cultural milieu: a cognitive-developmental curriculum intervention through psychological education. *Dissertation Abstracts International* 38(10-A) (Apr 1978):6030.

Uhlemann, Max R.; Margaret T. Hearn; and David R. Evans. Programmed learning in the microtraining paradigm with hotline workers. *Amer J Community Psych* 8(5) (Oct 1980):603–12.

Washington, Craig S. A method for developing self-esteem and authenticity in paracounselors and counselors. *Dissertation Abstracts International* 37(9-A) (Mar 1977):5618.

Zahner, Carl J. Moral judgment: a comparison of training effects on professional and paraprofessional counselors. *Dissertation Abstracts International* 38(7-A) (Jan 1978):4067-68.

Zerega, William D. et al. Comparison of cognitive and participant modeling on counselor interview discrimination. *Academic Psych Bull* 2(1) (Mar 1980):103-15.

TRAINING

Aldridge, Ernest E., and Allen E. Ivey. The microcounseling paradigm in the instruction of junior high school students in attending behavior. *Canadian Counsellor* 9(2) (Apr 1975):138-44.

Alssid, Lawrence L. and William R. Hutchison. Comparison of modeling techniques in counselor training. *Counselor Educ & Supervision* 17(a) (Sep 1977):36-41.

Arnold, Bill R. Effectiveness of microcounseling as a supervisory model for teaching interviewing skills. *Dissertation Abstracts International* 37(6-A) (Dec 1976):3506.

Authier, Jerry, and Kay Gustafson. Application of supervised and nonsupervised microcounseling paradigms in the training of paraprofessionals. *J Counseling Psych* 22(1) (Jan 1975):74-78.

Avery, A. W. Communication skills training for paraprofessional helpers. *Am J Community Psych* 6(6) (Dec 1978):583-91.

Ayal, Haviva, and Rivka Bekerman. Peer counselling: a means of actualising adolescents' helping potential. *Brit J Guid & Counseling* 6(2) (Jul 1978):204-14.

Bailey, K. G.; P. Deardorff; and W. R. Nay. Students play therapist: relative effects of role playing, videotape feedback, and modeling in a stimulated interview. *J Consult Clin Psych* 45(2) (Apr 1977):257-66.

Baldwin, B. A., and R. E. Staub. Peers as human sexuality outreach educators in the campus community. *J Am Coll Health Assoc* 24(5) (Jun 1976):290-93.

Bath, Kent E. A comparison of three brief empathy training programs. *Dissertation Abstracts International* 35(10-B) (Apr 1975):5098.

Bauer, J. The hotline and its training problems for adolescent listeners. *Adolescence* 10(37) (Spr 1975):63-69.

Beers, Thomas M., and Milton E. Foreman. Intervention patterns in crisis interviews. *J Counseling Psych* 23(2) (Mar 1976):87-91.

Belle, Robert L. The effects of microcounseling on attending behavior of counseling trainees. *Dissertation Abstracts International* 37(5-A) (Nov 1976):2626.

Bernard, Harold S.; Allen M. Roach; and Harvey Resnick. Training bartenders as helpers on a college campus. *Personnel & Guid J* 60(2) (Oct 1981):119-21.

Bernard, H. S., and B. S. Yudowitz. Inservice training of nonprofessional counselors in a correctional institution setting. *Bull Am Acad Psychiatry Law* 3(3) (1975):175–84.

Brandenburg, J. B. Peer counseling for sex related concerns: a case study of a service in a college medical setting. *J Am Coll Health Assoc* 24(5) (Jun 1976):294–300.

Brown, J. E., and J. S. O'Shea. Improving medical student interviewing skills. *Pediatrics* 65(3) (Mar 1980):575–78.

Bry, Brenna H. et al. A pilot course for the training of peer counselors for educationally disadvantaged students. *Teaching of Psychology* 2(2) (Apr 1975):51–55.

Butler, Cynthia. Peer mediated social skills training with withdrawn children. *Dissertation Abstracts International* 39(12-B) (Jun 1979):6111.

Canada, Richard M., and Michael L. Lynch. Systems techniques applied to teaching listening skills. *Counselor Educ & Supervision* 15(1) (Sep 1975):40–47.

Carr, Barbara A. An evaluation of the generalizability of five interviewing skills taught to first-year baccalaureate nursing students using the microcounseling paradigm. *Dissertation Abstracts International* 37(3-B) (Sep 1976):1427.

Carson, Stephen L. Training psychiatric outpatients in active listening skills via the microtraining paradigm. *Dissertation Abstracts International* 35(12-B, pt. 1) (Jun 1975):6066.

Carter, Larry G. Counseling effectiveness following treatment of counselor state anxiety. *Dissertation Abstracts International* 36(8-A) (Feb 1976):5035–36.

Cassata, D. M.; R. M. Conroe; and P. W. Clements. A program for enhancing medical interviewing using videotape feedback in the family practice residency. *J Fam Pract* 4(4) (Apr 1977):673–77.

Christian, P. L., and L. S. Smith. Using videotapes to teach interviewing skills. *Nurse Educ* 6(4) (Jul–Aug 1981):12–14.

Comeau, Louise H. The effect of teaching counseling skills and concepts to women college student advisors. *Dissertation Abstracts International* 38(4-B) (Oct 1977):1948.

Cooke, G. Training police officers to handle suicidal persons. *J Forensic Sci* 24(1) (Jan 1979):227–33.

Cooker, Philip G., and Peter J. Cherchia. Effects of communication skill training on high school students' ability to function as peer group facilitators. *J Counseling Psych* 23(5) (Sep 1976):464–67.

Copeland, Elaine J. Training advanced educational-opportunity program students as peer-group counselors for freshman students. *J Nonwhite Concerns in Personnel & Guid* 7(2) (Jan 1979):62–66.

Corn, Roger. Aiding adjustment to physical limitation: a peer counselor training program. *Cat Selected Documents in Psych* 9(9) (Feb 1979): ms. 1811.

Dalali, Isobel D.; V. Charuvastra; and J. Schlesinger. Training of paraprofessionals: some caveats. *J Drug Educ* 6(2) (1976):105–12.

DeVol, T. I. Does level of professional training make a difference in crisis intervention counseling? *J Comm Health* 2(1) (Fall 1976):31–35.

Dixon, M. C., and J. Burns. The training of telephone crisis intervention volunteers. *Am J Comm Psych* 3(2) (Jun 1975):145–50.

Donahue, Michael J. Peer counseling for police officers: a program for skill development and personal growth. *Dissertation Abstracts International* 38(4-A) (Oct 1977):1992–93.

Dorosin, D.; V. D'Andrea; and R. Jacks. A peer counselor training program: rationale, curriculum, and evaluation: an initial report. *J Am Coll Health Assoc* 25(4) (Apr 1977):259–62.

Edwards, Susan S. Student helpers: a multilevel facilitation program. *Elem School Guid & Counseling* 11(1) (Oct 1976):53–58.

Elias, Burger S. F. et al. Teaching interview skills to mentally retarded persons. *Am J Ment Defic* 85(6) (May 1981):655–57.

Engler, C. M. et al. Medical student acquisition and retention of communication and interviewing skills. *J Med Educ* 56(7) (Jul 1981):572–79.

Evans, David R.; Max R. Uhlemann; and Margaret T. Hearn. Microcounseling and sensitivity training with hotline workers. *J Comm Psych* 6(2) (Apr 1978):139–46.

Fain, Charlotte A. A comparison of the effectiveness of microtraining, positive verbal reinforcement via immediate feedback, and traditional parent skill groups in teaching specific parent skills and improving parent attitudes. *Dissertation Abstracts International* 37(6-A) (Dec 1976):3416–17.

Flaherty, J. A., and B. F. Sharf. Using communication specialists in the teaching of interview skills. *J Med Educ* 56(12) (Dec 1981):1021–23.

Fyffe, A. E., and T. P. Oei. Influence of modelling and feedback provided by the supervisors in a microskills training program for beginning counsellors. *J Clin Psych* 35(3) (Jul 1979):651–56.

George, Gary O.; Ray E. Hosford; and C. Scott Moss. Using videotape programs for training inmates in peer counseling techniques. *Teaching of Psych* 5(4) (Dec 1978):205–07.

Goade, Gary J. A high school peer counseling program: training and effects. *Dissertation Abstracts International* 40(12-A, pt. 1) (Jun 1980):6151.

Guggenheim, F. G., and S. O'Hara. Peer counseling in a general hospital. *Am J Psychiatry* 133(10) (Oct 1976):1197–99.

Gumaer, Jim. Training peer facilitators. *Elem School Guid & Counseling* 11(1) (Oct 1976):27–36.

Hannay, D. R. Teaching interviewing with simulated patients. *Med Educ* 14(4) (Jul 1980):246–48.

Hearn, Margaret T. Three modes of training counselors: a comparative study. *Dissertation Abstracts International* 37(10-B) (Apr 1977):5353–54.

Hinterkopf, Elfie, and Les Brunswick. Promoting interpersonal interaction among mental patients by teaching them therapeutic skills. *Psychosocial Rehab J* 3(1) (Win 1979):20–26.

Hodge, Elaine A. Supervision of empathy training: programmed vs. individual and peer vs. professional. *Dissertation Abstracts International* 37(7-A) (Jan 1977):4134.

Hunt, D. D. "Bug-in-the-ear" technique for teaching interview skills. *J Med Educ* 55(11) (Nov 1980):964–66.

Hunt, D. D. et al. Live versus videotaped interviews. *J Med Educ* 56(11) (Nov 1981):916–18.

Hutter, M. J. et al. Interviewing skills: a comprehensive approach to teaching and evaluation. *J Med Educ* 52(4) (Apr 1977):328–33.

Jewett, L. S. A comparison of structured and self-directed approaches to teaching interviewing and interpersonal skills to pediatric residents. *Annu Conf Res Med Educ* 19 (1980):70–75.

Junek, W.; P. Burra; and P. Leichner. Teaching interviewing skills by encountering patients. *J Med Educ* 54(5) (May 1979):402–07.

Kapp, R. A., and S. D. Weiss. An interdisciplinary, crisis-oriented graduate training program within a student health service mental health clinic. *J Am Coll Health Assoc* 23(5) (Jun 1975):340–44.

Katsky, Patricia O. The training and growth of therapists: a social-psychological study. *Dissertation Abstracts International* 36(5-A) (Nov 1975):3142–43.

Kauss, D. R. et al. The long-term effectiveness of interpersonal skills training in medical schools. *J Med Educ* 55(7) (Jul 1980):595–601.

Keat, Donald B. Training as multimodal treatment for peers. *Elem School Guid & Counseling* 11(1) (Oct 1976):7–13.

Kent, G. G.; P. Clarke; and Smith D. Dalrymple. The patient is the expert: a technique for teaching interviewing skills. *Med Educ* 15(1) (Jan 1981):38–42.

Kimberlin, Carole, and Deloss Friesen. Effects of client ambivalence, trainee conceptual level, and empathy training condition on empathic responding. *J Counseling Psych* 24(4) (Jul 1977):354–58.

Kress, Golub E., and D. Caldwell. Teaching history-taking and interviewing skills to PNPs. *Pediatr Nurs* 7(1) (Jan–Feb 1981):41–45.

Lamonica, Elaine L. et al. Empathy training as the major thrust of a staff development program. *Nurs Research* 25(6) (Nov–Dec 1976):447–51.

Laskow, Gregory B. Evaluation of four training techniques for paraprofessional telephone counselors. *Dissertation Abstracts International* 35(9-B) (Mar 1975):4653.

Leff, M. et al. Interviewing the adolescent patient: an educational program for health professionals. *J Med Educ* 54(11) (Nov 1979):899–901.

Levin, E. M.; M. T. Scurry; and D. A. Bosshart. The teaching of interviewing and counseling skills to internal medicine residents. *J Med Educ* 54(10) (Oct 1979):819–21.

Lochman, J. E. et al. Interviewing skills training in a family practice residency program. *J Fam Pract* 12(6) (Jun 1981):1080–81.

Long, B. E.; C. M. Harris; and P. S. Byrne. A method of teaching counseling. *Med Educ* 10(3) (May 1976):198–204.

McInroy, John D. A comparative study of three microcounseling models. *Dissertation Abstracts International* 36(8-A) (Feb 1976):5052–53.

McKay, S. R. A peer group counseling model in nursing education. *J Nurs Educ* 19(3) (Mar 1980):4–10.

McKenzie, D. J. Training for crisis therapy. *Aust Nurs J* 4(9) (Apr 1975):24–27.

Maguire, P. et al. The value of feedback in teaching interviewing skills to medical students. *Psych Med* 8(4) (Nov 1978):695–704.

Malstrom, Edward A. Counselor empathic response training utilizing physiological data feedback techniques. *Dissertation Abstracts International* 37(5-A) (Nov 1976):2747–48.

Margolis, C. G. et al. Brief hotline training: an effort to examine impact on volunteers. *Am J Comm Psych* 3(1) (Mar 1975):59–67.

Mass, Irene E. The effect of paraprofessional training on the self-esteem of the trainees. *Dissertation Abstracts International* 37(12-B, pt. 1) (Jun 1977):6306–07.

O'Brien, Donald E. An investigation of the effects of videotape feedback in the training of interviewers. *Dissertation Abstracts International* 37(8-A) (Feb 1977):5361.

Paur, Roman M. An Assessment of an intensive forty-hour counselor skills-building program entitled "Counselor training: short-term client systems for paraprofessional volunteer trainees." *Dissertation Abstracts International* 37(2-A) (Aug 1976):891–92.

Pepe, E. A.; C. G. Hodel; and D. A. Bosshart. Use of peers to teach interviewing and clinical problem-solving. *J Med Educ* 55(9) (Sep 1980):800.

Price, S. et al. Training family planning personnel in sex counseling and sex education. *Public Health Rep* 93(4) (Jul–Aug 1978):328–34.

Restad, Raymond O. A training model for self-help, using peer counseling, with college-age students who have a chronic health problem: diabetes. *Dissertation Abstracts International* 39(11-A) (May 1979):6551.

Reutlinger, Ellen F. The effectiveness of lay helpers in working-class parent-training programs. *Dissertation Abstracts International* 37(4-A) (Oct 1976):1996–97.

Roach, William L. A comparative study of two models of communication skills training. *Dissertation Abstracts International* 37(9-A) (Mar 1977):5711.

Robbins, A. S. et al. Interpersonal skills training: evaluation in an internal medicine residency. *J Med Educ* 54(11) (Nov 1979):885–94.

Roberts, Wesley K., and Betty K. Hart. Technique for training paraprofessionals in rape-crisis counseling procedures. *Cat of Selected Documents in Psych* 6 (May 1976):46–47.

Ruhf, Lawrence. A training program in peer-oriented drug and crisis counseling: design, implementation, evaluation. *Dissertation Abstracts International* 38(4-A) (Oct 1977):1904.

Sage, Robert E. A comparison between two different approaches to teaching counseling skills: a modified human relations training model vs. a traditional approach. *Dissertation Abstracts International* 37(8-A) (Feb 1977):4872–73.

Sawyer, Horace W., and Conrad M. Allen. Microcounseling as a training model for the rehabilitation initial interview. *J Applied Rehab Counseling* 7(3) (Fall 1976):170–75.

Settles, Carl E. The effects of two training modes on lay and professional therapy with black adolescent males. *Dissertation Abstracts International* 37(5-A) (Nov 1976):2704.

Shaw, Leonard W. A study of empathy training effectiveness: comparing computer-assisted instruction, structured learning training, and encounter training exercises. *Dissertation Abstracts International* 39(10-A) (Apr 1979):5957–58.

Singleton, Nolan C. Training incarcerated felons in communication skills using an integrated IPR (interpersonal process recall) videotape feedback/affect simulation training model. *Dissertation Abstracts International* 36(9-A) (Mar 1976):5957–58.

Skula, A. et al. The impact of paraprofessional alcoholism counselor training. *Int J Addict* 15(6) (1980):931–38.

Smith, C. K.; R. R. Hadac; and J. H. Leversee. Evaluating the effects of a medical interviewing course taught at multiple locations. *J Med Educ* 55(9) (Sep 1980):792–94.

Spiro, J. H.; M. Roenneburg; and B. J. Maly. Teaching doctors to treat doctors: medical peer counseling. *J Med Educ* 53(12) (Dec 1978):997.

Stillman, P. L.; D. L. Sabers; and D. L. Redfield. The use of paraprofessionals to teach interviewing skills. *Pediatrics* 57(5) (May 1976):769–74.

————. Use of trained mothers to teach interviewing skills to first-year medical students: a follow-up study. *Pediatrics* 60(2) (Aug 1977):165–69.

Stillman, S. M. Trainee-centered explanation for response to training in therapeutic skills. *Psych Rep* 42(1) (Feb 1978):198.

Sutnick, M. R., and J. G. Carroll. Using patient simulators to teach clinical interviewing skills. *J Am Diet Assoc* 78(6) (Jun 1981):614–16.

Thompson, Anthony J. A study of the effect of having a trainee co-counsel with a live model during a microcounseling practice session. *Dissertation Abstracts International* 37(10-A) (Apr 1977):6285.

Toler, Hayward C. The relative effectiveness of programmed instruction, cued-videotape modeling, and behavioral feedback on the acquisition and use of interview skills. *Dissertation Abstracts International* 36(9-A) (Mar 1976):5960–61.

Tosi, D. J., and D. M. Eshbaugh. A cognitive-experiential approach to the interpersonal and intrapersonal development of counselors and therapists. *J Clin Psych* 34(2) (Apr 1978):494–500.

Tucker, Anita F. Empathy training for undergraduate college students in a cross-cultural milieu: a cognitive-developmental curriculum intervention through psychological education. *Dissertation Abstracts International* 38(10-A) (Apr 1978):6030.

Uhlemann, M. R.; M. I. Hearn; and D. R. Evans. Programmed learning in the microtraining paradigm with hotline workers. *Am J Comm Psych* 8(5) (Oct 1980):603–12.

Vaughan, M., and J. N. Marks. Teaching interviewing skills to medical students: a comparison of two methods. *Med Educ* 10(3) (May 1976):170–75.

Veatch, D. J. A videotape series for teaching job interviewing skills. *Am Ann Deaf* 125(6) (Sep 1980):747–50.

Wallace, M. A., and F. B. Schreiber. Crisis intervention training for police officers: a practical program for local police departments. *J Psychiatr Nurs* 15(2) (Feb 1977):25–29.

Waters, Elinor et al. Strategies for training adult counselors. *Counseling Psych* 6(1) (1976):61–66.

Wehler, R., and H. Hoffmann. Personal Orientation Inventory scores of female alcoholism counselors before and after training. *Psych Rep* 43(2) (Oct 1978):500–02.

Welch, Cecil A. Counsellor training in interviewing skills: interpersonal process recall in a microcounseling model. *Dissertation Abstracts International* 37(11-A) (May 1977):6963.

Whitney, Karen K. Short-term interview behaviors training for residence hall counselors and its effect on their in-residence activity and interview performance. *Dissertation Abstracts International* 37(3-A) (Sep 1976):1417.

Wright, A. D. et al. Patterns of acquisition of interview skills by medical students. *Lancet* 2(8201) (Nov 1980):964–66.

Zapka, J. M., and R. M. Mazur. Peer sex education training and evaluation. *Am J Public Health* 67(5) (May 1977):450–54.

Zwibelman, Barry B., and James J. Hinrichsen. Effects of training on peer counseling responses to human sexuality problems. *J Counseling Psych* 24(4) (Jul 1977):359–64.